The Tastes & Traditions
of
Troy State University

A Collection of Recipes from the TSU Family

Volume II

Presented to _____Jackie_____

By _____Dad_____

About the Artist Nall

"Alabama Pansy 2000," the painting which graces the cover of "The Tastes and Traditions of Troy State University, Volume Two," is the creation of internationally acclaimed painter and sculptor Nall Hollis.

A native of Troy, Nall was born in April 1948. His roots firmly planted in Troy -- besides growing up a Trojan, his grandmother, Lucy Trotman Nall, graduated from Troy State Normal School in 1920 -- Nall is also an integral part of TSU. Serving as artist-in-residence for the College of Communication and Fine Arts in spring 2001, he has also displayed his work in the university's Malone Gallery of Art.

Educated in Alabama, Nall also studied in Paris at the Ecole des Beaux Arts, where he worked under Salvador Dali. His work has since been displayed in shows and galleries around the world and has also earned him a Fulbright Scholar Grant.

With his wife Tuscia, Nall founded the N.A.L.L. (Nature Art and Life League) Art Association in Vence, France in 1991 to sponsor the arts, help young artists and promote cultural exchange between France and the United States. In 1997, the N.A.L.L. Art Foundation was created in the United States to further support those goals.

Nall currently lives in Vence and Huntsville, Alabama.

Be sure to look for Nall's family recipes -- from grandmother Lucy Nall, mother Mary Hollis, and wife Tuscia -- throughout "The Tastes and Traditions of Troy State University, Volume Two."

Troy State University

Troy State University traces its origin to February 26, 1887, when it was established as the Troy Normal School by an act of the Alabama Legislature.

The school grew steadily, becoming the Troy State Teachers College in 1929 and Troy State College in 1957 before being named Troy State University in 1967.

Located in Troy in the Wiregrass region of southeast Alabama, Troy State University is the main campus of the Troy State University System, which also consists of a branch campus in Phenix City; University College, which offers degree programs at more than 50 military installations and metropolitan locations throughout the United States and the world; and two other independently accredited universities, Troy State University Dothan and Troy State University Montgomery. The System serves nearly 18,000 students worldwide, including more than 5,000 at the main campus.

TSU offers its students an array of academic programs -- some 70 majors, more than 30 minors and 10 pre-professional areas of study -- in small-class settings. Students pursue degrees at the associate, bachelor's, master's and education specialist levels.

TSU offers its students an array of athletic, philanthropic and social opportunities. The university fields athletic teams in seven men's and seven women's sports, and students participate in dozens of service and professional organizations, honor societies, social fraternities and sororities.

Alumni of the TSU System number approximately 70,000. They live in all 50 states and in some 50 nations worldwide.

Greetings, Troy State University family and friends, and welcome to "The Tastes and Traditions of Troy State University, Volume Two."

In this edition you will find a sampling of foods to satisfy the tastes of all Trojans. There are traditional recipes and favorites from volume one as well as quick-and-easy recipes submitted by the university's most important treasure, our students. At TSU, students are known by name, not by number, a philosophy which has influenced the composition of this cookbook. Our students have provided dozens of recipes which contrast with the contributions of the more experienced chefs within the TSU family and add a unique dimension to this volume of "The Tastes and Traditions." Collectively, our unique diversity is reflected in a most delectable way.

Our students were the inspiration for another special feature of "The Tastes and Traditions." As part of our leadership development curriculum, I lead a session on etiquette in a business luncheon or dinner setting. We have listed our students' most popular questions from these sessions – perhaps the answer to a question of yours is included.

You should know that like its predecessor, volume two of "The Tastes and Traditions" is used by many TSU groups and organizations as a fund-raising tool. The Lady Trojans basketball team paid its way to a tournament in Hawaii in 1995 by selling cookbooks, and our alumni chapters have used them to raise money for scholarships. The book you are now holding is more than likely benefiting a TSU student in some way, so remember "The Tastes and Traditions" on gift-giving occasions. It especially makes a great wedding present for TSU graduates.

We owe a very special "thank you" to native Trojan and renowned artist Nall Hollis, who donated his beautiful painting, "Alabama Pansy, 2000" for the cover of this book. Nall's generosity has been a splendid gift for TSU. He continues to be a special friend to this university.

Thank you for your recipes, photos, information and support for this effort. We love and appreciate each one of you and look forward to seeing you at Troy State University again soon!

God bless and keep you.

Janice Hawkins

Janice Hawkins
TSU First Lady

The Hawkins family: Jack, Janice, Kelly (back left), Katie and Jo Jo.

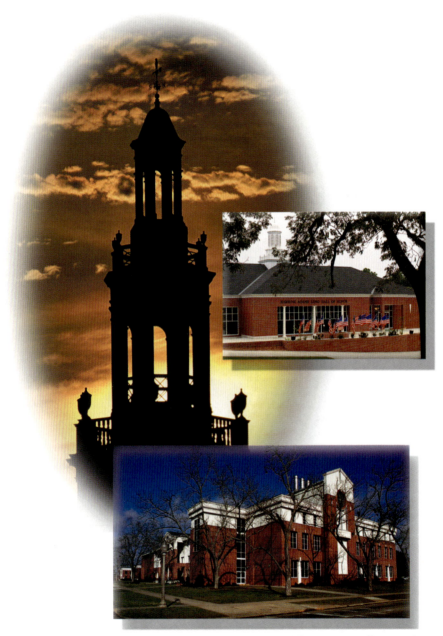

The Palladium, pictured here at sunset, sits atop Bibb Graves Hall, Troy State University's oldest building. The tiered spire, named for a similar feature of the Pallos Athens in ancient Greece, overlooks the University's academic quad. The TSU Science Center (above), constructed in 1999, and the Hawkins Adams Long Hall of Honor (top right), constructed in 1997, are two of the newest structures on the quad.

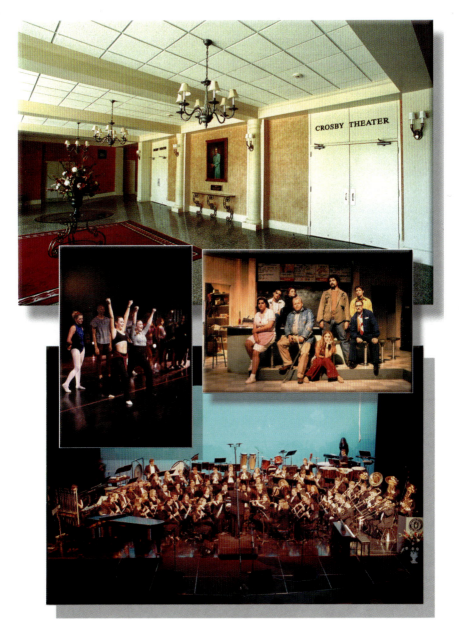

The Claudia Crosby Theater, named in honor of Troy arts patron Claudia Graves Crosby, opened in February 2000. Located in C.B. Smith Hall, the Crosby Theater gives the University's drama, choral and music students a Broadway-caliber forum in which to hone their skills. In addition to providing a home for TSU's nationally-recognized fine arts programs, the theater plays host to a variety of campus and community events.

The world comes to Troy State University and the University, in turn, reaches out to the world. While TSU students hail from more than 50 foreign countries -- and alumni reside in 46 different nations -- the University's programs transcend borders as well. A University-led photo safari in June 2000 gave students a bird's-eye view of Kenyan wildlife and a chance to fashion the traditional wedding outfit of the Masai people (above). Dozens of international students displayed the flags of their native lands prior to a fall 1999 football game; TSU's students comprise the most racially diverse student body in Alabama (opposite, top and right).

Trojan athletic teams ascended to the highest level of collegiate competition -- NCAA Division I -- during the 1990's. Coinciding with their transition was a series of dramatic improvements to the University's athletic facilities. Male and female athletes benefited from a number of new and upgraded facilities, including (clockwise from left) the Elizabeth Mills Rane Learning Center in Davis Fieldhouse; Richard M. Scrushy Field at Memorial Stadium; and Trojan Arena.

An end and a beginning, commencement has been a signal moment in the lives of the more than 75,000 people who have earned diplomas from Troy State University. At top right, a new graduate makes a point with best-selling author W.E.B. Griffin, who served as commencement speaker in June 1999.

As it points toward a new century, Troy State University promises to build on its traditions of service, leadership and educational excellence.

Table of Contents

Beginnings
Margaret Pace Farmer 16
Appetizers 17
Beverages 49
Soups & Sauces 54
Salads 74
Breads & Breakfast 94

Main Events
Claudia Crosby 116
Main Dishes 117
Student Etiquette 125
Vegetables & Side Dishes 189

Finishing Touches
Rosa Parks 220
Desserts 221
Index 319
Order Form 327

Thank you to the special people who made this cookbook a reality:

Steve Knockemus (staff writer), Helen Ricks (design/layout),
Bonnie Money (layout), Donald Norsworthy (photography),
Reba Allen (design), Debbie Sanders and Margaret Pace Farmer
(special assistance), and all who contributed recipes, photographs
or other information.

Key to cookbook symbols

Denotes recipe from   Denotes traditional recipe   TSU "tidbit"
Tastes & Traditions Vol. I

The Tastes & Traditions of Troy State University
Volume II

Copyright © 2000
Troy State University Foundation
Troy, Alabama

ISBN 0-916624-45-5

First Printing   5,000 copies   October 2000

Proceeds from *The Trastes and Traditions of Troy State University* will be returned to the Troy State University Foundation for scholarships and other academic development uses.

Printed in the USA by
WIMMER
The Wimmer Companies
Memphis

Beginnings

Appetizers
Beverages
Soups & Sauces
Salads
Breads & Breakfast

Margaret Pace Farmer

Margaret Pace Farmer has participated, observed, documented and chronicled as the Troy State Normal School developed from a two-year teacher's school to a worldwide university system. Born in Troy in 1912, Mrs. Farmer grew up with close ties to the institution: her father, Dr. Matthew Downer Pace, was a member of the college faculty for five decades and served as its president in 1936-37. Mrs. Farmer attended elementary, junior high and high school at the normal school campus, and earned her bachelor's degree from Troy State Teachers College in 1932.

An insatiable learner, writer and teacher, Mrs. Farmer is the de facto historian of Troy, Pike County and their people. Her first book, "History of Pike County, 1821-1900," was published in 1951; she later complemented that with "One Hundred Fifty Years in Pike County, Alabama, 1821-1971." Mrs. Farmer was a founding member and first president of the Pike County Historical Society and was the first woman to serve as president of the Alabama Historical Society. She and her husband, Curren, founded the Pike Pioneer Museum in 1971. Mrs. Farmer continues to write a weekly column for The Pike County Citizen and has given her collected writings to the Troy Public Library.

As avid a cook as a writer, Mrs. Farmer's recipes are spiced with bits and pieces of local history.

Look for Mrs. Farmer's recipes throughout "The Tastes and Traditions of Troy State University, Volume Two."

Appetizers

Appetizers

Sausage Grabbies

This recipe was given to me by Mary Ann Wiley when she heard we were having several family members spend Thanksgiving holidays with us. It was, and still is, a favorite of my family.

1 pound bulk sausage
2 jars Old English cheese spread
1/2 stick margarine, softened
1/4 - 1/2 teaspoon pepper
1/2 teaspoon garlic powder
2 packages English muffins

Crumble sausage, fry lightly and drain. Stir in remaining ingredients. Spread on English muffin halves. Cut into quarters, halves or leave whole. Freeze. When ready to serve, cook under broiler until bubbly and lightly browned .

Kathy Omasta
TSU

Artichoke Dip

1 (8 1/2 ounce) can artichoke hearts, drained and chopped
1 cup Parmesan cheese
1 cup mayonnaise
1/2 teaspoon lemon juice
1 can chopped green chiles, optional

Preheat oven to 400 degrees. Place all ingredients in a food processor and puree, using chiles if a hotter dip is desired. Turn into a greased ovenproof dish and bake 15 minutes. Serve with toast wedges for dipping.

Jessica Armstrong
TSUD '96

Judy Morgan
TSU

Helen McKinley
TSU Friend

Officers of the U.S. Navy are pursuing their master of business administration degree while traveling the world's seas, thanks to the unique Executive MBA program designed by the Sorrell College of Business.

Tastes and Traditions

Crab Dip

1 pound white crabmeat
1/4 cup finely chopped green onions
1/4 cup finely chopped celery
1 cup mayonnaise
1 egg
1 teaspoon Old Bay seasoning
Dash of Tabasco
Parmesan cheese

Mix all ingredients except Parmesan together. Pour into buttered small casserole and sprinkle with Parmesan. Bake at 350 degrees for 20 minutes. Serve with bagel chips or crackers.

Bobby Ross Phillips
TSU '59

TSU's conversion to the semester system in fall 1999 gave the university the opportunity to begin another tradition: the annual lighting of a campus Christmas tree. A living Christmas tree, planted on the Bibb Graves Quad that fall, is decorated each December by student organizations while hot chocolate and other refreshments are passed around. Traditional carols are sung after the ceremonial lighting of the tree. The special festivities are a prelude to the annual Christmas program presented by the John M. Long School of Music. Students, faculty and staff enjoyed the inaugural Christmas-tree-lighting ceremony in December 1999.

Appetizers

Hot Mexi-Corn Dip

This recipe was a favorite of the parents for tailgating during the "wonderful" 1999 football season. It's a favorite of our son, Brock Nutter, TSU quarterback.

8 ounces cream cheese, softened
1 stick butter, softened
3 cans Mexi-corn, well drained
1 small can chopped green chiles, well drained
1 (12 -16 ounce) jar chunky picante sauce
1 1/2 cups grated Jack/Cheddar cheese, divided

Combine cream cheese and butter until smooth and well blended. Add corn and green chiles. Stir in picante sauce and 1 cup of grated cheese, mixing well. Pour into 9 x 13-inch pyrex dish and bake 45 minutes at 350 degrees. Sprinkle with reserved cheese and bake until cheese is melted, 5 to 10 minutes more. Serve warm with corn chip scoops.

Vicki Nutter
TSU Parent

TSU quarterback Brock Nutter was joined by parents Vicki and Jack following the Trojans' victory at Southwest Texas State in October 1999.

Tastes and Traditions

Shrimp Dip

This is a quick and easy appetizer that is great for tailgating or late night snacks.

1 can shrimp, rinsed and drained
1 package cream cheese, softened
3 green onions, chopped
Dash of pepper

Gently fold shrimp into the cream cheese. Add onions and pepper. Mix well (shrimp is very tender and will fall apart). Refrigerate for about 3 hours before serving.

Lisa Bennett
TSU Student
Alpha Gamma Delta Sorority

Chicken Dip

This recipe came from my daughter in Birmingham. It has always been a hit. I especially get comments from men about how good it is.

1 package slivered almonds, divided
8 ounces cream cheese, softened
1 can white chicken, drained and broken up
1 can cream of mushroom soup
1 small jar chopped mushrooms, drained, optional
1 tablespoon Worcestershire sauce
Garlic salt, pepper, and salt to taste

Toast half of the almonds and reserve. Place remaining ingredients in a small crock pot. Heat well. (If you're in a hurry, you can heat ingredients in microwave before placing in crock pot.) When ready to serve, sprinkle with reserved almonds. Serve with tortilla chips.

Mary G. Taylor
TSU

During the 1990s, all of TSU's athletic programs jumped -- or were in the process of jumping -- to NCAA Division I competition.

Appetizers

Chicken Party Dip

2 (8 ounce) packages cream cheese, softened
1 large can chicken breast meat, drained
1 package Ranch seasoning

Mix all ingredients together. This mixes easier if you use your hands. Serve with crackers.

Christi Green
TSU '96

Black-eyed Pea Dip

1 small onion, chopped
2 tablespoons butter
1 can black-eyed peas, rinsed and drained
1 can artichokes, drained and chopped
1/2 cup mayonnaise
1/2 cup sour cream
4 tablespoons Parmesan cheese
1 package Hidden Valley salad dressing mix
Grated mozzarella cheese

Sauté onion in butter. Add all other ingredients except mozzarella. Bake at 350 degrees 20 minutes or until hot and bubbly. Sprinkle with cheese. Return to oven and brown cheese. Serve with Melba petite crackers or tortilla chips.

Brock Nutter
TSU Student

Music professors Robert Smith and Ralph Ford worked with world-renowned composer John Williams on the score for the 1999 blockbuster movie, "Star Wars: The Phantom Menace."

Tastes and Traditions

Spinach Dip

1 (10 ounce) package frozen chopped spinach, thawed and drained
1 (16 ounce) container sour cream
1 cup mayonnaise
1 package vegetable soup, dip & recipe mix
1 (8 ounce) can water chestnuts, drained and chopped
3 green onions, chopped

In medium bowl stir all ingredients until well mixed. Cover; chill 2 or more hours to blend flavors. Stir well before serving. If desired, spoon into round bread bowl. Serve with cut up vegetables, crackers, or corn chip scoops. Note: For Spinach & Cheese Dip: Add 1 cup shredded cheese with spinach.

Jennifer Handke King
TSU Student

Hot Cheese Dip

This dip is a great appetizer that all will enjoy. Good for tailgating and other gatherings!

8 ounces shredded mozzarella cheese
8 ounces shredded sharp cheese
2 cups mayonnaise
1 medium onion, chopped fine
1 can chopped mild green chiles, drained
Black olives, optional
1 (1 1/2 ounce) package sliced pepperoni

Combine all ingredients except pepperoni and spread in a baking dish. Arrange pepperoni on top. Bake at 325 degrees for 25 minutes. Serve with king-size Fritos.

Amy Shively
TSU Student

Dozens of top executives in Hong Kong are enhancing their professional training through a master of business administration degree program developed and maintained by the Sorrell College of Business and University College.

Appetizers

Creamy Cheese Dip

2 pounds processed cheese
1 can Rotel
1 pound sausage
1 pound ground turkey or ground beef
1 can cream of chicken soup
1 can cream of mushroom soup
1/4 cup milk

Cube cheese and place over low heat in large saucepan; add Rotel. Brown sausage and beef or turkey and add to cheese mixture. Add soups and milk. If you wish you may leave this to warm in crockpot. Serve hot with chips, sour cream, and jalapeños.

Jamie Fallin
TSU '00

Corn Chip Dip

Great for tailgating!! Better if it sits overnight (about 8 hours) so the dressing soaks in.

1/2 - 1 small bundle of green onions, finely chopped
1 can Trappey's black-eyed peas with jalapeño peppers
1 can shoepeg corn, drained
1 green bell pepper, chopped
1 small bottle Zesty Italian Dressing

Combine all the ingredients. You may only need to use half of the bundle of scallion onions. Mix together. Serve with large corn chips.

Candi Phillips
TSU Student
Kappa Delta Sorority

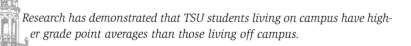

Research has demonstrated that TSU students living on campus have higher grade point averages than those living off campus.

Tastes and Traditions

Layered Mexican Dip

In October 1999, the Kappa Gamma chapter of Phi Mu held its first annual Greek Fiesta to promote Panhellenic relations on the TSU campus. Each sister invited a girl from another sorority over for a Mexican dinner. This dip was a huge success with everyone.

8 ounces sour cream
1 package taco seasoning mix
16 ounces refried beans
1/2 cup sliced pickled jalapeño peppers
1 cup shredded monterey jack cheese
1 cup shredded Cheddar cheese
1 1/2 cups shredded lettuce
1 large tomato, chopped

Combine sour cream and taco seasoning. Spread refried beans onto a 9-inch round serving plate; spoon sour cream mixture evenly over beans. Layer with jalapeño peppers and remaining ingredients. Serve with tortilla chips.

Phi Mu Sorority

Greek Week, an annual event, highlights TSU's 21 fraternities and sororities and their contributions to the campus and local community. Here, two sorority members prepare to take a cold seat in the "musical ice buckets" competition.

Appetizers

Mexican Cheese Dip

For 10 years, TSU's chapter of Phi Mu has been enjoying this treat on bid day. Alumni bring it by the gallon and there is never a drop left. Can be refrigerated and warmed at any time.

1/2 pound hamburger meat
1 package taco seasoning, optional
1 pound Velveeta cheese
1 can Rotel

Cook hamburger and drain. Add taco seasoning, if desired. Melt cheese in large bowl in microwave; add Rotel to cheese and mix; add hamburger mixture. Stir well and heat in microwave. Serve with corn chips scoops.

Phi Mu Sorority

Kristin Fountain
Troy State Student
Alpha Gamma Delta Sorority

Cheddar Curry Spread

2 cups grated sharp Cheddar cheese
1 small can chopped or sliced black olives, drained
1/2 cup mayonnaise
1/2 teaspoon curry
2 green onions, chopped fine
1 small clove garlic, minced

Combine all ingredients until blended. Serve in hollowed-out squash, at room temperature, with your favorite crackers.

Reba Davis
TSU

Chapters of the Troy State University Alumni Association can be found in Kirov, Russia, and Hong Kong, China.

Tastes and Traditions

Beef Cheese Ball

While my husband was in the Marine Corps we lived in many different places. Each time we moved, I left with some great recipes. This one was given to me when we lived in California. Now, every time I pull out a recipe it brings back wonderful memories of places we called home and of all our dear friends.

4 ounces beef stick
2 tablespoons mayonnaise
8 ounces cream cheese, softened
1 tablespoon minced onion
4 teaspoons chopped olives
2 tablespoons Worcestershire sauce

Grate beef stick. Add mayonnaise to cream cheese. Then add onions, olives, Worcestershire sauce and half of the beef. Chill in freezer 15 to 20 minutes and shape in a ball. Sprinkle with rest of beef. Refrigerate. Serve with crackers.

Vicki Schmidt
TSU

Cheese Ball

1 (3 ounce) package cream cheese, chilled
3 ounces blue or roquefort cheese, chilled
1 small jar Old English cheese, chilled
8 ounces American cheese, chilled
Garlic clove
Chili powder

Put cheese in a meat grinder in the order given. About half-way through add garlic to the grinder. Mix the ground cheese well with a fork or hands. Mold into a ball and roll in chili powder. Wrap in wax paper, then in foil and refrigerate for at least an hour. Serve with any kind of crackers. Keeps a long time.

Beth Jetton
Troy State Student
Alpha Gamma Delta Sorority

Appetizers

Sausage-Stuffing Balls

In my family, with a Southern mother and a British/Westerner father, food was sometimes a matter of compromise. At Thanksgiving, the turkey stuffing had to be cornbread -- but it also had to have little sausage balls in it. This was our favorite part of Thanksgiving dinner. As an adult, I thought once or twice a year was too seldom for this treat, and devised this hors d'oeuvre.

1 pound sausage meat
1 1/4 cups water or chicken broth
1 tablespoon butter
2 tablespoons dried minced onion
1 (8 ounce) package corn bread stuffing mix, lightly crushed
1 egg, lightly beaten
3 tablespoons melted butter

Form sausage into 48 small balls. Fill medium-size sauce pan half full with water. Add sausage balls, bring to a boil, reduce heat and cover pan. Simmer for 30 minutes. Drain sausage balls and refrigerate while preparing next step. Bring water or broth, butter and onion to a boil. Add stuffing mix and stir, as directed. Cool slightly and stir in egg.
Wrap small amount of stuffing mix around each sausage ball. Roll the 48 covered sausage balls in the melted butter. These may be frozen at this point. Bake at 375 degrees for about 15 minutes, or until lightly brown. If frozen, allow another 10 to 15 minutes. (These can also be frozen after baking and heated in the microwave.) These are best served hot, but also good if served at room temperature.

Tuny Jennings
TSU-Florida Region

The Anna Green Gitenstein Memorial Rose Garden, situated in front of Smith Hall, is a colorful part of the Bibb Graves Quad.

Tastes and Traditions

Sausage Cheese Balls

2 pounds uncooked sausage
4 cups shredded sharp Cheddar cheese (16 ounces)
1 1/2 cups all-purpose baking/biscuit mix
1/2 cup finely chopped onion
1/2 cup finely chopped celery
1/2 teaspoon garlic powder

Preheat oven to 375 degrees. Combine all ingredients. Form into 1-inch balls. Bake 15 minutes on ungreased cooking sheet until golden brown. Makes about 6 dozen sausage balls. Sausage balls may be frozen.

Judy Morgan
TSU

Sheree Huner
TSU Student
Phi Mu Sorority

Trojan guard Eugene "Tote" Christopher drives to the basket against Jacksonville State in 2000. The Trojan men captured the Trans America Athletic Conference regular-season title in 1999-2000.

Appetizers

Pepperoni and Cheese Crescents

1 (8 ounce) can crescent rolls
24 slices pepperoni
1/2 cup shredded mozzarella cheese
1 egg, lightly beaten

Separate dough into triangles. Put 3 slices of pepperoni in each triangle. Sprinkle with mozzarella cheese. Roll up into crescent and curve into half-moon shape. Brush with beaten egg and bake at 375 degrees for 8 to 10 minutes.

Kristen Nelson
TSU Student
Phi Mu Sorority

Mary's Cheese Straws

This is my version. I worked a long time getting the right amount of ingredients. When I serve them I am asked to share my recipe. So here it is!

8 ounces grated sharp Cheddar cheese, room temperature
8 ounces grated extra sharp Cheddar cheese, room temperature
3 sticks margarine, softened
4 cups all-purpose flour
1/2 teaspoon salt
1/2 teaspoon red pepper

Blend margarine and cheese; add other ingredients. Mix well. Press through cookie press and arrange on an ungreased baking sheet. Bake at 350 degrees for 20 minutes.

Mary G. Taylor
TSU

Many of the leaders of the U.S. military have been trained by Troy State University. More than 50 active, flag-rank and general officers in the Navy, Marines, Army and Air Force have earned degrees from TSU.

Tastes and Traditions

Bay Crab Quiche

My sister, Cathy Flynn (TSU), baits the traps, catches, cleans and picks the crabs. I cook them. My husband, George (TSU '81), loves this recipe as a main dish served with salad.

1/2 cup mayonnaise
2 tablespoons flour
2 eggs, beaten
1/2 cup milk
1 (7 1/2 ounce) can crabmeat, drained or 1 (6 ounce) package frozen
    crabmeat, or meat from 13 crabs, cleaned, cooked, and picked.
8 ounces shredded marbled Monterey Jack and Colby Cheese or 4 ounces
    shredded Monterey Cheese and 4 ounces shredded Colby Cheese
1/3 cup red onion, diced fine
1 (9 inch) unbaked pastry shell

Preheat oven to 350 degrees. Combine mayonnaise, flour, eggs, and milk. Mix until blended. Stir in crabmeat, cheese, and onion. Pour into pastry shell and bake at 350 degrees for 45 minutes.

Anne-Charlotte Embling
TSU '81

Quiche

2 deep-dish pie shells
1 pound bacon, diced, fried and drained
2 onions, chopped and sautéed in butter
Swiss cheese, grated
6 eggs, beaten
2 cups half and half
Salt, pepper, and nutmeg

Pierce pie shells with a fork and bake about 5 minutes at 350 degrees to prevent sogginess. Place bacon, onion, and cheese in this order in shells. Sprinkle with cheese. Mix eggs, half and half, salt, pepper and nutmeg together and pour over cheese. Bake at 375 degrees for approximately 30 minutes.

Anna Smith
TSU

Economic studies have shown that TSU has an annual impact of some $200 million on southeast Alabama.

Appetizers

Peach Salsa

A different and refreshing change from the same old salsa. Men love it.

1 (16 ounce) can peaches, drained and cut in bite-size pieces
4 Roma Tomatoes, drained and cut in bite-size pieces
4 green onions, finely chopped
2 tablespoons chopped pickled jalapeños
1 tablespoon chopped cilantro
1 tablespoon lime juice
1 teaspoon honey
1/4 teaspoon salt
1/4 teaspoon pepper

Mix all ingredients together. Refrigerate 2 to 3 days ahead. Serve with tortilla chips.

Vicki B. Nutter
TSU Parent

Black Bean Salsa

Wonderful salsa!

2 (15 ounce) cans black beans, drained
1 (16 ounce) can whole kernel corn, drained
1 (16 ounce) can tomatoes, chopped
1 (10 ounce) can tomatoes and chiles (mild or hot), chopped
1/2 cup chopped cilantro
6 tablespoons lime juice
1/2 cup picante sauce
3 tablespoons vegetable oil
1/2 cup finely chopped red onion
1/2 teaspoon cumin

Mix all ingredients and refrigerate overnight for flavors to blend. Serve with chips.

Jodi Ward
TSU Friend

The Alabama Supreme Court visited TSU in November 1991, holding a special session and hearing arguments on campus. TSU-TV aired the session live, the first such broadcast of the state's highest court.

Tastes and Traditions

One Minute Salsa

1 (10 ounce) can Rotel
1 (14.5 ounce) can stewed tomatoes
1/2 teaspoon garlic salt
1/2 teaspoon pepper

Pour ingredients into blender and process 5 seconds. Serve with tortilla chips.

Jonna Davis
TSU

Pimento Cheese 1

We take this to our Trojan football tailgating parties.

1 pound processed cheese, cubed
1/3 cup milk
1/4 cup vinegar
1 medium jar pimento, drained
1 egg, lightly beaten
Garlic salt, lots
1 cup mayonnaise

Mix all ingredients except mayonnaise in a double boiler. Cook for 30 minutes. stirring often. Let cool, then add mayonnaise and mix thoroughly.

Alan Boothe
TSU
Alabama House of Representatives

The only place in the United States where the country's greatest bandmasters can be found under one roof is at the National Bandmasters Hall of Fame, located in TSU's Hawkins Adams Long Hall of Honor.

Appetizers

Pimento Cheese 2

Serve with crackers. It also makes great sandwiches.

8 ounces grated sharp Cheddar cheese, room temperature
8 ounces grated medium Cheddar cheese, room temperature
1 small jar pimento, drained and mashed
8 ounces cream cheese, softened
1/4 cup mayonnaise
1/4 teaspoon cayenne pepper

Combine Cheddar cheeses. Add pimento. Mix softened cream cheese and mayonnaise and add to Cheddar cheese mixture. Add cayenne pepper. Mix well. Chill. This will be very firm and should be served at room temperature. To make a cheese ball, chill for 1 hour; shape into a ball, roll in 2 cups toasted pecans.

Jean S. Helms
TSU Friend

Boursin Cheese Spread

Save money and make your own boursin!

8 ounces cream cheese, softened
2 tablespoons butter, softened
1/2 teaspoon minced garlic
1/4 teaspoon dill
1/4 teaspoon thyme
2 tablespoons chopped parsley
1 tablespoon chopped chives
Freshly ground pepper

Blend all ingredients except pepper together and form into 2 small balls. Roll in ground pepper. Wrap in plastic wrap and chill. Enjoy with crackers.

Mamie Mason
TSU Friend

Dr. and Mrs. Hawkins play host to graduates and their families for breakfast at the Chancellor's Home prior to each graduation ceremony.

Tastes and Traditions

Dill and Cream Cheese Appetizer

This is really a simple and good recipe. Every time I serve it, people make positive comments. It's great served at parties.

8 ounces cream cheese
Dill weed
1 (8 count) package refrigerated crescent rolls
1 egg yolk, optional

Roll cream cheese in dill weed. Unroll crescent rolls and press seams together. Place cream cheese in center. Wrap dough around cream cheese and seal all edges. Brush top with egg yolk, if desired. Bake at 425 degrees for 15 to 17 minutes or until brown. Serve hot with party crackers.

Mary G. Taylor
TSU

Cream Cheese and Caviar

Dish may be frozen or prepared early in the day, except for decorating with egg mixture. Red caviar may be substituted for the black.

1 (8 ounce) package cream cheese, softened
4 tablespoons grated onion, divided
2 tablespoons chives
Dash of Worcestershire sauce
Dash of Tabasco sauce
1 tablespoon lemon juice
3 tablespoons mayonnaise
Salt and pepper to taste
1 (3 1/2 ounce) jar black caviar
2 hard-cooked eggs
2 teaspoons grated onion
Mayonnaise to blend
Olives, thin lemon slices and parsley

Blend cream cheese, 2 tablespoons onion, chives, Worcestershire, Tabasco, lemon juice, mayonnaise and salt and pepper to taste. Mold into a ball. Cover with caviar. Chop eggs and blend with remaining onion, mayonnaise, salt and pepper. Using a pastry bag with star tip, decorate the caviar mold around edges with the egg mixture. Garnish with olives, lemon slices and parsley. Serve with Triscuits.

Elizabeth Lent
TSU Student
Kappa Delta Sorority

Appetizers

Bacon-Wrapped Dates

This appetizer has a surprising combination of flavors and causes people who try it to ask what it is. They always want the recipe.

1 pound bacon slices, cut into thirds
1 box whole, pitted dates

Spread bacon slices in a single layer on a jelly roll pan and broil until slightly cooked but still soft. Drain well on paper towels until cooled. Wrap each bacon slice around a date and secure with a toothpick. Place on jelly roll pan or broiler pan and broil, turning until evenly browned. Drain well and serve warm or at room temperature.

Deb Davis
TSU Spouse

Roll-Ups

This recipe can be prepared the night before.

2 (8 ounce) packages cream cheese, softened
1/2 small onion, chopped
2 - 3 tablespoons lemon juice
2 tablespoons -1/4 cup chopped jalapeño pepper, to taste
1/4 cup salsa
1 - 2 teaspoons Worcestershire
1/2 pint sour cream
1 1/2 teaspoons garlic
1 small can chiles, chopped, optional
2 - 3 tablespoons hot sauce
1 package large flour tortillas

Combine cream cheese and remaining ingredients except tortillas in a bowl. Spread thin layer of mixture on each tortilla. Roll up, cover and refrigerate for at least 2 hours but preferably overnight. When ready to serve, slice tortillas into bite-size pieces and serve with salsa.

Hope Tillery
TSU Student
Kappa Delta Sorority

The executives of the nation's largest rehabilitation hospital system -- the HealthSouth Corporation -- are enhancing their education through TSU's specially designed HealthSouth-Executive Master of Business Administration program.

Tastes and Traditions

Grated Carrot Sandwiches

This recipe freezes well and makes excellent tea sandwiches.

2 (8 ounce) packages cream cheese, softened
4 small carrots, finely grated
1 tablespoon onion juice or 1 tablespoon minced onion
Salt and white pepper to taste
Mayonnaise
1/2 cup chopped pecans
Bread

In mixer, beat cream cheese, grated carrots, onion juice, salt, pepper, and enough mayonnaise to make mixture spreadable. Add chopped pecans. Spread on bread slices. (For tea sandwiches, brown or white trimmed bread may be used.) Cut into desired shapes. Another option is to spread filling on trimmed bread and roll-up like a jelly roll. Chill or freeze and slice bread into round, spiral-shaped sandwiches. Ribbon sandwiches may be made by alternating brown and white bread; then slice into strips. Tip: Use electric knife for cutting and trimming bread.

Peggy Blount Wood
TSU '86

"Come Back" Sandwiches

These sandwiches may be a Troy original – I've never tasted them anywhere else.

1 tablespoon butter
2 tablespoons flour
1 cup milk
1 cup grated cheese
1 cup chopped nuts
2 pimentos, chopped
1/2 green pepper, finely chopped
1/2 cup celery, finely chopped
Sprinkle of onion
1 cup mayonnaise
White bread

To make cream sauce, combine first three ingredients and cook until thick. Remove from stove and add cheese, nuts, pimentos, green pepper, celery and onion. When you are ready to assemble sandwiches, add mayonnaise and spread on white bread.

Margaret Pace Farmer
TSU '32

Appetizers

Sweet Snack Mix

This has a "more-ish" taste – the more you eat, the more you want! Good for tailgating, snacking or anytime you need a bite of something.

1 (12 ounce) box Rice Chex
1 (12 ounce) box Corn Chex
1 (12 ounce) box Crispix
1 pound mixed nuts
1 pound butter
2 pounds brown sugar
1 cup light corn syrup
1 teaspoon salt
2 teaspoons vanilla

Mix cereals and mixed nuts together. Pour in large baking pan. (It may take two.) Put aside. Bring butter, brown sugar, corn syrup and salt to a boil. Simmer for 5 minutes without stirring. Remove from heat and add vanilla. Pour this mixture over cereal mixture. Bake at 200 degrees for one hour, stirring every 15 minutes.

Sherry J. Dye
TSU Spouse

BBQ Chicken Pizza

1 pizza crust
8 ounces chicken strips
1 can mushrooms, drained
1/4 cup barbecue sauce
1/2 cup onion slices
1 cup grated mozzarella cheese.
Jalapeño peppers, optional

Make pizza crust as directed on package. In nonstick pan coated with nonstick cooking spray, sauté chicken strips, mushrooms and barbecue sauce. Arrange chicken strips and mushrooms on crust and top with onion slices and cheese. Top with jalapeño peppers, if desired. Bake as directed on pizza crust package.

Bonnie, Kari Ann, Kendra and Missy
TSU Students
Kappa Delta Sorority

Tastes and Traditions

Angels on Horseback

This recipe comes from Beaufort, South Carolina. Growing up along the seashore and river, I learned to love to fish and crab. Sunburned and tired, no matter, the evening soon turned into feasts. But bringing in the oysters was something else; more work. Digging the hole to roast the oysters and of course, searching for the pearl before you ate -- life at its best. The original recipe came from Mrs. Carl Dorr.

Oysters, drained and unwashed
Fresh garlic
Pepper
Bacon
Toasted bread, cut into triangles
Fresh lemon (no plastic allowed)
Garnish (scallion, parsley, or chive)

Clean oysters. Rub gently with fresh garlic and sprinkle with pepper. Place on cookie sheet under broiler, covering each with small piece of bacon. (Use toothpicks to hold bacon around oysters if you like.) Broil until bacon is cooked. Turn, watching carefully until done. Place on toasted bread. Serve with slices of fresh lemon. If serving from platter, place toasted bread first, place angels on top of bread, lemon slice to go with each. Garnish of your choice. Serve immediately.

Linda Stewart
TSU Parent

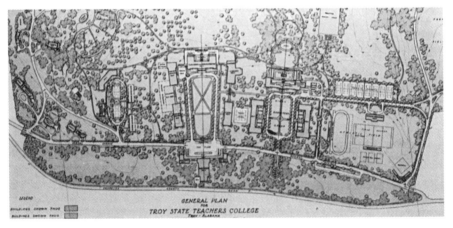

The Olmsted Brothers, the same architects who designed New York's Central Park and the Biltmore Estate, also designed the TSU campus, which covers close to 600 acres. The Olmsted Brothers' campus plan included two quadrangles as well as a plaza where Smith Hall is now located.

38

Appetizers

Bread and Butter Pickles

1 gallon sliced cucumbers
8 medium onions, sliced
1/2 cup salt
4 cups vinegar
4 cups sugar
1/2 teaspoon cloves
1 1/2 teaspoons turmeric
2 teaspoons celery seed
2 tablespoons mustard seed

Mix cucumbers, onions and salt together and cover with 1 quart crushed ice. Let stand for 3 hours. Drain well. Bring remaining ingredients to a boil. After mixture has been heated to a boil, drop cucumbers into mixture (but do not let them boil). Pour cucumbers and mixture into jars and seal.

Chandra Myrick
TSU Student

Watermelon Rind Sweet Pickles

I was the second home economics teacher at Troy State. I worked until my children were born.

1 watermelon rind
Alum
7 1/2 pounds sugar
2 quarts vinegar
1 teaspoon cloves
Few pieces ginger
1 small piece stick cinnamon
1 tablespoon black peppercorns
1 tablespoon allspice
Lemon peel

Use thick rind only. Peel all green from outside and all pink from inside. Cut into shapes. Soak in strong brine 3 days. Freshen by putting in very cold water which has had small pieces of alum dropped into it. Wash rind and bring to boil in fresh water. Boil until tender. Combine remaining ingredients and bring to a boil. Add rind and boil until clear.

Lucy T. Nall
TSU '20

Tastes and Traditions

Green Tomato Pickles

This recipe was given to me by Erin Trotman Helton, the first home economics teacher at Troy State. Dr. E.M. Shackelford (president of Troy State Normal 1899-1936) called her and offered the job to her. She told him she didn't have a degree and he told her if she only taught the students to make biscuits like she made them, he wanted her to have the job. She was the best cook in the world.

7 pounds green tomatoes
3 gallons lime water
Ginger
4 pints white vinegar
6 pounds sugar
1 teaspoon mace
1 teaspoon cinnamon
1 teaspoon whole cloves
1 teaspoon allspice
1 teaspoon celery seed

Slice 7 pounds green tomatoes and soak in lime water for 24 hours. Wash in fresh water. Soak in ginger and 2 gallons of water. Make syrup of remaining ingredients. Add tomatoes and boil 1 hour. Seal in jars while hot.

Lucy T. Nall
TSU '20

Orange Marmalade

4 cups chopped oranges
2 chopped lemons, optional
1 pound fruit jell or sun jell
6 1/2 cups sugar

Peel oranges and save peeling. Scrape about half of white pith from peel and discard. Thinly slice peel. Chop oranges. Combine peel, oranges and chopped lemon, if desired. Bring to a boil, add fruit jell and boil for about 1 minute. Add sugar and boil to 200 count down. Ladle in jars and seal.

Mary Mitchell
TSU Friend

_____ *Appetizers*

Pashka

4 (8 ounce) packages cream cheese, softened
1 cup butter, softened
2 cups powdered sugar
3 egg yolks
2 teaspoons vanilla
Grated lemon peel
1 cup slivered almonds

Combine cream cheese and butter, beating until smooth. Add powdered sugar, egg yolks, vanilla and lemon peel, mixing until smooth. Fold in almonds. Pour mixture into 7-cup mold lined with dampened cheesecloth. Chill or freeze overnight; if frozen, let stand to thaw before serving. Invert mold to remove and serve with fresh fruit such as apples or strawberries.

Debbie Fortune
TSU

The Phi Mu Recipe

1 tablespoon creativity
1 teaspoon good taste
1 teaspoon time
Dash of charm

Blend ingredients together. Add one tablespoon of fun. Mix with a sprinkle of skill. Serve proudly.

Phi Mu Sorority

Phi Mu sisters gathered outside their house on Sorority Hill on "bid day," August 1999.

Tastes and Traditions

Hot Wings With Veggies

First Edition Favorite

Anyone who knows about living with a coach and three teenage girls knows you have to be ready to feed unexpected guests at a minute's notice. One of Coach Blakeney's favorites is the following:

20 - 24 pieces chicken drumettes
Oil for deep fat frying
1/2 cup Louisiana or Durkee hot sauce
1/2 cup margarine
1 1/2 teaspoons Lowry's seasoned salt
24 carrot sticks
24 celery sticks
Ranch dressing

Preparation time - 1 hour.

Wash and pat dry individual drumettes. Drop in hot oil and fry about 15 minutes or until wings are brown and crispy. Drain on a rack until all wings are cooked. In a small saucepan, heat margarine, hot sauce, and salt. Just before serving, place chicken in a container with a lid and pour the hot sauce over all. Replace lid and shake until all pieces are coated. Arrange on a platter with carrot and celery sticks and a bowl of ranch dressing for dipping. Delicious!!!

Janice Blakeney
TSU Spouse

French Bread Garlic Shrimp

1 loaf French bread, cut in 1-inch slices
1 1/2 pounds fresh, peeled shrimp
1 stick butter
3 - 4 cloves garlic, chopped fine
1/2 pound provolone cheese, sliced

Line casserole dish with bread slices. Top with shrimp. Melt butter and use to sauté garlic, then pour over shrimp. Bake in 400 degree oven until shrimp turn pink, about 5 to 8 minutes, depending on size of shrimp. Cover with slices of cheese and return to oven until cheese melts.

Mary Pinckard
TSU Friend

Appetizers

Water Chestnut Dip

First Edition Favorite

This dip looks beautiful served in a hollowed-out red cabbage head. Lightly steamed and chilled asparagus spears are wonderful with this dip.

1 (8 ounce) carton sour cream
1 cup real mayonnaise
1 (8 ounce) can water chestnuts, drained and chopped
2 tablespoons soy sauce
1/2 cup chopped fresh parsley
3 dashes Tabasco sauce
1 - 2 green onions, chopped

Combine all ingredients except green onions in food processor. Pulse to blend. Stir in onions just before serving. Serve chilled with raw vegetables.

Janice Hawkins
TSU First Lady

Cheese Rounds

Traditional Recipe

This recipe came from the family of Dr. J.O. Colley who donated Beard Hospital to Troy State and thus helped start the TSU Foundation.

1/2 cup butter
1 cup flour
1 teaspoon salt
1/4 teaspoon red pepper
2 cups grated sharp cheese
Pecan halves

Cream butter and add sifted dry ingredients and cheese. Form into 2 rolls and chill. Slice thin and place pecan half on top of each round. Bake at 325 degrees for 10 minutes.

Margaret Pace Farmer
TSU '32

Tastes and Traditions

Bacon and Tomato Party Sandwiches

First Edition Favorite

This has been my most requested recipe, so here it is. It's also one of Jack's favorites.

1 tablespoon Durkee's Sauce
1 cup real mayonnaise
1 tablespoon fresh lemon juice
1/2 pound bacon, cooked and crumbled (no bacon bits)
1/4 cup chopped fresh parsley
Pinch of sugar
Fresh tomatoes, room temperature
White bread
Creole seasoning

Mix Durkee's, mayonnaise, lemon juice, bacon, parsley and sugar. Thinly slice tomatoes. Using biscuit cutter about the same size as the tomatoes, cut rounds out of white loaf bread. Spread mayonnaise mixture over bread rounds. Top with tomato slice and season lightly with Creole seasoning.

Janice Hawkins
TSU First Lady

Members of the Brundidge Alumni chapter enjoyed tailgating during 1999 Homecoming.

Appetizers

Hot Broccoli Dip

2 packages frozen broccoli, chopped
1 stick butter
1 medium onion, chopped fine
2 stalks celery, chopped
2 tablespoon flour
1 can mushroom soup
1 (4 ounce) can sliced mushrooms
dash of red pepper
1 (6 ounce) roll garlic cheese, diced
melba toast rounds

Cook broccoli according to directions. Melt butter in large saucepan. Add onions and celery, cook until onions are tender. Add flour, mushroom soup, mushrooms, red pepper and diced cheese. Cook over low heat, blending well. Drain broccoli, add to cheese mixture. Cook over low heat for 20 minutes. Remove from saucepan and place in chafing dish to keep warm while serving. Serve with melba toast rounds. Make ahead and refrigerate till ready to serve.

Teresa Wares
TSU

Delicious Hot Mustard

12 ounce "Coleman's" dry mustard
1/4 teaspoon red pepper
1/2 teaspoon white pepper
1/2 teaspoon black pepper
4 cups sugar
3 cups cider vinegar
2 teaspoon salt
6 eggs
1 stick butter

Mix mustard and peppers with enough water to make a thick paste. Set aside. Mix sugar, vinegar and salt together, boil until sugar melts. Remove from burner and pour into mustard mixture. Beat until smooth, return to pan. In a separate bowl beat six eggs very well, Pour eggs into mustard mixture and mix well. Return to heat, bring to boil, stirring frequently (careful not to scorch). Boil until mixture begins to thicken, remove from heat. Add 1 stick butter, stir until melted. Cool slightly and bottle. Yield: 8 pints.

Cheryl Dichiara
TSU '74

Tastes and Traditions

Spinach & Mushroom Quiche

Great for a large party. Bake on cookie sheet (with sides) and cut into 70-80 squares! Can also be made ahead and frozen. Thaw and warm.

Pastry Shell
1 1/2 sticks butter
5 tablespoons margarine
3 1/2 cups flour
1 tablespoon salt
ice water

Cut butter and margarine into flour and salt, add ice water gradually until pastry forms a ball (not sticky). Wrap in plastic wrap, chill 1 hour. Roll pastry on floured board into a rectangle (to fit large cookie sheet). Press into pan and flute edges. Chill 30 minutes. Line with foil and fill with dried beans. Bake for 15 minutes at 350°. Take out foil and beans. Bake 5 minutes longer. Sprinkle 1 cup grated swiss or gruyere cheese over crust before adding spinach mixture. Fill with filling and bake till lightly colored, puffed and set, about 30-40 minutes. Do not overcook.

Filling
6 green onions, chopped
1 pound mushrooms sliced thin
6 tablespoons butter
2 (10 ounce) packages frozen, chopped spinach
9 eggs
3 cups heavy cream
salt and pepper
1 teaspoon nutmeg
red pepper to taste

Sauté onions, mushrooms in butter. Thaw and squeeze out water in spinach, then add to mushrooms and onions. Mix together the eggs, cream, salt, pepper, nutmeg and red pepper and pour over cheese in crust to bake. Bake at 450°. This is a good appetizer or as a luncheon quiche. The spinach filling can also be served over rice or angel hair pasta with the cheese sprinkled on top.

Mamie Mason
TSU Friend

Appetizers

X Y Zucchini Appetizer

3 cups (4-small) zucchini, sliced
1 cup Bisquick baking mix
1/2 cup onion, finely chopped
1/2 cup Parmesan cheese
2 tablespoons parsley, snipped
1/2 teaspoon salt
1/2 teaspoon oregano
dash of pepper
1 clove garlic, mashed
1/2 cup vegetable oil
4 eggs, slightly beaten

Mix all ingredients together and spread in greased 9 x 13 inch baking dish. Bake at 350 degrees for 25 minutes until golden brown. Cut into bite size pieces. Makes 4 dozen.

Troy Bank and Trust
TSU Friend

Frozen Cucumber Pickles

This recipe is a favorite at our restaurant. When it isn't on the menu our diners are all anxious to know when it will return.

4 cups thinly sliced cucumbers
2 cups thinly sliced onions
1 tablespoon salt
2 tablespoons water
1 cup sugar
1/2 cup cider vinegar

In glass or stainless steel bowl, combine cucumbers, onions, salt and water. Let stand for 2 hours. Add sugar and vinegar. Stir. Pack lightly in glass or plastic container leaving space at top. Cover with juice and freeze.

Debbie Deese
TSU Friend
Red's Little Schoolhouse Restaurant
Grady, Alabama

Tastes and Traditions

Crab Mornay

1 stick butter
1/4 cup chives, chopped
2 tablespoons flour
1 pint half and half cream
1/2 pound swiss cheese, grated
1/2 cup parsley, chopped
1 tablespoon sherry wine
Red pepper and salt to taste
1 pound fresh white crabmeat

Melt butter in heavy pot and sauté onions. Blend in flour, cream and cheese until cheese is melted. Add other ingredients and gently fold in crabmeat. Serve in chafing dish with bagel chips or in patty shells.

Janice Hawkins
TSU First Lady

Crawfish & Eggplant Appetizer

Good as an appetizer in smaller portions or as an entrée. Men love it!

1 eggplant
Salt (to taste)
Flour
1 pound crawfish meat
Butter
Green onions
Garlic salt (to taste)
1 can cream of shrimp soup

Slice eggplant into 1/4 inch to 1/2 inch thick rounds. Salt and flour. Pan fry on each side (until crispy). Put on rack in warm oven. Sauté in pan; crawfish meat, small amount of butter, green onions and garlic salt to taste. Put crawfish mixture on top of eggplant. Heat soup and pour on top.

Harold and Carolyn McCray
TSU Friends

Beverages

Coffee Punch

This punch will serve around 40 people and needs no ice.

8 tablespoons instant coffee
2 cups sugar
3 quarts hot water
2 quarts milk
1 tablespoon vanilla
1 small can chocolate syrup
2 quarts vanilla ice cream
2 quarts coffee ice cream

Mix first three ingredients until the instant coffee and sugar are dissolved. Add the milk, vanilla, and chocolate syrup and mix well. Stir in the ice creams.

Mary Frances Parker
TSU

Springtime Punch

2 cups sugar
2 1/2 cups water
1 cup fresh lemon juice (3 - 4 lemons)
1 cup fresh orange juice (2 - 3 oranges)
1 (6 ounce) can frozen pineapple juice concentrate, thawed
2 quarts ginger ale, chilled

In a saucepan, bring sugar and water to a boil. Boil for 10 minutes; remove from heat. Stir in lemon, orange, and pineapple juices. Refrigerate. Just before serving, combine with ginger ale in a large punch bowl. Make 3 quarts.

Jean S. Helms
TSU Friend

Tastes and Traditions

Punch

This is great for parties.

1 small package cherry gelatin
2 cups hot water
1 cup sugar
1 1/2 quarts cold water
1 large can pineapple juice
2 bottles ginger ale

Combine cherry gelatin, hot water, and sugar. Mix until sugar dissolves. Add cold water. Keep this in refrigerator until ready to serve. Add pineapple juice and ginger ale just before serving. Serves 30.

Janis W. Stewart
TSU Friend

Old Hotel Vicksburg Punch

First Edition Favorite *This recipe was passed down by word of mouth until 1946, when it was tasted by Gen. Dwight D. Eisenhower at a reception in Vicksburg, Mississippi. He requested the recipe for Mamie because he enjoyed it so much.*

2 cups boiling water
1 cup sugar
1/2 - 1 cup lemon juice
3 (12 ounce) cans frozen orange juice, prepared according to directions
1 (46 ounce) can pineapple juice
1 (20 ounce) can crushed pineapple, with juice
1 (6 ounce) jar maraschino cherries, with juice
1 (32 ounce) bottle ginger ale

Boil water; add sugar and lemon juice. Boil for 5 minutes. Set aside to cool. Add orange juice, pineapple juice, pineapple and cherries. Chill. Just before serving, add ginger ale.

Carol W. Wright
TSUM '92

Beverages

Champagne Punch

First Edition Favorite

This may be the best punch recipe I've ever sampled. TSU graduate Van English gave me this wonderful recipe.

2 containers raspberry or pineapple sherbet
2 large bottles Ocean Spray pure cranberry juice
1 can jellied cranberry sauce with whole cranberries
1/2 cup lemon juice
2 bottles pink champagne
1 bottle Canada Dry ginger ale

Soften sherbet and place in punch bowl. Take spatula and spread sherbet to coat edges of bowl. Slowly pour in cranberry juice. Add cranberry sauce to center of bowl. Add lemon juice. Pour champagne while whipping sherbet with wire beater. While still whipping, add ginger ale. Serves 25.

Janice Hawkins
TSU First Lady

Mecosta Fruit Punch

First Edition Favorite

This is a punch with body and flavor.

2 quarts of tea (made with loose tea, not tea bags)
12 oranges
12 lemons
1 quart strawberry halves, fresh or frozen
1 jar maraschino cherries, halved, with juice
1 can crushed pineapple or pineapple chunks, with juice
1/2 bottle rum and 1/2 bottle Cointreau, optional

When tea cools, pour into punch bowl. Squeeze oranges and lemons, and pour juices into punch bowl. Add cherries, strawberries and pineapple, with their juices. (According to taste, 1/4 cup of sugar may be added at this time). Add about 60 ice cubes and stir thoroughly. Then if alcoholic but temperate punch is desired, add rum and Cointreau and stir again. Allow punch to stand at least 20 minutes before beginning to serve. The rum and Cointreau blend smoothly and almost imperceptibly with the fruit juices.

Russell A. Kirk
TSU Friend

Tastes and Traditions

Mint Tea

6-8 cups boiled water
6 mint tea bags
1 cup sugar
2 cups ginger ale
3/4 cup fresh lemon juice
1 cup pineapple juice

Steep tea in boiled water. Add sugar to hot tea. Add remaining ingredients and mix. Serve with ice ring. Garnish with fresh mint.

Janey Adams
TSU Parent

Christmas Instant Spiced Tea

This recipe can be made well in advance. Just keep it in your cabinet, and when you want a spicy hot drink, heat a cup of water and mix in the mixture to taste.

1/2 cup instant tea
2 cups Tang instant orange drink
1 cup sugar
1 tablespoon cinnamon
1 teaspoon ground cloves
1 package lemonade mix

Mix well. Store in an airtight container. Use 2 heaping teaspoons per cup of hot water.

Ray Smith
TSU

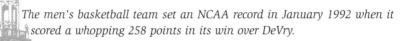

The men's basketball team set an NCAA record in January 1992 when it scored a whopping 258 points in its win over DeVry.

Beverages

Sangria

First Edition Favorite

Some friends from Portugal gave this recipe to me.

1/2 gallon red "fruity" wine (Chianti, Piasno, etc.)
Assorted fruit slices (apples, oranges, lemons, pears, etc.)
2 cups sugar
1 cup brandy
1 quart 7-Up or ginger ale
Cinnamon to taste

Combine wine, fruit slices, sugar and brandy in a large bowl. Let stand a minimum of 4 hours, stirring occasionally. Just prior to serving, add 7-Up or ginger ale and cinnamon to taste. May be served chilled or at room temperature.

Tips: Play with the fruit combinations a little. Pulpy fruits like apples and peaches make it a little sweeter; citrus fruits make it a little more dry.

The longer it stands (ferments) the better. For the holidays, I mix the basics in large, wide-mouth glass jars and cover with a cloth. I let it stand at least overnight, then use the jars as I need them for entertaining. It only gets better as it sits longer.

By the way, the fruit makes a great treat by itself.

Charlie Colvin
TSUM

TSU Chancellor Jack Hawkins, Jr. meets with Trojan football players Shawn Stuckey, left, and Maurice Stringer prior to the Division I-AA national semi-final playoff game against the University of Montana on December 14, 1996. The game, which was played in Missoula, took place on a field of solid ice. (Note: Shawn Stuckey now plays with the Buffalo Bills of the National Football league.)

Tastes and Traditions

Soups & Sauces

Taco Soup

Excellent substitute for chili on those cold nights.

1 1/2 pounds ground beef or ground turkey
1 package taco seasoning
1 package ranch dressing mix
1 can pinto beans, undrained
1 can kidney beans, undrained
1 can Rotel tomatoes or 1 can diced tomatoes, undrained
1 can whole kernel corn, undrained
Grated cheese
Fritos or tortilla chips

Brown meat, drain and add other ingredients. If on top of stove, simmer, stirring often, until well heated. If in crock pot, heat on low for 4 to 5 hours or on high 2 to 4 hours. Served topped with grated cheese over Fritos or tortilla chips.

Andrea Howell
TSU Student
Phi Mu Sorority

Mary G. Taylor
TSU

Deedee Hughes
TSU '92

Deborah Armstrong
TSU '73

Sara Jones
TSU Spouse

The Department of Speech and Theatre's production of Shakespeare's "A Midsummer Night's Dream" in fall 1998 was well received on campus and elsewhere. It was one of only six collegiate plays invited to participate in the Kennedy Center American College Theatre Festival regional competition in Richmond, Virginia.

Soups & Sauces

Steven's Gumbo

Steve loves to catch his crabs, clean, cook and pick the meat for this delicious gumbo! I like to go to the local fish market and purchase the already picked meat.

1 cup chopped onions
1 cup chopped green bell peppers
1 cup chopped celery
2 tablespoons vegetable oil
1/3 cup flour
1/2 teaspoon minced garlic
3 cups chicken broth
2 cups cooked rice
1 package smoked sausage
1 pound shrimp, shelled
1 pint oysters
1 pint crabmeat

Seasoning Mix:
1 teaspoon salt
1/4 teaspoon red pepper, black pepper and white pepper
1 bay leaf
1/4 teaspoon thyme and oregano leaves

Combine chopped onions, peppers and celery in bowl. Set aside. Mix together seasoning mix and set aside. Heat the oil in a large heavy skillet over medium high heat until it begins to smoke. Gradually add flour, whisking constantly, until the roux turns dark red-brown. Add half of vegetables and cook 2 minutes. Add rest of vegetables and cook 2 minutes more. Add minced garlic and seasoning mix. Cook 2 minutes. Place broth in large pan and bring to a boil. Add roux mixture by spoonfuls until all has been added and dissolved. Add the sausage. Cook 15 minutes. Add seafood and cook about 10 minutes. Serve over rice.

Mamie Mason
TSU Friend

TSU was named one of the top Southern regional universities by U.S. News & World Report 1999 College Guide.

Tastes and Traditions

Mammaw's Turkey Soup

As long as I can remember, my mother has made this soup using the turkey bones left over from Thanksgiving and Christmas dinners. All the girls in the family fight over a container to take home.

All turkey bones
2 large onions
3 stalks celery or more
2 - 3 large cans tomatoes
1 can tomato herb sauce
1 can tomato paste
1 can water to each can tomatoes

Begin by boiling the turkey bones until the remaining meat falls off the bone. Add other ingredients and boil together for several hours. Add celery salt, parsley flakes, whole oregano flakes, a pinch of basil leaves and crushed red pepper to the soup for seasonings. Add corn and drained butter beans or your favorite vegetables to the soup mixture. Spaghetti may also be added if you are not going to freeze it.

Mary Beth Green
TSU Friend

Cheddar Chowder Soup

This recipe can be prepared ahead of time and frozen until ready to serve. You may want to double the portions for best results!

2 cups water
2 cups diced potatoes
1 teaspoon salt
1/4 teaspoon pepper

White sauce:
1/4 cup butter
1/4 cup flour
2 cups milk
2 cups grated Cheddar cheese

1 cup cubed ham

Combine water, potatoes, salt and pepper in large kettle. Boil 10 to 12 minutes. Meanwhile, in a small saucepan, make white sauce by melting butter. Add flour and stir until smooth, about 1 minute. Slowly add milk and cook until thickened. Add grated cheese to white sauce and stir until melted. Add white sauce and cubed ham to kettle, heat through and enjoy!

Ashley A. Malchow
TSU Student
Kappa Delta Sorority

Soups & Sauces

Santa Fe Soup

This can be prepared ahead of time and frozen. The recipe makes enough for a large group. It's great for parties and football season. Delicious served with chips or cornbread.

2 pounds ground beef
1 large onion, chopped
2 packages taco seasoning
2 packages ranch dressing mix
2 cans shoepeg corn, drained
2 cans diced tomatoes
2 cups water
1 can Rotel tomatoes, undrained
1 can Black Beans, undrained
1 can pinto beans, undrained
1 can kidney beans, undrained

Toppings:
Grated cheese
Chopped green onions
Salsa
Sour cream

Tostitos, Fritos or cornbread

Brown and drain the ground beef in pot. Add chopped onion to meat and brown. Add taco seasoning, ranch dressing mix, shoepeg corn, diced tomatoes and water. Add Rotel tomatoes, black beans, pinto beans and kidney beans to pot and mix. Simmer all ingredients for approximately 2 hours. Garnish with grated cheese, green onions, salsa and sour cream. Serve with Tostitos, Fritos, or cornbread.

Denise Waddell
TSU '88, '90

Janice Blakeney
TSU Spouse

TSU's Department of Athletic Training is accredited by the prestigious Commission on Accreditation of Allied Health Education Programs. Graduates of this program have worked with sports teams across the country, including the New York Yankees.

Tastes and Traditions

Potato Soup

1 large onion, chopped
1/2 cup margarine
8 cups diced potatoes, cooked and drained
1 (10 3/4 ounce) can cream of mushroom soup, undiluted
1 (10 3/4 ounce) can cream of chicken soup, undiluted
Salt and black pepper to taste
Milk

Sauté onion in margarine until tender. Place onion and potatoes in stockpot. Stir in soups, season with salt and black pepper and add milk to preferred consistency. Bring to a boil, reduce heat and simmer until flavors are blended. Yield: 8 to 12 servings

Variation: Sauté 6 slices turkey bacon, remove from skillet, drain and crumble. Sauté onion in margarine added to bacon drippings. Sprinkle bacon bits on individual servings of soup. Cream of broccoli soup may be substituted for other cream soups.

Debbie Fortune
TSU

The TSU campus was a veritable boomtown during the 1990s. Buildings renovated and constructed during the decade include the Pace Hall Rotary International Center, Scrushy Field at Memorial Stadium, the TSU Science Center, Trojan Arena and Sartain Hall, Shackelford Hall, the Claudia Crosby Theater in Smith Hall, the Hawkins Adams Long Hall of Honor and the Adams Student Center. Smith Hall, shown here undergoing renovation in July 1999, was one of many buildings refurbished during the 1990s.

Soups & Sauces

Baked Potato Soup

My fiance's father gave me this recipe two years ago. Since then, I have added things and omitted things and now I make it better than he does, but don't tell him I said that!

1 medium onion, chopped
2 medium carrots, peeled and chopped
5 medium baking potatoes, peeled
1 can cream of potato soup
2 tablespoons butter
1/3 cup milk or cream
Salt and pepper to taste

Toppings:
Chopped scallions, bacon pieces and shredded Cheddar cheese

Place onion and carrots in stew pot with enough water to cover. Cube three potatoes and add to stew pot. Boil until tender. Meanwhile, cube remaining potatoes, place in a separate pot and boil until tender. Drain two-thirds of water from carrots, onion, and potatoes mixture. Pour remaining water along with vegetables into blender. Blend until smooth. Return to stew pot. Drain all water from other pot and add potato cubes to stew pot with blended mixture. Add canned soup and warm through. Finish with butter and milk and stir until creamy. Serve with warm cheese biscuits and toppings.

Holly Hudson
TSU Student

Broccoli Soup

1 onion, chopped
1 stick butter
1 can cream of celery soup
2 cans cream of mushroom soup
3 soup cans of milk
8 ounces Velveeta Mexican cheese, cubed
2 packages frozen chopped broccoli
Salt and pepper to taste

Sauté onions in butter. Add celery and mushroom soups and milk and mix until smooth. Stir in cheese and broccoli. Simmer 30 minutes. Be careful not to cook too long!

Heather Moran
TSU Student
Phi Mu Sorority

Tastes and Traditions

Vegetable Soup

My husband always likes soup on Sunday night for supper, served with my quick cornbread.

1 package stew meat, fat removed, chopped
1 large onion, chopped
4 stalks celery, chopped
4 large carrots, chopped or sliced
1 large can tomatoes, undrained
1 can chicken broth
3 medium potatoes, peeled and quartered
1 can mixed vegetables or 1 small can English peas and 1 small can
    butterbeans, drained

Place meat in soup pot and add enough water to cover. Bring to a boil, reduce heat and simmer. Add onion, celery, carrots, and tomatoes. Add chicken broth and potatoes. A few minutes later add canned vegetables. Cook slowly until meat and vegetables are done. For a thicker soup, add small amounts of macaroni. Variation: use chicken and beef broth.

Frances Cox Jones
TSU Friend

Pea Soup

One year, we were hosting the state convention for the American Association of University Women here at Troy State. I was a bit unstrung from trying to coordinate the activities, but Dr. Eloise Kirk invited me to her home and served me this soup. It soothed me. This is her recipe.

1 pound (2 1/2 cups) split peas
2 - 3 pounds of ham
1 carrot sliced
1 stalk celery sliced
1 - 2 potatoes, quartered
1/4 teaspoon pepper
Salt to taste

Wash and soak peas overnight. Place peas and ham in 3 quarts water, bring to boil, then reduce heat and simmer. Remove ham; dice and return to soup. Add carrot, celery, potatoes, pepper and salt. Cook 3 1/2 to 5 hours until it is thick.

Margaret Pace Farmer
TSU '32

Soups & Sauces

Williamsburg Tasty Turkey Soup

This recipe takes advantage of leftover holiday turkey or can be made with a whole chicken. Serve with French bread or cornbread. It makes enough to feed a crowd.

1 turkey carcass or whole chicken
4 quarts water
1 cup butter or margarine
1 cup all-purpose flour
3 onions, chopped
2 large carrots, diced
2 stalks celery, diced
1 1/2 cups long-grain rice, uncooked
2 teaspoons salt
3/4 teaspoon pepper
2 cups half and half

Place turkey carcass or whole chicken and water in large Dutch oven; bring to a boil. Cover, reduce heat, and simmer 1 hour. Remove turkey or chicken from broth, and pick meat from bone. Set broth and meat aside. Measure broth and add water, if necessary, to measure 3 quarts. Heat butter in a large Dutch oven; add flour, and cook over medium heat, stirring constantly, 5 minutes. (Roux will be a very light color.) Stir onion, carrots and celery into roux; cook over medium heat 10 minutes, stirring often. Add broth, turkey or chicken, rice, salt and pepper; bring to a boil. Cover, reduce heat and simmer 20 minutes or until rice is tender. Add half and half, and simmer until thoroughly heated. Makes 4 1/2 quarts.

Faye and Gerald Dial
TSU Board of Trustees

The Trojan Express Food Court, located in the Adams Student Center, opened to rave reviews from students, faculty and staff in September 1999.

Tastes and Traditions

Michele's Spaghetti Sauce

1 cup chopped onion
Vegetable oil
3 large cans crushed tomatoes, undrained
Black pepper
1 1/2 teaspoons oregano
2 teaspoons sugar
1/2 teaspoon baking soda
1 pound ground beef
1 pound smoked sausage

Sauté onion in small amount of oil. Add tomatoes and spices. Bring to a boil, reduce heat and simmer one hour. Brown ground beef and sausage. Drain. Add to tomato sauce. Simmer one hour. Serve over noodles.

Michele Armstrong Andrews
TSU '72

Beer Cheese Spaghetti Sauce

I acquired this recipe in the early '90s while I was visiting friends stationed in Belgium. It's one of my favorite dishes to serve guests. It passed the test of my family years ago during a Christmas vacation. My husband and I cooked what we call "dueling spaghettis" -- a red sauce and this sauce. It was a hit, even with the skeptics!

1 cup finely chopped celery
1 cup grated carrots
2 cups chicken broth
6 tablespoons butter
6 tablespoons flour
1/4 cup chopped onion
1 (13 ounce) jar processed cheese
Milk
Beer

Cook celery and carrots in broth until tender. Sauté onion in butter. Add flour and cook, stirring, until smooth. Add to carrots and celery. Stir in cheese. Add 1 part milk to 1 part beer until desired thickness (usually about a half to two-thirds a can of beer). Cook over medium heat until hot. This is best when served along with a red sauce, with half red and half beer cheese on top of pasta. You can use any bottled or canned spaghetti sauce, but for the absolute best flavors, prepare Graham's Spaghetti Sauce.

Lt. Col. Rebecca Graham Abraham
TSU '81

Soups & Sauces

Graham's Spaghetti Sauce

In the summer of 1953, my family went on a picnic at Camp Grist, just outside Selma, Alabama. Upon their return home, their neighbor, Sgt. Larry Garcia, brought over a pot of his family recipe spaghetti sauce. That recipe became our family's favorite, and has now traveled the world. The recipe is easily doubled or tripled, so it's great for crowds.

1 - 1 1/2 pounds ground beef
1 large bell pepper, diced
1 large onion, diced
3 stalks celery, diced
1 ounce olive oil
1/2 teaspoon oregano
1/2 teaspoon curry powder
2 - 3 bay leaves
1 (16 ounce) can tomato sauce
1 clove garlic, minced, or equivalent garlic powder
1 package sliced pepperoni
1/2 teaspoon Kitchen Bouquet
Salt and pepper to taste

Sauté onions, pepper, and celery in olive oil until wilted. Brown meat; drain. Add wilted vegetables and remaining ingredients. Use as much of the pepperoni as you want; I recommend at least half the package. If sauce appears too thin, add more tomato sauce. Cook on low 1 to 2 hours. Serve over hot pasta.

Lt. Col. Rebecca Graham Abraham
TSU '81

Orange Sauce

This was served at Forty-Niners Study Club meetings.

1/2 cup milk
2 tablespoons flour
1 1/2 tablespoons butter, melted
Juice of 1 1/2 lemons
1 small can orange juice, undiluted
1/2 pint whipping cream

Combine all ingredients except whipping cream and chill. When ready to serve, whip cream and fold into sauce. Serve on slices of angelfood cake.

Frances Cox Jones
TSU Friend

Tastes and Traditions

Adelaide's White Cream Sauce

This is a family favorite. Good and easy. Just add a salad or green vegetable and enjoy a full meal.

3 tablespoons butter
3 tablespoons flour
2 cups milk
Salt and pepper to taste

Melt butter in saucepan. Blend in flour. Pour milk in slowly and stir constantly until sauce thickens.

Add any one of the following: salmon, cheese, chicken, turkey, chipped beef. Serve over toast points or rice.

Sherry J. Dye
TSU Spouse

Orange Sauce for Meat

This is the recipe of Holly Farmer Barnard. She used this sauce for chicken as well as duck. It will work for any poultry.

1/3 cup brown sugar
1/3 cup white sugar
1 tablespoon cornstarch
1 tablespoon orange rind
1 cup orange juice
1/4 teaspoon salt

Stir ingredients over low heat until sugars dissolve. Simmer until transparent and thick, about 3 minutes. Makes 1 1/2 cups.

Margaret Pace Farmer
TSU '32

The Miss TSU Pageant was named the "best large pageant" in the state in 1999. The winner of Miss TSU competes for the Miss Alabama crown each year.

Soups & Sauces

Homemade Barbeque Sauce

This recipe was created by Jessie Mae Hillery, the great-grandmother of TSU student Clovia Shanae Jackson, and given to her by her grandmother, Gussie Daniels.

1 medium onion, grated
1 cup canned tomatoes
1/4 cup vinegar
1/4 cup Worcestershire sauce
1/4 cup brown sugar
2 teaspoons mustard
1 teaspoon salt
1 teaspoon lemon juice
2 tablespoons margarine

Combine all the ingredients in a saucepan, bring to a boil, reduce heat and simmer for 30 minutes.
Yield 2 cups.

Clovia Jackson
TSU Student

Some 350 young women gathered at TSU in June 2000 for Girls State, the annual mock legislative and leadership forum for Alabama's top female high school seniors. The event marked the first time in 50 years that Girls States had been held outside of Montgomery.

Tastes and Traditions

Pear Relish

8 quarts pears, peeled and quartered
5 green bell peppers, quartered and seeds removed
5 red bell peppers, quartered and seeds removed
3 hot peppers
5 large onions
5 cups apple cider vinegar
5 cups sugar
1 teaspoon salt

Grind pears in food processor (or coarse food grinder or chopper, the old way). Drain in cheese cloth or strainer until excess juice is removed. Grind peppers and onions. Combine all ingredients, bring to a boil and cook 45 minutes. Place in scalded half pint jars. Seal.

Dr. J. Allen Jones' mother made pear relish when he was growing up. He started making his own pear relish in 1952 and has been making it ever since.

Frances Cox Jones
TSU Friend

My mother, Amorette Brabham Harrison, used this recipe she got from Auburn University's Food Preservation book. (I omit the boiling and haven't died yet.)

Allene Snider
TSU Friend

Greek Week festivities traditionally culminate with the fraternity tug-of-war. Here, members of Sigma Chi put their backs--and--faces to work in the 2000 competition.

Soups & Sauces

Cream of Peanut Soup

For all you peanut lovers out there, you've got to try this!

1 tablespoon butter
2 tablespoons finely chopped onion
1 tablespoon flour
1 quart milk
1/2 cup peanut butter
1/4 teaspoon celery salt
1/2 cup finely chopped dry roasted peanuts (optional)

Melt butter, add onion, sauté until soft but not brown. Add flour and cook until foamy. Add milk, peanut butter and celery seed. Cook in double boiler until creamy. You may strain through a fine sieve or serve as is. Add peanuts, taste for seasonings. Serves 4.

Michael Aul
TSU Student
AFROTC

Curried Cream Cheese Soup

4 (3-ounce) packages cream cheese
2 cups canned beef consommé
3/4 teaspoon curry powder
1/2 medium garlic clove
salt and pepper

Put in blender and purée on full speed until smooth. Taste for seasonings. Refrigerate and serve very cold. Add shrimp or slivered chicken, if you like.

Tom Strother
TSU

All of the TSU System's Alabama campuses are equipped with electronic distance education classrooms. Two-way video and audio systems in these high-tech facilities allow the System's students and faculty to meet with each other without traveling the miles that separate the System's campuses.

Tastes and Traditions

Cream of Mushroom Soup

Simply the best mushroom soup you will ever have.

1 1/2 pounds fresh mushrooms
1 stick unsalted butter
2 finely chopped shallots
6 tablespoons flour
6 cups chicken stock, fresh or canned (low salt if you use canned)
2 egg yolks
3/4 cups heavy cream
salt and pepper (white pepper is best)
1/4 cup sherry

In a large stainless-steel skillet melt 4 tablespoons of the butter over moderate heat. Add the sliced mushrooms and shallots and cook them, tossing them constantly with a wooden spoon, for 2 minutes or until they are lightly colored. With a slotted spoon, transfer them to a bowl and set them aside. In a heavy 4 to 6 quart saucepan, melt the remaining butter over moderate heat. Remove the pan from the heat and whisk in the 6 tablespoons of flour, then cook over low heat, stirring constantly, for 1 or 2 minutes. Do not let this roux brown. Remove the pan from the heat, let cool a few seconds. then pour in the chicken stock, beating constantly with a wire whisk to blend stock and roux. Return to heat and stir until this cream soup base comes to a boil, thickens and is perfectly smooth. Then add the chopped mushrooms and shallots and simmer, stirring occasionally, for 15 minutes. (Note: If you don't like chunky soup, pureé soup base in food processor at this point. You can pureé half or all depending on your taste) With a wire whisk, blend the egg yolks and the cream together in a bowl. Whisk in some of the hot soup, 2 tablespoons at a time, until 1/2 cup has been added. Then reverse the process and slowly whisk the now-warm egg-yolk-and-cream mixture into the soup. Add sherry. Bring to a boil, and boil for 30 seconds, stirring constantly. Remove the pan from the heat. Taste and season with salt and pepper. Serves 6.

Dick Pridgen
TSU Friend

An unwelcome visitor came to Troy in October 1995 when Hurricane Opal ripped through campus. The storm uprooted many of the university's hallmark pecan trees and caused some $1 million in damage to the campus.

Soups & Sauces

Carrot Soup

2 tablespoons butter
3/4 cup finely chopped onion
3 cups finely chopped carrots
1 quart chicken stock, fresh or canned (low salt, if canned)
2 teaspoons tomato paste
2 tablespoons plain white rice, uncooked
Salt
White pepper
1/2 cup heavy cream
1 tablespoon unsalted butter, softened

In a heavy 3- to 4-quart saucepan, melt the butter over moderate heat. Stir in the onions and cook, stirring occasionally for 5 minutes, or until they are soft but not browned. Add the carrots, chicken stock, tomato paste and rice, and simmer gently, uncovered for 30 minutes. Pureé the soup in food processor and put back into pan. Season it with salt and white pepper, and stir in the cream. Before serving, return the soup to low heat and bring it to a simmer. Remove the pan from the heat and stir in the tablespoon of soft butter. Ladle the soup into a tureen or into individual soup bowls and garnish with chopped parsley.

Cheryl Colley Dichiara
TSU '74

Quick Crab Bisque

Delicious! People will think you have worked all day.

1 cup crabmeat, fresh or frozen
1 can cream of mushroom soup, undiluted
1 can cream of asparagus soup, undiluted
1 cup light cream
1 3/4 cups milk
1/2 teaspoon Worcestershire sauce
1/2 teaspoon Tabasco
1/3 cup dry sherry

Mix all ingredients in a saucepan and heat on low heat until hot. Do not boil. Serves 6

Doug and Rachel Hawkins
TSU Board of Trustees

Tastes and Traditions

Corn and Shrimp Chowder

You may substitute crawfish or chicken for shrimp. Also, try leaving out tomato and cheese if you want true corn chowder. This is a wonderful soup.

1/4 cup butter
1 medium onion, chopped
1 large tomato, peeled and chopped
1/4 cup all-purpose flour
4 cups water
3 chicken bouillon cubes
2 cups fresh or canned whole kernel corn or 1 (10-ounce) package frozen corn
1 (14 3/4 ounce) can cream style corn
8 ounces shrimp, peeled and deveined
4 ounces shredded smoked cheddar cheese
1 cup half and half or light cream
2 tablespoons snipped chives or parsley

Melt butter in a 4 to 5 quart Dutch oven. Cook onion until tender but not brown. Stir in tomato and flour. Cook and stir over medium heat for 3 minutes. Stir in the water, bouillon cubes, and corn. Bring to boil; reduce heat. Cover and simmer about 20 minutes. Add shrimp. Return to boil; reduce heat. Simmer, uncovered, for 3 minutes or until shrimp is pink. Stir in the cheese and cream. Heat and stir until cheese is melted. Top with chives or parsley. Season to taste with cracked black pepper.

Allen and Annette Owen
TSU Board of Trustees

Curry Dressing

A wonderful change from the same old salad dressings. Great served on Alabama sliced tomatoes, sliced eggs and bibb lettuce.

1 cup sour cream
2 cups mayonnaise
1 tablespoon grated onion or juice
1 tablespoon fresh lemon juice
1 teaspoon curry powder

Combine all ingredients and chill before serving.

Rachel Rodgers
TSU Student

Soups & Sauces

Divine Dressing for Fruit Salad

This was given to me many years ago by my lovely 90-year-young neighbor.
It is an old-fashioned recipe but delicious.

1 package (3 ounces) cream cheese, softened
3 tablespoons mayonnaise
1 cup heavy cream, whipped
2 tablespoons fresh lemon juice

Combine all ingredients and chill. Serve over tropical fruit (canned or a jar
of fresh tropical fruit from produce department) thoroughly drained of
juices. Mix fruit with dressing and chill overnight. This is so good.

Janice Hawkins
TSU First Lady

Fruit Salad Dressing

This recipe came from the Stork Club in New York City.

1/2 cup sugar
1 teaspoon paprika
1 teaspoon celery salt
1 cup vegetable oil
2 tablespoons lemon juice
1 teaspoon celery seed
1 teaspoon onion juice
1 teaspoon dry mustard
2 tablespoons vinegar
2/3 teaspoons salt

Mix dry ingredients and liquid separately. Pour liquid over dry ingredients
very slowly. Beat hard. Start with a few drops of vinegar and lemon juice,
then start oil. It should be thick and look like fig jam.

Janie Ketchum
TSU '73

Tastes and Traditions

Mango Vinaigrette Salad Dressing

2 cups mango puree (found in produce department)
4 limes - squeezed
1/2 teaspoon fresh grated ginger
4 tablespoons fresh cilantro, chopped
2 shallots, finely chopped
1 cup olive oil
1 teaspoon salt and pepper
1/2 teaspoon cayenne

Process everything but olive oil. Slowly add oil. Serve over crisp spring greens.

Tom Davis
TSU

Cucumber Sauce

Mix and season to taste. Serve with red snapper or whole salmon.

3 cups chopped cucumbers, peeled and seeded
1/3 cup chopped green onion
1 1/2 teaspoons lemon juice
1 1/2 cups sour cream
2 tablespoons mayonnaise
few drops worcestershire sauce
salt and white pepper

Reba Allen
TSU

Mustard Sauce for Shellfish

3 1/2 teaspoons dry Coleman's mustard
1 cup mayonnaise
2 teaspoons Worcestershire sauce
1 teaspoon A1 sauce
1/8 cup half and half cream
1/8 teaspoon salt

Blend and chill. Serve with stone crab claws or other shellfish.

Donald Norsworthy
TSU

Soups & Sauces

Marinade for Beef Tenderloin 1

1 cup red wine
1/2 cup soy sauce
1 cup orange juice
1 tablespoon thyme
1 tablespoon rosemary
1/4 cup Worcestershire sauce
1 cup onions, chopped
6 cloves garlic, chopped
1 tablespoon black pepper

Marinate for up to 3 days in refrigerator. Cook tenderloin at 450 degrees for 30 minutes (don't open oven door).

Sharon Litchfield
TSU Friend

Marinade for Beef Tenderloin 2

1/4 cup olive oil
1 cup red wine
1/4 cup soy sauce
4 cloves garlic, crushed
2 bay leaves
lots of black pepper

Put meat in zip lock bag and marinate overnight in refrigerator.

Mamie Mason
TSU Friend

Apricot Pork Tenderloin

This can be used on the grill but it makes a mess, so I usually cook it in the oven. Men love this recipe.

1/4 cup olive oil
1/2 cup white wine Worcestershire sauce
1/2 jar apricot preserves
1 tablespoon minced garlic
Pork tenderloin

Combine all ingredients except pork and bring to a boil. Pour sauce over pork tenderloin and cook 30 minutes per pound at 350 degrees.

Nancy Bradshaw
TSU Friend

Tastes and Traditions

Salads

Endive and Pear Salad with Gorgonzola Cream Dressing

This was served at a luncheon honoring award-winning actress Polly Holliday in April 1999.

4 tablespoons apple cider vinegar, divided
3 tablespoons olive oil
1 tablespoon honey
4 large heads Belgian endive, sliced
1 large pear, halved, cored and sliced
1/3 cup sour cream
1/3 cup plain yogurt
1 1/4 cups crumbled Gorgonzola cheese
1/2 cup hazelnuts, toasted and husked
Chopped fresh chives

Whisk 3 tablespoons vinegar, oil and honey in large bowl to blend. Add endive and pear and toss to coat. Blend sour cream, yogurt and remaining 1 tablespoon vinegar in medium bowl; mix in cheese. Season dressing to taste with salt and pepper. Mound pear salad on platter. Top with dressing, then nuts and chives.

Sodexho-Marriott
TSU

Golden Globe award-winning actress Polly Holliday – perhaps best known as Flo in the sitcom "Alice" – served as visiting professor of theatre in April 1999.

= Salads

Caesar Salad

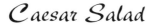

First Edition Favorite *This is Jimmy's favorite recipe. Jimmy has enjoyed being the "Team Doc" for Troy State for more than 25 years. It is a family tradition to attend TSU football games.*

1 large clove garlic
1 tin flat anchovy fillets
1/2 teaspoon salt
1/4 teaspoon black pepper
1 teaspoon Dijon mustard
1 whole egg
2 tablespoons Worcestershire sauce
6 tablespoons olive oil
4 tablespoons tarragon vinegar
Juice of 1 lemon
2 large bunches Romaine lettuce
1/2 cup grated Parmesan cheese
1 1/2 cups croutons

Rub wooden bowl with garlic clove. With a spoon, mash the anchovies to a pulp in bottom of bowl. Add salt, pepper, and mustard; mix well. Break egg into bowl and mix well. Add Worcestershire, oil, vinegar and lemon juice. Allow this to set for 3 minutes in refrigerator. When ready to serve, tear lettuce into bowl. Add cheese, croutons, and dressing and toss. Serve on salad plates.

James and Jenelle Andrews
TSU Board of Trustees

The remodeled Richard M. Scrushy Field at Memorial Stadium opened in September 1998. The first-class facility was made possible by gifts of $4.5 million from the City of Troy and $1 million from Richard M. Scrushy.

Tastes and Traditions

Royal Curried Chicken Salad

1/2 cup sliced almonds, toasted
2 cups cooked chicken, chopped
1/4 cup chopped water chestnuts
1/2 pound seedless green grapes, halved
1 (8 ounce) can pineapple chunks, drained
1/2 cup chopped celery
3/4 cup mayonnaise
1 teaspoon curry powder
2 teaspoons lemon juice
2 teaspoons soy sauce
2 avocados

Combine first 6 ingredients in a large bowl; set aside. Combine mayonnaise, curry powder, lemon juice and soy sauce in a bowl; spoon mixture over chicken mixture, and toss gently to coat. Cover and chill at least 4 hours. Peel and chop avocados; sprinkle over salad, and serve immediately. Yield: 6 servings.

Carla (Musgrove) Meadows
TSU Friend

The International Student Cultural Organization (ISCO) promotes friendship and cultural exchange between TSU's international and American students. Each year, ISCO sponsors a festival in which students prepare foods and dress in traditional costumes from their native countries.

Salads

Chicken Salad

4 chicken breasts, boiled and chopped
1 cup chopped pecans
1 cup chopped celery
1 cup chopped apple
2 hard-cooked eggs, chopped
1 tablespoon chopped onion
2 tablespoons chopped sweet pickles
Salt and pepper to taste
Mayonnaise

Combine all ingredients, using enough mayonnaise to achieve desired moistness. Cover and refrigerate.

Torri West
TSU Student
Alpha Gamma Delta Sorority

West Indies Salad

First Edition Favorite

This recipe is a favorite dish in my hometown of Mobile.

Prepare at least 24 hours in advance.

1 medium onion, chopped very fine
1 stalk celery, chopped very fine, or 1 teaspoon celery seed
4 ounces ice water
2 bay leaves
Salt and pepper to taste
1 pound white lump crab meat
4 ounces salad oil
3 ounces cider vinegar
Green leaf lettuce
1/2 ripe cantaloupe, sliced into thin wedges
Lemon wedges
1/2 cup chopped parsley

Mix onions, celery, water, bay leaves, seasonings, and crab meat; toss lightly. Mix oil and vinegar. Pour to cover crab meat. Do not break up crab meat. It should remain in lumps. Turn gently into a glass bowl. Cover and refrigerate. To serve, arrange a bed of leaf lettuce. Place the melon wedges in a circle on the lettuce. Use a slotted spoon to lift crab meat from marinade and place in the center of the melon. Garnish with lemon wedges and sprinkle chopped parsley over crab meat. Serves four.

J. Gary Cooper
TSU Friend

Tastes and Traditions

Hot Chicken Salad

2 cups diced chicken
2 cups sliced celery
1/2 cup broken pecans or slivered almonds, toasted
1/2 teaspoon Accent
2 teaspoons lemon juice
2 teaspoons grated onion
1 cup mayonnaise
3/4 cup crushed potato chips

Combine all ingredients except potato chips. Spoon into a greased baking dish and cover with potato chips. Bake at 400 degrees for 18 to 20 minutes.

Jean W. Laliberte
TSU

Smoked Chicken Salad

Tired of the same old chicken salad? Try this for a different taste. Smoke your own chicken or purchase one already smoked. Great way to use leftover holiday turkey also!

4 whole fryers or 2 turkey breasts, smoked
1 cup chopped celery
1 cup chopped green onions
1 cup chopped pecans, toasted
1/2 cup chopped fresh parsley
1/2 cup chopped fresh basil
1 cup chopped sun-dried tomatoes
Liberal sprinkle lemon pepper and salt
Dressing:
2 cups mayonnaise
1 cup Durkee's Dressing
1/2 cup red wine vinegar
1/2 cup sugar

Combine chicken or turkey with remaining salad ingredients. Mix dressing ingredients, blending well. Pour dressing over salad and mix thoroughly. Cover and refrigerate overnight to mingle flavors. Fills about 100 small tart shells or use for sandwiches or salads.

Mamie Mason
TSU Friend

Salads

Pasta Salad

1 (16 ounce) package pasta shells
1 1/2 pounds crab or "sea legs"
1/2 cup sliced green onions
1 package frozen peas, slightly cooked
1 tomato, chopped
1/2 cup mayonnaise
1/2 cup sour cream
1 tablespoon Dijon mustard
1 teaspoon vinegar
1 teaspoon salt
1/4 teaspoon pepper
1/2 cup black olives

Cook shells according to package directions and drain. Add crab meat,
onions, peas and tomato. Blend mayonnaise, sour cream, mustard, vinegar
and salt and pepper. Pour over pasta mixture and toss to coat. Make 12
cups.

Vicki Schmidt
TSU

Colonial Cranberry Salad

*My late sister-in-law, Susan Varner of Augusta, Georgia, liked to make this
for Thanksgiving. My own family has adopted the same tradition.*

1 cup sugar
2 cups fresh cranberries
1 (6 ounce) package strawberry gelatin
2 tablespoons lemon juice
1 tablespoon brandy
1 (3 ounce) package cream cheese, cut in small cubes
1/2 cup chopped nuts (walnuts go well)
1 cup chopped celery
1 cup chopped apples

Combine 1 cup water, sugar and cranberries in a medium saucepan. Bring
to a boil. Remove from heat, cover and let cool 5 minutes. Combine 1 cup
boiling water and gelatin. Add 1 cup cold water, cranberry mixture and
lemon juice. Chill until partly set. Fold in remaining ingredients. Chill until
firm.

Jane Varner
TSUM '98

Tastes and Traditions

Cranberry Salad

This recipe had to be doubled for our family of 11 since the small grandchildren decided they liked it. My mother, Evelyn Upchurch Cox of Carrollton, Alabama, tripled this recipe for all of us and our college friends when we were growing up.

1 cup ground, raw cranberries (measure after putting through blender)
1/4 cup sugar
1 package raspberry gelatin
1/2 cup boiling water
3/4 package plain gelatin with enough cold water to dissolve
1/4 cup fresh orange juice or fresh orange pieces
1 teaspoon grated orange rind
Juice of 3 fresh lemons
1 (9 ounce) can crushed pineapple, drained
1/2 cup chopped celery
1/2 cup chopped nuts

Mix ground cranberries and sugar. Add raspberry gelatin to boiling water. Add plain gelatin to a little cold water. Stir and add to hot gelatin. Add other ingredients and pour into one large mold or into individual molds that are lightly oiled. Makes 5 or 6 custard cups. When ready to serve, run knife around edge of mold and salad comes out easily. Serve on lettuce with mayonnaise.

Frances Cox Jones
TSU Friend

Seven Cup Salad

1 cup crushed pineapple, drained
1 cup chopped pecans
1 cup fruit cocktail, drained
1 cup cottage cheese
1 cup coconut
1 cup mayonnaise
1 cup sour cream
Lettuce cups

Combine first five ingredients in medium bowl. Blend mayonnaise and sour cream in small bowl. Add to pineapple mixture and mix lightly. Chill in refrigerator for 30 to 45 minutes. Serve in lettuce cups.

Leigh Tranum
TSU Student
Phi Mu Sorority

Salads

Strawberry Pretzel Salad

1 (10 ounce) bag (2 2/3 cups) pretzels, crushed to fine crumbs
3/4 cups margarine, melted
1 cup plus 3 tablespoons sugar, divided
1 (8 ounce) package cream cheese, softened
1 (1 1/2 ounce) package whipped topping mix or 2 cups frozen whipped
   topping, thawed
1 (6 ounce) package strawberry gelatin
3 cups boiling water
1 (16 ounce) package frozen strawberries

Combine pretzels, margarine and 3 tablespoons sugar. Press into a 9 x 13-
pan and bake at 350 degrees for 10 minutes. Cool. Mix cream cheese with
remaining sugar and whipped topping. Spread over the cooled crust.
Dissolve gelatin in boiling water; drop frozen strawberries into gelatin and
let thicken slightly in the refrigerator. Pour over topping mixture. Chill until
set. Yield: 12-20 servings.

Mildred Finlay
TSU

Charlotte Hall
TSU '69

Salad Dressing

*A family friend, Mrs. Margaret Hendrie, gave me this recipe many years
ago. The amazing thing is that she did not cook, but this salad dressing is
wonderful. Use on fresh spring greens, thoroughly dried so the dressing will
cling to the leaves. Add your favorite salad ingredients. We like blue cheese
and sunflower seeds.*

1 1/2 teaspoons salt
3 dashes of Tabasco
1/4 teaspoon Worcestershire sauce
1 tablespoon malt vinegar
1 tablespoon tarragon vinegar
1 tablespoon cider vinegar
1 tablespoon lemon juice
1/2 teaspoon garlic salt
11 tablespoons cooking or olive oil

Combine all ingredients and blend well.

Janice Hawkins
TSU First Lady

Tastes and Traditions

Gazpacho Salad

This is a wonderful form of the old tomato aspic. Try it.

3 packages unflavored gelatin
2/3 cup cold water
1 1/2 cups tomato juice
1 1/2 cups V-8 juice
3 - 4 fresh tomatoes
1 small green pepper
1 cup celery
1 cup radishes
1 small cucumber
1 green onion
3 tablespoons red wine vinegar
2 tablespoons fresh lemon
1 teaspoon hot sauce
2 - 3 dashes Worcestershire sauce and red pepper
Roquefort Dressing

Dissolve gelatin in water. Heat to boiling tomato juice and V-8 juice and stir in gelatin. Mince tomatoes, peppers, celery, radishes, cucumber and onion and add to mixture. Add red wine vinegar, lemon juice, hot sauce, Worcestershire and red pepper. Top with dressing.

Eloise Hood
TSU Friend

Taco Salad

1 pound hamburger meat
1 small can tomato sauce
1 package taco mix plus water according to package directions
1 package Frito's scoops
Shredded mozzarella, Cheddar or American cheese, optional
Optional toppings: lettuce, tomato, etc.

Brown meat, drain. Add tomato sauce, taco mix and water and heat to boil. Line 9 x 13-inch casserole dish with half of chips. Top with beef mixture. Add remaining chips. Bake till heated through. Top with cheese, if desired, and return to oven until cheese is melted. Before serving at lettuce and tomato if desired.

Carrie Rogers
TSU Student

Salads

Blueberry Congealed Salad

Our family loves this salad. Aunt Sharon Goff has a standing obligation to prepare it at Thanksgiving, Christmas and any other holiday or family gathering.

1 large can crushed pineapple, drained and juice reserved
1 large can blueberries, drained and juice reserved
2 packages blackberry Jello
2 cups cold water
1/2 cup chopped nuts
Topping:
1 (8 ounce) package cream cheese
1 cup sour cream
1/3 cup sugar

Heat reserved juices. Dissolve Jello in juice, add cold water and let thicken. Add fruits and nuts and congeal. Mix topping and spread over salad. Refrigerate.

Amy Shively
TSU Student

Lime Congealed Salad

This makes a great summer meal when accompanied by other salads.

1 (6 ounce) package lime gelatin
1 large can crushed pineapple in heavy syrup, drained and juice reserved
1 (8 ounce) package cream cheese, softened
1/2 cup crushed pecans or walnuts

Dissolve gelatin in 2 cups boiling water. Add enough cold water to reserved juice to make 2 cups. Stir into gelatin. Chill gelatin in refrigerator or freezer until slightly jelled. Combined cream cheese, pineapple and nuts and beat until smooth consistency. Add mixture to slightly jelled gelatin and whip until well blended. Pour into mold and chill until set. Enjoy.

Micki Sims
TSU '00 .

TSU was Alabama's fastest-growing university in the 1990s, when enrollment jumped by 32 percent. Enrollment at the rest of the state's universities decreased over that same period.

Tastes and Traditions

Shoepeg Corn Salad

1 can English peas, drained
1 can shoepeg corn, drained
1 can French-style green beans, drained
1 onion, chopped
1 small jar pimentos, drained
1 bell pepper, chopped
3/4 cup sugar
2/3 cup vinegar
1/3 cup salad oil
1 teaspoon salt
1/4 teaspoon pepper

Combine vegetables in a large salad bowl. Mix remaining ingredients and pour over vegetables. Toss to coat, cover and refrigerate overnight.

Rosa Seymour
TSU Parent

Marinated String Bean Salad

This recipe is a favorite of my husband, head football Coach Larry Blakeney, and our girls.

4 celery sticks, diced
3 small onions, diced
1 green bell pepper, cut in small strips
1 (20 ounce) can small English peas, drained
1 (20 ounce) can French-style string beans, drained
1 small jar pimento, drained

Marinade:
1 cup sugar
1 cup white vinegar
1/2 cup salad oil
1 tablespoon water
1 tablespoon salt
1/4 teaspoon black pepper

Place all salad ingredients in a large bowl. Mix marinade and pour over salad. Cover and chill in refrigerator at least overnight.

Janice Blakeney
TSU Spouse

Salads

Calico Slaw

First Edition Favorite

This recipe keeps well in the refrigerator. It can be prepared a day or two ahead. Leftovers last a couple of weeks. This goes well with sandwiches as well as full meals. This recipe was given to me by my mother who loves to cook and once owned Holley's Restaurant in Elba.

6 cups shredded green cabbage
2 cups shredded red cabbage
1 red pepper, chopped
1 green pepper, chopped
2 carrots, shredded
1 cup vinegar
3/4 cup oil
1 cup sugar
Salt and pepper to taste
1 tablespoon celery seed
1 teaspoon dry mustard

Place cabbages, peppers and carrots in large bowl with lid. Combine remaining ingredients in small saucepan and bring to boil. Let mixture cool. Pour over cabbage mixture; mix thoroughly, cover and refrigerate at least overnight. Stir again before serving.

Jimmy Holley
TSU
Alabama Senate

Onion Slaw

My brother Henry makes the best slaw! The secret to this recipe is the tomatoes. I laughed the first time I saw him making it, but after tasting it I knew it was the best! Mine isn't as good as his, but it's close.

1 head cabbage, chopped
1/2 onion, chopped
2 - 3 tablespoons mayonnaise
Salt and pepper
1 tomato, chopped

Place cabbage, onion and mayonnaise in a bowl and mix. Add salt and pepper to taste. Stir in tomatoes, cover and chill.

Helen Ricks
TSU

Tastes and Traditions

English Country Salad

This recipe was prepared for the luncheon honoring former Georgia governor Zell Miller, who gave the commencement address at graduation ceremonies in March 1999.

3 unpeeled Winesap or Granny Smith apples, sliced
1/2 pound Belgian endive
1 bunch watercress or mustard cress
4 ounces black walnuts or English walnuts
1/4 pound Stilton cheese, crumbled

Vinaigrette:
2 tablespoons Grand Marnier
1 tablespoon white wine vinegar
2 tablespoons honey
1 tablespoon Dijon mustard
1/4 cup best-quality olive oil
1/4 cup vegetable oil
1 teaspoon lemon juice

Slice apples crosswise into 1/4-inch-thick round slices to reveal star pattern of core. Arrange endive leaves in a spoke pattern on chilled individual salad plates. Place one round slice of apple in center of plate and dice remaining apples. Make a circle of watercress around the apple slice. Sprinkle nuts, cheese and diced apples on top of watercress. Drizzle with vinaigrette.
For Vinaigrette: combine all ingredients and mix well.

Sodexho-Marriott
TSU

At the Winter Commencement ceremony in March 1999, Dr. Hawkins was joined by Alabama Gov. Don Siegelman, second from left, and former Georgia Gov. Zell Miller, far right.

Salads

Rice Salad

This recipe has been in my family for many years. I have made it for my own family with great success.

2 (4 ounce) packages chicken-flavored rice
1 (16 ounce) can artichoke hearts, drained and sliced
1/2 cup vinaigrette dressing
4 green onions with tops, sliced
8 stuffed green olives
1/2 green pepper, chopped
1/3 cup mayonnaise
1/2 teaspoon curry powder

Cook rice according to directions, omitting butter. Cool. Marinate artichokes in vinaigrette dressing at least 2 hours. Add artichokes with half the marinade to rice. Add other ingredients and toss well. Serve well chilled.

Jane G. Varner
TSUM '98

Turkey, Mandarin and Poppy Seed Salad

5 cups torn red leaf lettuce
2 cups torn spinach leaves
1/2 pound honey roasted turkey, cut into 1/2-inch julienne strips
1 (10 1/2 ounce) can mandarin oranges, drained
1/4 cup orange juice
1/4 cup vinegar
1 1/2 tablespoons poppy seeds
1 1/2 teaspoons olive oil
1 teaspoon Dijon-style mustard
1/8 teaspoon black pepper
Red grapes and strawberries

In large bowl, combine lettuce, spinach, turkey and oranges. In small bowl, whisk together orange juice, vinegar, poppy seeds, oil, mustard and pepper. Pour dressing over turkey mixture, toss to coat evenly. Garnish plate with red grapes and strawberries. Serve immediately.

Sherri (Musgrove) Wenick
TSU '87

Tastes and Traditions

Broccoli and Cauliflower Salad

This salad adds a festive touch to a buffet table. Serves eight to ten people.

2 bunches broccoli
1 head cauliflower
1 cup cubed apples
1/2 cup chopped walnuts
1/2 cup raisins

Dressing:
1 cup mayonnaise
1/3 cup sugar

Cut florets from broccoli and break into bite-sized pieces. Peel stems and cut into 1-inch lengths. Place in a large salad bowl. Break cauliflower into florets and add to bowl. Add apples, nuts and raisins and toss.
For Dressing: Mix mayonnaise and sugar until sugar is dissolved. Add to salad and toss to coat. Cover and chill.

Faye and Gerald Dial
TSU Board of Trustees

Pasta and Chicken Salad

1 3/4 cups uncooked macaroni shells
1/2 cup mayonnaise
1/2 cup sour cream
2 tablespoons cider vinegar
1/4 teaspoon dill weed
1 1/2 tablespoons Dijon mustard
1 teaspoon sugar
1/2 teaspoon white pepper
1/4 teaspoon seasoned salt
2 cups chopped cooked chicken
2 cups seedless white grape halves
1/2 cup chopped green onions

Cook macaroni according to directions and drain. Combine mayonnaise, sour cream, vinegar, dill weed, mustard, sugar, white pepper and seasoned salt in bowl; mix well. Combine macaroni, chicken, grapes, and green onions in a large bowl; mix well. Stir in dressing. Chill, covered, for 6 hours to overnight.

Doug and Rachel Hawkins
TSU Board of Trustees

Salads

Nina Fraser's Salad

I got this recipe from Nina Fraser, whose husband, Tinny, taught at Troy State for many years.

2 (3 ounce) packages cream cheese, softened
1 small can pimentos, drained and chopped
1/2 cup finely chopped celery
2/3 cups chopped nuts
1 small can crushed pineapple, drained and juice reserved
Salt to taste
1 (3 ounce) package lemon Jello

Mash cream cheese with chopped pimentos. Add celery, nuts, pineapple, and salt. Dissolve Jello in one cup of boiling water. Use the juice from the pineapple and cold water to make 1 cup and add to Jello mixture. Mix dissolved Jello with cream cheese mixture. Place in molds and chill until set. Serve with whipped cream or mayonnaise.

Margaret Pace Farmer
TSU '32

Since 1954, the Pike County Chamber of Commerce has sponsored the TSU Homecoming Appreciation Day Parade. Troy's George O'Neal has served as parade marshal for nearly 50 years.

Tastes and Traditions

Green Bean Salad

A cool salad for a summertime lunch. Serves 10 people.

1 can Blue Lake green beans, drained
1 can English peas, drained
1 bell pepper, chopped or sliced
2 - 3 small onions, chopped or sliced
1 jar chopped pimento, drained
1 1/2 cups chopped celery (about 4 stalks)
1 cup sugar
3/4 cup wine vinegar
1 teaspoon salt
1/2 cup oil

Mix all ingredients. Chill for several hours or overnight before serving.

Faye and Gerald Dial
TSU Board of Trustees

Bing Cherry Salad Mold

A very rich and delicious salad. Serves eight to 10 people.

3 (3 ounces) packages black cherry gelatin
2 1/4 cups hot water
3 (1 pound) cans Bing cherries, drained and 2 1/4 cups syrup reserved
1 1/2 cups dry sherry
1 1/2 cups sour cream
1 1/2 cups thinly sliced almonds, crumbled
Lettuce

Dissolve gelatin in hot water. Add sherry and reserved cherry syrup. Chill until slightly thickened. Add cherries, sour cream and almonds. Pour into a large mold and chill. Unmold on a bed of lettuce.

Faye and Gerald Dial
TSU Board of Trustees

Salads

Wilted Spinach Salad

2 bunches of spinach (washed and dried thoroughly)
1 pound thick sliced bacon (fried until crisp)
4 Boiled eggs (sliced)
1 package fresh mushrooms (sliced thin)
1 package frozen green peas (defrosted)
1 cup vinegar
1 cup water
salt and pepper to taste
1/2 cup sugar

Wash and dry thoroughly spinach. Drain bacon on paper and crumble. Mix vinegar, sugar, water, salt & pepper with bacon grease. You may not want to use all the bacon grease but most of it. Stir and heat until boiling point. Toss all fresh ingredients with spinach. Pour hot dressing over salad and toss lightly. Serves 6-8

Sharon Higdon
TSU Friend

Mandarin Romaine Salad with Praline Pecans

Serve this delicious salad with beef tenderloin and rice.

1 head romaine lettuce
1/2 cup green onions, chopped
1/2 cup celery, chopped
1 (11 ounce) can mandarin oranges, drained
3 3/4 oz. package sliced almonds
2 teaspoons sugar
1 tablespoon butter

Combine lettuce, onions, celery and oranges. Keep refrigerated until ready to serve. In skillet over low heat (watch closely), saute' butter, sugar, and almonds. Cool, then crumble in baggie. Add to salad mixture.

Dressing:
1/4 cup wine vinegar
1 tablespoon sugar
1/2 cup salad oil
2-3 drops Tabasco
salt and pepper, to taste
1 teaspoon almond extract

Mix well and pour over salad mixture just prior to serving; toss well.

Sharon Litchfield
TSU Friend

Tastes and Traditions

Snow Pea Salad

This salad gets rave reviews whenever I serve it.

1 large head iceberg lettuce, shredded
1 pound snow peas, steamed 30 seconds, cooled
1/2 cup chopped parsley
cherry tomatoes, halved
pine nuts, toasted

Sesame Seed Dressing

1/2 cup sesame seeds, lightly browned in oven
2/3 cup salad oil
2 tablespoons lemon juice
2 tablespoons vinegar
2 tablespoon sugar
1 clove garlic, crushed
1 1/2 teaspoons salt

Put all ingredients in a blender except sesame seeds and mix well. Add seeds. This dressing will store well. Toss salad with dressing. Lightly pile this salad on red lettuce leaves for color.

Janice Hawkins
TSU First Lady

Avocado and Grapefruit Salad

2 cups salad oil
1 cup cider vinegar
1/2 cup catsup
2 teaspoons salt
6 tablespoons sugar
1 small onion, grated
black pepper

Blend all ingredients in blender or food processor on high speed. Chill long enough for flavors to blend. When ready to serve, pour dressing over orange slices, grapefruit sections and sliced avocado on romaine lettuce.

Mary Gibson
TSU Friend

Salads

Creamy Congealed Salad

This is my daughter Kay's favorite recipe.

1 small can evaporated milk
1 cup grated cheddar cheese
1 small can crushed pineapple
1/2 cup mayonnaise
1 cup boiling water
1 small package orange gelatin

Whip evaporated milk until fluffy. Dissolve gelatin in boiling water. Fold whipped milk into gelatin. Add cheese, pineapple, and mayonnaise. Mix well. Refrigerate until firm.

Betty Chancellor
TSU

The Sound of the South Marching Band added to the festive atmosphere when the Curry Commons were dedicated at Troy State University Montgomery in September 1999. The TSUM Clock Tower, the central feature of Curry Commons, is in the background.

Tastes and Traditions

Breads & Breakfast

Yeast Rolls

This recipe was given to me by my great-grandmother, Lucy Nall.

1 package yeast
1/2 cup lukewarm water
2 eggs
1/2 to 3/4 cup sugar
1 cup shortening
1 1/2 cups water
3 - 4 cups bread flour
1 teaspoon salt

Dissolve yeast in the lukewarm water, stir, and set aside. In large bowl, beat eggs and sugar. Melt shortening in 1 1/2 cups water and add to egg mixture. Add 2 to 3 cups flour to mixture; stir, then add dissolved yeast. Batter should be consistency of lumpy waffle batter. Cover and let rise 2 hours at room temperature in draft-free place. Next, stir down risen batter and add 1 teaspoon salt and enough flour (about 1 cup) to make sticky dough. Cover and chill for at least 4 hours. Roll out on floured board; cut circles and dip in melted butter; fold in half and pinch closed; put in pan and let rise for 2 hours at room temperature. Bake in 400 degree oven for 10 to 15 minutes. Serve immediately. Freeze leftover rolls. When ready to serve, thaw, wrap in foil and rewarm in a medium oven.

Ricky Mora
TSU Friend

Lucy T. Nall

The senses of taste and smell -- and the aromas of any kitchen or dining room table -- can serve as great spurs of memory, as palpable pathways to the past. Those principal traits of food considered, the contributions of **Lucy Trotman Nall** to this cookbook are culinary time machines to the days when Troy State University was still a normal school and meals were still eaten around a communal table.

Born in Troy in 1900, Lucy Trotman Nall matriculated to Troy State Normal School, sharing many laughs with the self-titled "Dirty Dozen" -- a happy-go-lucky group of female students -- before receiving her teaching degree in 1920. She then began a colorful series of careers: selling insurance, recruiting young people for summer camps, recruiting for and leading tour groups to Europe, and serving as Troy State Normal's second home economics teacher. She also initiated a Troy institution when she began taking in boarders in her Murphree Street home.

The reputation of the meals Mrs. Nall served in her home grew quickly, and she soon was receiving additional "boarders" at mealtime. Her patrons were regulars and included college faculty, doctors, dentists, pharmacists and other Troy professionals. She usually served 15 people at breakfast, 20 at lunch and 30 for Sunday dinner, spreading the meals over two long tables set with family linens, silver, crystal and china. Mrs. Nall's home and meals were an important part of Troy's culture for many years. *(Editor's note: Mrs. Nall is the grandmother of artist Nall Hollis, whose work decorates the cover of this book).*

Breads & Breakfast

Dinner Rolls

1 cup self-rising flour
1/2 cup milk
3 heaping tablespoons mayonnaise

Mix ingredients well. Fill greased muffin tins thee-quarters full. Bake 15 minutes in 400 degree oven.

Adrian Odom
TSU Student
Alpha Gamma Delta

Jean's Famous Rolls

My mother, Jean Gordon of Little Rock, makes these for every holiday meal. Note that you start them the day before.

1/2 cup boiling water
1/2 cup butter
1/2 cup sugar
1 teaspoon salt
1 1/4 tablespoons dry yeast
1/2 cup lukewarm water
1 egg
3 cups flour
Garlic powder
Sesame seeds

Pour boiling water over butter, sugar and salt in a large bowl. Stir to dissolve and cool. Dissolve yeast in the lukewarm water and beat in eggs. Add to cooled mixture. Add flour, 1 cup at a time, beating after each addition. Cover the bowl and let sit overnight in the refrigerator. Take out 2 hours before baking. Roll out on a lightly floured board. Cut in rounds, crease with a knife and fold over. Place close together in a buttered baking pan and brush tops with melted butter. Sprinkle a few grains of garlic powder on top and then sprinkle with sesame seeds. Bake in a 425 degree oven about 12 to 15 minutes or until well browned.

Jane Varner
TSUM '98

Tastes and Traditions

Spoon Rolls

Traditional Recipe

My mother, Stella Grindley, got this recipe from the famous Stockton Hotel in California where she worked (and met my dad) in the early 1930s. They were known for these rolls, as was my mom.

Janice Hawkins

1 package dry yeast
2 cups warm water
1 1/2 sticks margarine, melted
1/4 cup sugar
1 egg, beaten
4 cups self-rising flour

Dissolve yeast in the warm water. Mix margarine with sugar in a large bowl. Add egg. Add dissolved yeast to creamed mixture. Add flour and stir until well mixed. Place in airtight container and keep in refrigerator. To cook: Drop by spoonfuls into well-greased muffin tin and bake at 350 degrees for 20 minutes or until browned. This dough will keep in the refrigerator for two weeks.

Stella Grindley
TSU Friend

Cheese Biscuits

Make these bite-sized and they're great for parties or tailgating.

2 3/4 cups all purpose baking mix (Bisquik)
1/2 teaspoon crushed red pepper or cayenne pepper
3/4 teaspoon garlic powder, divided
1 cup milk
1 to 2 cups shredded cheese
2 tablespoons butter, melted
1 pound sausage, cooked and drained, optional

Preheat oven to 425 degrees. Combine baking mix, red pepper and 1/2 teaspoon garlic powder. With a fork, stir in milk and cheese until mixture forms a soft dough. Add sausage, if desired. Drop dough by 1/4 cupful onto greased cookie sheet. Combine butter and remaining garlic powder; brush on dough tops. Bake 10 to 12 minutes or until golden brown. Makes 12 biscuits or about 50 small.

Hope Tillery
TSU Student
Kappa Delta Sorority

Breads & Breakfast

Dawn's Biscuits

After hearing my husband laugh about our Basset Hound, Odell, burying my biscuits in the front yard, I vowed never to make them again. Then that ole Trojan Spirit got me, and being a transplanted Yankee with a stubborn streak, I decided to try again. I finally arrived at the following recipe. Hope you guys enjoy.

4 cups self-rising flour
1 tablespoon sugar
2 tablespoons baking powder
1 teaspoon baking soda
2 cups buttermilk
2/3 cup shortening
Pinch of garlic powder

Sift flour, sugar, baking powder and baking soda together. Mix in remaining ingredients. Fold out to a floured surface and turn several times. Roll out to one inch thick. Cut and place close together in greased cake pans. Brush tops with buttermilk and bake at 400 degrees for 10 minutes, and another 10 minutes at 450 degrees.

Dawn Pfeiffer Andress
TSU

Cheddar Apple Bread

Great anytime, morning or night. Not so sweet and freezes well.

2 1/2 cups all-purpose flour
3/4 cup sugar
1 tablespoon baking powder
1/2 teaspoon salt
1/2 teaspoon cinnamon
2 eggs
3/4 cup milk
1/3 cup melted butter
2 cups shredded Cheddar cheese
1 1/2 cups chopped peeled apples
3/4 cup chopped pecans

Preheat oven to 350 degrees. Combine all dry ingredients and mix. Combine eggs, milk, and melted butter; mix well. Pour into dry ingredients and mix well. Stir in remaining ingredients. Spoon into a greased and floured 9 x 5-inch loaf pan. Bake 1 hour and 15 minutes. Let stand in pan for 5 minutes. Remove from pan and allow to cool completely before cutting.

Susan Culwell Delenne
TSU '79

Tastes and Traditions

Easy Apple Bread

Wrap in Saran wrap and place in a decorative basket for a great Christmas gift!

1 1/3 cups all-purpose flour
3/4 teaspoon baking soda
1/2 teaspoon salt
1 teaspoon cinnamon
1/4 teaspoon ground cloves
1 cup sugar
1/2 cup cooking oil
2 eggs, beaten
1 teaspoon vanilla
2 - 3 apples, coarsely chopped
1/2 cup raisins
1/2 cup chopped nuts

Combine flour, soda, salt, cinnamon and cloves. In a separate bowl, mix together sugar and oil. Add eggs and vanilla; beat well. Add the apples and mix well. Stir in the raisins and nuts. Add the flour mixture; mix well. Turn into a greased 9 x 5 x 3-inch loaf pan. Bake in a preheated 350 degree oven for 1 hour. Remove to a wire rack. Cool for 10 minutes. Remove loaf from pan and cool completely. Makes 1 loaf.

Cameron Martindale
President, TSUM

Dr. Cameron Martindale became Troy State University Montgomery's third president on April 13, 2000. An expert in adult education, Dr. Martindale joined TSUM in 1986.

Breads & Breakfast

Banana Loaf

1 cup sugar
1/2 cup shortening
2 eggs
2 cups self-rising flour
3 ripe bananas, mashed
1/2 cup chopped nuts
1 teaspoon vanilla

Cream sugar and shortening. Add eggs, one at a time. Add flour. Add bananas, nuts and vanilla. Turn into a greased loaf pan and bake at 350 degrees for 40 minutes or until done.

Hope Hobdy
TSU Student
Kappa Delta Sorority

Louise's Banana Bread

This recipe was a banana cake originally. It is simply the best banana bread you will ever eat! It also freezes well.

1 cup shortening or 1 stick butter and 1/2 cup shortening
3 cups sugar
4 eggs
6 very ripe bananas, well-mashed
2 teaspoons vanilla
3 1/2 cups all-purpose flour
2 teaspoons soda
Pinch salt
1 cup buttermilk
2 cups chopped pecans, optional

Cream together shortening and sugar. Add eggs and mix well. Add bananas and vanilla. Mix together flour, soda and salt. Add to banana mixture alternately with buttermilk. Mix all very well. Stir in pecans, if desired. Grease and flour loaf pans (5 small or 3 medium). Evenly divide dough. Bake at 350 degrees for 30 to 45 minutes or until set in middle. Enjoy! Good with Orange Cream Cheese: Mix together 1 (8 ounce) package cream cheese, softened, 1/2 teaspoon orange flavoring, and grated rind of 1 orange. Mix and spread over bread.

Louise Meyer
TSU Friend

Tastes and Traditions

Pear Bread

1 cup vegetable oil
2 cups granulated sugar
3 eggs
2 1/2 cups peeled and chopped fresh pears
1 cup chopped pecans
2 teaspoons vanilla extract
3 cups all-purpose flour
1 teaspoon baking soda
1/2 teaspoon salt
1 teaspoon ground cinnamon
1/2 teaspoon ground nutmeg

Preheat oven to 300 degrees. In a medium mixing bowl, combine oil, sugar, and eggs, blending well. Stir in pears, pecans, and vanilla. In another bowl, combine remaining ingredients. Stir dry ingredients into the pear mixture. Pour the batter into 2 greased loaf pans. Bake loaves 1 hour. Cool loaves 10 minutes, them remove from pans and cool on wire rack.

Mary Mitchell
TSU Friend

Homemade Cornbread Fritters

1/4 cup self-rising corn meal
1 tablespoon self rising flour
Salt to taste
Vegetable oil

Combine corn meal, flour, salt and enough water to make a thick batter. Heat vegetable oil in a skillet over medium-high heat. Drop batter in spoonfuls into skillet. Brown one side and remove. Add more oil to skillet, return fritters and brown other side.

Hayden Mitchell
TSU Student
Phi Mu Sorority

Since 1989, the Tropolitan, TSU's weekly student newspaper, has won 32 regional and national awards in the Society of Professional Journalists Mark of Excellence competition.

Breads & Breakfast

Corn Light Bread

Traditional Recipe

This is a very old recipe made by my great-grandmother. She made this all her life and passed it on. Make it a tradition in your family.

2 cups white corn meal
1/2 cup all-purpose flour
1/2 cup sugar
1 teaspoon baking soda
2 cups buttermilk
1/2 teaspoon salt
1 tablespoon bacon drippings

Mix all ingredients together and cook at 350 degrees for 60 minutes.

Leigh Ann Jones
TSU Friend

Hush Puppies

These are great served with fish or seafood. The jalapeño peppers add just enough kick.

1 cup cornbread mix
1 cup biscuit mix
1 can cream-style corn
1 onion, chopped
1 egg
1 jalapeño pepper, chopped

Mix all together. Drop by teaspoonfuls into hot oil; cook until brown.

Hope Hobdy
TSU Student
Kappa Delta Sorority

Growth was a hallmark of the Troy State University System during the 1990s, made evident by the increase in value of the System's physical plant. The value of the System's buildings and other properties grew from $55.2 million in 1989 to $85.3 million in 1999, an increase of more than 50 percent.

Tastes and Traditions

Date Bread

The secret ingredient in this recipe is the mace. It's the secret to good pound cakes, too.

3 cups Bisquik
3/4 cup brown sugar
1 egg
1 1/4 cups milk
1 1/2 cups chopped dates
1/2 teaspoon cinnamon
1/4 teaspoon mace

Mix all the ingredients together. Transfer to a greased loaf and and cook at 350 degrees for 45 to 50 minutes.

Margaret Pace Farmer
TSU '32

Irish Brown Bread

This is a recipe that has been passed down for generations in my Irish family. My cousins still cook this brown bread daily! My grandfather, Papa Eddie, brought the recipe to the United States with him when he immigrated here. I have to say, when comparing my Irish cousins' version of the bread to my mother's version, my mom definitely wins! Enjoy!

3 cups whole wheat flour
1 cup unbleached white flour
1 1/2 teaspoons salt
1 teaspoon baking soda
3/4 teaspoon baking powder
2 cups buttermilk (you may add more if dough is too stiff)
1 tablespoon sugar

Mix all ingredients and knead on floured board for 2 to 3 minutes, until smooth and elastic. Form in round loaf and place in well-greased pan. Cut a 1/2-inch-deep "X" on top of bread with knife dipped in flour. Bake at 375 degrees for 50 to 60 minutes. Bread should be lightly browned and sound hollow with thumped. Serves 12.

Katie Hawkins
TSU Student
Phi Mu Sorority

Breads & Breakfast

Sweet Potato Muffins

This recipe came from Christiana Campbell's Tavern in Williamsburg, Virginia. Janice and I had a memorable meal there on our wedding trip. I requested this recipe so she could make it for me at home!

1 stick butter
1 1/4 cups granulated sugar
1 1/4 cups canned or fresh sweet potatoes, mashed
2 eggs
1 1/2 cups all-purpose flour
2 teaspoons baking powder
1 teaspoon cinnamon
1/4 teaspoon nutmeg
1/4 teaspoon salt
1 cup milk
1/2 cup chopped raisins
1/4 cup chopped pecans or walnuts

Have all ingredients at room temperature. Cream butter, sugar and sweet potatoes until smooth. Add eggs. Blend well. Sift flour, baking powder and spices and add alternately with milk to batter. Do not over mix. Fold in nuts and raisins last. Sprinkle a little cinnamon-sugar on top before baking. Bake in greased muffin tins at 400 degrees for approximately 25 minutes or until done. Makes about 2 dozen small muffins. They may be frozen and reheated.

Jack Hawkins, Jr.
Chancellor, TSU System

Sour Cream Biscuit

This is a great party biscuit.

2 cups self-rising flour
1 cup sour cream

Blend flour and sour cream, knead lightly, roll, cut with biscuit cutter (any size) and bake at 450° for 15 minutes.

Janice Hawkins
TSU First Lady

The Olympic Torch Relay passed through campus on its way to the Centennial Olympic Games in Atlanta in July 1996.

Tastes and Traditions
Fluffy Gingerbread

2 cups all-purpose flour
1 1/2 teaspoons soda
1 teaspoon cinnamon
1/2 teaspoon cloves
2 teaspoons ginger
1/2 cup shortening
1/2 cup sugar
2 eggs
3/4 cup syrup
1 cup boiling water

Lemon Sauce:
1/2 stick margarine
3/4 cup sugar
1/4 cup flour
Juice of 1 lemon
Boiling water

Mix all dry ingredients. Cream shortening and sugar well. Add eggs and beat. Stir in syrup, then add the dry ingredients, beating well. Add boiling water, stirring thoroughly. Pour batter into a greased and floured 8 x 12 x 2-inch pan and bake at 375 degrees until sides of gingerbread leave pan. Serve hot with a Lemon Sauce poured over.

For Sauce: Combine all ingredients except water in top of double boiler; mix well. Add boiling water and cook until desired thickness, stirring constantly.

Deloria Musgrove
TSU Parent

Research by chemistry professor Moore Asouzu – a method of computer-based chemical analysis that helps the paper industry make its products more efficiently – resulted in TSU's first patent. Prof. Asouzu, second from left, was presented a special copy of the patent in June 2000 by Chancellor Jack Hawkins, Jr., third from left, and Dr. Robert Pullen, dean of the College of Arts and Sciences. Gwanda Asouzu also attended the ceremony.

Breads & Breakfast

Spinach Cornbread

Good with vegetable soup.

1 box Jiffy cornbread mix
1 onion, chopped
1 box chopped spinach, thawed
3/4 cup cottage cheese
1 stick margarine, melted
2 eggs, beaten
1/2 teaspoon salt
1/3 cup buttermilk

Grease skillet and preheat. Squeeze spinach dry. Mix all ingredients together. Pour into hot skillet and cook at 400° for 30 minutes or until brown on top.

Troy Bank and Trust
TSU Friend

Dill Bread

1 package yeast
1/2 cup lukewarm water
1 cup cottage cheese
1 tablespoon butter, melted
1 egg
2 tablespoons onion, chopped
2 tablespoons dill weed
2 tablespoons sugar
1 teaspoon salt
1/4 teaspoon soda
2 1/2 cups flour

Sprinkle yeast over water and stir til dissolved. Heat cottage cheese to lukewarm. Combine all ingredients except flour; add flour gradually. Cover. Let rise until double. Stir down. Put in greased 1 1/2-quart casserole. Let rise until light - about 40 minutes. Bake at 350 degrees for 50 minutes. Brush with additional melted butter. Sprinkle with salt.

Shirley Rollins
TSU Parent

Tastes and Traditions

Bread Sticks

Try these variations of bread sticks.

1/4 cup butter or margarine
1 package commercial bread sticks
1/2 cup sugar
1 teaspoon cinnamon

Melt the butter and pour over the bread sticks that are one deep in a flat pan. Roll the buttered bread sticks in the mixture of cinnamon and sugar. Place on a cookie skeet and bake for 10 minutes in a 350 degree oven. Remove, cool and wrap in foil or wax paper until ready to use. You can freeze them, then put back in the oven to heat.

Variations: Always pour melted butter over breadsticks first and then roll in Parmesan cheese, or paprika and oregano, or finely chopped almonds, or sprinkle garlic powder on top of buttered bread sticks.

Donna Massey
TSU

Croutons

These are so good! They're easy, too.

1 loaf 1/4 inch, sliced bread
1 stick butter, softened
1 teaspoon Crazy salt

Mix butter and Crazy salt and spread on bread slices. Score bread in quarters so it will break evenly when done. Put bread on cookie sheets and bake at 200 degrees for about 2 hours or until very crisp. Eat with soup or salad.

Katie Hawkins
TSU Student
Phi Mu Sorority

Since 1971, many TSU students have received leadership training and career preparation through the university's detachment of the Air Force Reserve Officer Training Corps. Students earn a commission as a second lieutenant in U.S. Air Force upon graduation.

Breads & Breakfast

Gingerbread Muffins

Makes three dozen small muffins.

2 cups flour
1 1/2 teaspoons soda
1 1/2 teaspoons powdered ginger
1/2 teaspoon salt
1 cup molasses or sorghum syrup
1/3 cup butter or margarine
1/2 cup buttermilk
1 egg
1/2 cup raisins
1/2 cup chopped pecans

Sift the four, soda, ginger and salt. Set aside. Heat the molasses and butter until lukewarm. Pour in the buttermilk and slightly beaten egg. Beat thoroughly. Add the raisins and nuts to flour mixture, and stir in the molasses mixture only until blended. Drop into buttered muffin pans three-quarters full. Sprinkle top with cinnamon and sugar (1/2 teaspoon cinnamon, 1/2 cup sugar). Bake at 325 degrees for about 25 minutes.

Jackie McLeod
TSU Friend

Bran Muffins

3/4 cup Bran Flakes
1/4 cup brown sugar, packed
1/4 cup raisins
1 teaspoon cinnamon
1 (8 ounce) can biscuits
1 tablespoons margarine, melted
1/4 cup syrup

Combine cereal, sugar, raisins, and cinnamon and set aside. Place biscuits 2 inches apart in a greased 9" x 13" pan. Brush with margarine and sprinkle 1/2 cereal mixture on top. Drizzle with syrup and remaining margarine. Sprinkle with remaining cereal mixture. Bake at 450 degrees for 15 minutes or until brown. Invert on plate; remove pan.

Jane Weiss
TSU Friend

Tastes and Traditions

Tropical Muffins

2 cups all-purpose flour
2 teaspoons baking powder
1/2 teaspoons baking soda
1/2 teaspoon slat
1/2 cup brown sugar, packed
1 egg, beaten
1 cup sour cream
1 (83/4 ounce) can crushed pineapple, undrained
1/2 cup pecans, chopped
1/3 cup cooking oil

Mix together dry ingredients. In a separate bowl, combine egg and sour cream. Add pineapple, nuts, and oil. Add to dry ingredients and stir until moistened. Fill greased or paper lined muffin tins 2/3 full. Bake at 400 degrees about 20 minutes. For a sweeter muffin, more sugar may be added.

Jodi Ward
TSU Friend

Cinnamon Rolls

2 cups flour
2 teaspoons baking powder
1/4 teaspoon soda
3/4 teaspoon salt
1/4 cup shortening
2/3 cup buttermilk
1 stick margarine
1/2 cup sugar
Cinnamon
1/2 box confectioners' sugar
1/4 cup milk

Sift together dry ingredients. Cut in shortening until coarse like cornmeal. Stir in buttermilk until dough is soft. Roll out dough until very thin. Dot with margarine. Sprinkle with sugar and cinnamon. Roll dough, as for jelly roll, and cut into 3/4 inch slices. Place on greased cookie sheet. Bake at 450 degrees for 15 minutes or until brown. Mix confectioners' sugar with milk and glaze rolls.

Anne Boothe
TSU Friend

Breads & Breakfast

Danish

2 (8 ounce) packages refrigerator crescent rolls
2 tablespoons butter, softened
1 tablespoon melted butter
1 cup puréed cooked prunes or apricots
1 teaspoon lemon juice
1/4 cup finely chopped pecans
1/2 cup confectioners' sugar
2 or 3 teaspoons milk

Roll out 1 package of the rolls into a rectangle approximately 12 x 8 inches. Soften but do not melt the butter and spread abut 4 inches wide down center of rectangle. Unroll second package of rolls and place over the first, completely covering the butter. Brush top dough with melted butter. Spread puréed fruit and lemon juice down center of top dough.Sprinkle with nuts. Cut parallel pieces, about 2 inches long x 2 inches apart.. Fold dough pieces over filling. Place on a buttered cookie sheet and bake at 375 degrees until golden brown. Mix confectioners' sugar and milk and dribble over warm Danish. Cut and serve. Use same method but substitute marmalades, jams or butter for a richer and more flaky roll.

Dot Helms
TSU

Troy State Teachers College and area women contributed to the country's war effort in World War II in a number of ways, including the Radio School. Held on campus throughout the war years, the Radio School taught dozens of women to construct and maintain military radios. This group was photographed in July 1942.

Tastes and Traditions

Breakfast Casserole

6 slices buttered bread
1 pound sausage, browned and drained
1 1/2 cups grated Cheddar cheese
2 cups half and half
6 eggs, beaten

Place bread in 9 x 13-inch baking dish and top with sausage and cheese. Combine half and half and eggs and beat well. Pour mixture over other ingredients in baking dish. Cover with foil and refrigerate overnight. Remove from refrigerator 10 minutes before cooking. Bake 45 minutes in preheated 350 degree oven.

Debbie Sanders
TSU

Chandra Myrick
TSU Student

Breakfast Hot Dish

This dish is great for a brunch or if you want "breakfast for supper." It is a family favorite. Can be made ahead and frozen.

2 1/2 cups herb croutons
2 cups shredded sharp cheese
2 pounds sausage, cooked and drained
4 eggs
3/4 teaspoon dry mustard
2 1/2 cups milk
1 can cream of mushroom soup
1 small can mushrooms, drained

Arrange croutons in a greased large casserole dish and sprinkle with cheese Spread sausage over cheese. Beat eggs. Add remaining ingredients to eggs and pour over the casserole. Refrigerate overnight or freeze. Bake at 300 degrees for 1 1/2 hours.

Linda Curington
TSU Parent

TSU faculty and staff are also community leaders and volunteers. A 1998 study showed they give an average of 7,700 volunteer hours each month.

Breads & Breakfast

Brunch Ham and Cheese Casserole

Butter
Bread, crusts removed
3 eggs, lightly beaten
1 cup milk
1 cup chopped ham
1 cup grated sharp Cheddar cheese
2 - 3 dashes Tabasco
1 tablespoon dry mustard
2 teaspoons grated onion
Pepper to taste

Butter enough bread to line a casserole dish. Place in bottom of buttered dish. Mix remaining ingredients and pour over bread. Bake at 325 degrees for 35 to 40 minutes.

Lucy Baxley
TSU Friend
Alabama State Treasurer

Cream Cheese Breakfast Squares

My mother, Mary Shively, often surprises us with these on Sunday mornings. She makes an extra batch to take with her to Sunday School and everyone loves them!

2 (8 ounce) packages crescent rolls
1 1/2 cups sugar, divided
1 1/2 teaspoons vanilla
1 egg, separated
2 (8 ounce) packages cream cheese, softened
1/2 cup chopped nuts
1 teaspoon cinnamon

Roll out one package of crescent rolls and press seams together to make a rectangle. Put in bottom of a pyrex dish. Mix 1 cup sugar, vanilla, egg yolk and cream cheese together. Spread over crescent rolls. Roll out second package of rolls and press seams together. Place on top of cream cheese mixture. Brush egg white over top of rolls. Mix remaining sugar, cinnamon and nuts together. Sprinkle on top and push down lightly. Bake at 350 degrees for 30 minutes. Cool. Refrigerate. Cut in squares and serve cold. Makes 24 squares.

Amy Shively
TSU Student

Tastes and Traditions

Tramp Eggs

This is one of Kathryn Tucker Windham's recipes. It was a tradition in her family, and I think it soon will be in mine. It is expandable, so no amounts are given.

Eggs
Salt
Milk
Butter
Cheese

Butter a shallow baking dish, and break into it the number of eggs needed to serve the eaters. (I put 12 eggs in a 9 x 12-inch baking dish.) Sprinkle with salt and pour milk around them until the yellow tops are just peeping out. Dot with dabs of butter. Grate cheese over the top. Bake in slow (325 degree) oven until cheese is bubbly and eggs are of desired doneness. Serve atop toast or in a nest of grits.

Willetta Hatcher
TSU Friend

Renowned storyteller and folklorist Kathryn Tucker Windham – best known for her "13 Alabama Ghosts and Jeffrey" – shared stories with audiences during many visits to TSU during the 1980's and 1990's.

Breads & Breakfast

Sausage and Cheese Casserole

1/2 pound sausage
8 slices white bread, crusts removed and cut in 1/2-inch cubes
3/4 pound monterey jack cheese, grated
4 large eggs, beaten
1 1/2 cups milk
1/2 teaspoon salt
1 teaspoon Dijon mustard
1/2 teaspoon Worcestershire
3 tablespoons melted butter

Mix all ingredients and pour into a greased casserole dish. Bake in 350 degree oven for 45 minutes.

Lisa Henderson
TSU Student
Phi Mu Sorority

Sausage Grits

Good for breakfast or brunch.

1 pound bulk pork sausage
2 cups cheddar cheese, shredded
3 tablespoons oleo
3 cups hot, cooked grits
3 eggs, beaten
1 1/2 cups milk

Preheat oven to 350 degrees. Lightly coat a 9 x 13-inch baking dish with cooking spray. Cook sausage, breaking up and stirring until brown in heavy skillet. Drain and spoon into prepared dish. Add cheese and oleo to hot grits and stir until melted. Combine eggs and milk, then stir into grits. Pour over sausage. Bake uncovered for 1 hour. Serve hot. Serves 8.

Troy Bank and Trust
TSU Friend

Alumnus Kevin Kregel, who graduated from TSU-Florida Region in 1988, served as the mission commander for the space shuttle Endeavour when it embarked on a mission to map the earth in February 2000. Kregel, who joined NASA in March 1992, first piloted a space shuttle in 1995 and has logged hundreds of hours in space.

Tastes and Traditions

Cheese Grits Soufflé

Grits are no longer just for breakfast – they make a great side dish at dinner instead of rice or potatoes.

4 cups cooked grits
8 tablespoons butter
6 cups white cheddar cheese, grated
3/4 cup heavy cream
8 eggs, beaten separately
3/4 teaspoon Tabasco sauce
1/2 teaspoon salt
1/4 teaspoon powdered garlic

Mix butter and cheese with the hot grits until melted. Add remaining ingredients. Pour into a buttered 2-quart casserole and sprinkle with paprika. Bake at 375 degrees for 45-60 minutes. Freezes well but should defrost before cooking.

Dodie Pridgen
TSU Friend

Blueberry Muffins

1 cup milk
1/2 cup melted butter
1 egg, slightly beaten
2 cups all purpose flour
1/3 cup sugar
1 tablespoon baking powder
1 teaspoon salt
1 cup fresh or frozen blueberries
Topping:
1/4 cup melted butter
1/4 cup sugar

Preheat oven to 400 degrees. Combine milk, butter and eggs in large bowl. Add all remaining muffin ingredients except blueberries. Stir just until flour is moistened. Gently stir in blueberries. Spoon into greased 12-cup muffin pan. Bake for 24 to 28 minutes or until golden brown. Cool slightly; remove from pan. Dip tops of muffins in butter, then in sugar.

Jewel Flinn
TSU Spouse

Main Events

Main Dishes

Vegetables

Side Dishes

Mrs. Claudia Graves Crosby

Since February 2000, Troy State University's "main events" have taken place in the Claudia Crosby Theater. Located in C.B. Smith Hall, the Broadway-caliber theater and concert hall has seating for 930; state-of-the-art sound, lighting and stage-rigging systems and a "green room" for performers; a formal lobby with television-stage monitors; enhanced access and seating for handicapped visitors; and a revamped facade that brought aesthetic and architectural unity to the Bibb Graves Quad.

The Crosby Theater was made possible by the philanthropy of arts patron and special university friend Claudia Graves Crosby. A native of Troy, Mrs. Crosby spent the early years of her childhood in her hometown before moving to Washington, D.C. at the age of 12. She earned a degree from Wilmer Normal College and taught for several years in the nation's capital, where she also was an active supporter of the Theatre Guild and participated in amateur theater groups. With her husband of 51 years, Josiah D. Crosby, she also lived in Massachusetts and Florida, continuing her lifelong love of the theater.

Mrs. Crosby returned to Troy in 1994. When her gift to renovate the Smith Hall auditorium was announced in December 1998, it was the single-largest individual donation the university had ever received.

"Pike County is home and full of treasured memories of my youth, and Troy State University plays such an important role in making a difference in this community and region," Mrs. Crosby said at the time. "I believe in giving something back to a community and an institution that mean so much to me."

Mrs. Crosby died in June 2000. Her legacy of generosity and her affection for the theater will impact the community and university for generations, however. In addition to funding the facility that bears her name, Mrs. Crosby created TSU's own "Rhodes scholarship" -- the Marion Rhodes Scholarships, named for her grandfather -- to benefit students of theater and the fine arts.

The Claudia Crosby Theater

Main Dishes

Main Dishes

Favorite Meatloaf

*I have heard many say, "I never liked meatloaf before, but this is good!"
Even my finicky-eating husband likes it.*

4 ounces tomato sauce
1/3 cup brown sugar
1 teaspoon prepared mustard
1 egg, lightly beaten
1 small onion, minced
1/4 cup oats or cracker crumbs
1 1/2 - 2 pounds ground chuck
1 1/2 teaspoons salt
1/4 teaspoon pepper
Ketchup

Combine all the ingredients except ketchup in a bowl and mix thoroughly.
Place meat mixture in a 2-quart microwave-proof round casserole or ring
mold. Spoon ketchup over top and spread evenly. Cook in microwave,
uncovered, on high for 15 to 18 minutes. Let stand, covered, 5 to 10
minutes before serving.

Brenda Dennis
TSU Spouse

Little-Bit-Of-Texas Meatloaf

*Being a native Texan, I love spicy food. This dish is wonderful, but not too
spicy.*

1 (16 ounce) jar mild picante sauce, divided
3 pounds ground beef
1 1/2 cups chopped onion
1 cup chopped green pepper
1 teaspoon chili powder
2 teaspoons dried oregano
2 teaspoons ground cumin
1 teaspoon salt
1 cup seasoned dry bread crumbs
2 eggs

Preheat oven to 375 degrees. Set aside 1/4 cup picante sauce. Mix
remaining sauce with beef, onion, green pepper, chili powder, oregano,
cumin and salt; stir in bread crumbs and eggs until combined. Shape beef
mixture into loaf in roasting pan; spread with reserved picante sauce. Bake
for 1 hour and 15 minutes.

Carol Ann Ratcliffe
TSU Spouse

Tastes and Traditions

Marinated Flank Steak

Flank steak is frequently bypassed by most shoppers, yet with a little preparation, it could become a favorite steak. It is even good cold.

Flank steak
1 cup corn oil
1/2 cup vinegar
2 teaspoons dry mustard
1 teaspoon salt
1/4 teaspoon pepper
2 tablespoons Worcestershire sauce
1 garlic clove
Several drops hot sauce

Place steak in shallow pan. Mix remaining ingredients and pour over meat. Let marinate at least 3 hours. It's even better if you can marinate it overnight. Broil each side 3 to 4 inches below heat for 3 to 4 minutes per side. Cut in thin strips.

Scott Thornsley
TSU

Peachy Pork Tenderloin

This is a wonderful meat dish to take to a potluck or a family get-together. It is fast becoming popular in our family.

1/2 cup soy sauce
2 teaspoons minced garlic
Grated ginger root
1 (4 - 5 pound) pork tenderloin
3/4 cup peach preserves
2 tablespoons honey
Salt and pepper to taste

Combine soy sauce, garlic and ginger and pour over tenderloin. Marinate several hours or overnight. Pour off marinade and combine with peach preserves, honey, salt and pepper. Place tenderloin in baking pan and pour marinade mixture over top. Bake at 325 degrees until meat tests done with a meat thermometer.

Dinah Carlisle Kelsey
TSU '71

Main Dishes

Pork in Balsamic Vinegar

This dish can be prepared ahead of time and served warm or at room temperature.

1 1/2 pounds pork tenderloin
Salt and pepper to taste
2 tablespoons olive oil
2/3 cup dry white wine

Marinade:
1 medium onion, thinly sliced
1/4 cup cider vinegar
3 tablespoons fresh rosemary
2 tablespoons minced fresh sage
1 tablespoon chopped fresh parsley
2/3 cup balsamic vinegar
Juice of 1/2 lemon
1 tablespoon whole peppercorns
1/2 cup extra virgin olive oil

To make marinade: In a skillet, combine onion and cider vinegar and simmer until onion is soft. Add the rest of the marinade ingredients, remove from heat and set aside. Rub meat with olive oil and sprinkle with salt and pepper. Transfer meat to a baking dish, add marinade and wine. Roast meat at 375 degrees until cooked to 155 to 160 degrees . When finished, let cool and refrigerate in cooked marinade at least 3 hours, or up to 3 days. To serve, either bring to room temperature or reheat and slice. Spoon marinade over meat.

Elizabeth Ullery
TSU-Phenix City

Baba's Steak

3 tablespoons unsalted butter
4 filet mignons
3 tablespoons Dijon mustard
1 cup half and half cream
2 tablespoons Tabasco (less if you don't like hot)
1/4 cup brandy

Pan sear filéts in hot butter, add more butter as needed. Cook steaks to desired doneness and set aside. Put mustard in pan you cooked steaks in and stir to get meat particles. Add cream and Tabasco. Whisk and add brandy. Cook for 10 minutes to reduce. Place steak on serving plate and pour sauce over. Serve with salad and good red wine.

Baba Hendricks
TSU Friend

Tastes and Traditions

African Chop

This recipe was given to me by my sister, Jeannie Thomason Crowder, who was a Southern Baptist missionary to Nigeria, West Africa, from 1958 to 1968.

Chicken
Chicken broth
Curry powder
1/4 cup chunky peanut butter
Rice

Condiments:
Add or subtract any fruits or raw vegetables:
Celery, avocado, mangos, cantaloupe, raisins fluffed in hot water, red or green bell pepper, mandarin oranges, tomatoes, onions, hard-cooked eggs, bananas, crushed pineapple, dry-roasted peanuts, fresh coconut, ginger powder, green grapes

Boil chicken, allowing 1/4 cup per person. When done remove meat from bone and chop. Set aside. Make thick gravy from chicken broth. Add curry powder to taste. Stir in peanut butter and chopped chicken. Place rice on plate and top with chicken gravy. Chop vegetables and fruit and arrange as condiments in separate bowls. Sprinkle chicken with condiments as desired.

Eloise Thomason Kirk
TSU Friend

Kilby Hall, erected in 1924, was the first building constructed on the current TSU campus. Initially a training ground for Troy Normal students, Kilby stood on the site now occupied by the Adams Administration Building. It was a frequent subject of art students, including this class from the late 1930s.

Main Dishes

Orange-Cranberry Pork Chops

6 center-cut pork loin chops
1/4 teaspoon salt
Pepper to taste
1 tablespoon vegetable oil
1 (11 ounce) can mandarin oranges in light syrup, drained
1/2 cup dried cranberries
1/2 teaspoon ground cloves or ground allspice
1/2 cup chicken broth

Sprinkle the chops lightly with salt and pepper. Heat oil in a large skillet over medium-high heat. Add chops and brown on both sides, in batches if necessary. Top with oranges and cranberries, sprinkle with cloves and add broth. Bring to a boil Reduce heat to low; cover and simmer 15 minutes or until juices run clear when meat is pierced.

Amber Abercrombie
TSU Student
Phi Mu Sorority

Steamed Barbecued Spareribs

This recipe is good to cook ahead and freeze. If you like barbecue sauce a little on the hot side, add hot sauce to the recipe. Extra sauce is good served over rice. My family really likes this recipe.

3 pounds spareribs, cut in 2 or 3 inch lengths
1 medium onion, chopped fine
2 tablespoons vinegar
4 tablespoons lemon juice
2 tablespoons brown sugar
1 cup ketchup
3 tablespoons Worcestershire sauce
1 tablespoon prepared mustard
1 1/4 cups water
1 teaspoon salt
1/2 teaspoon black pepper

Brown spareribs on both sides in skillet and place in a saucepan. Mix remaining ingredients together and pour over ribs. Cook on high until steaming, reduce heat and simmer. Cook until ribs are tender, about 1 to 1 1/2 hours.

Edna Railey
TSU

Tastes and Traditions

Barbecued Spareribs and Sauce

1/2 cup cider vinegar
1/2 cup dry white wine
1 large onion, chopped
1 teaspoon dry mustard
2 tablespoons brown sugar
1/3 cup Worcestershire sauce
1 lemon, sliced
2 cloves garlic, minced
2 dashes Tabasco sauce
6 pounds loin ribs, cut in 8 to 10 rib pieces
3 teaspoons salt
1/4 teaspoon pepper
1 onion, quartered

Combine vinegar, wine, chopped onion, dry mustard, brown sugar, Worcestershire sauce, lemon slices, garlic and Tabasco in a saucepan. Bring to a boil, reduce heat and simmer, uncovered, for 1 hour. Place ribs in a large pan and cover with water. Add salt, pepper and quartered onion. Bring to a boil, reduce heat and simmer for 15 to 20 minutes. Drain. Place ribs bone-side-down over slow fire (250 to 300 degrees) to which soaked hickory chips have been added. Baste immediately with sauce. Broil 15 minutes. Turn meaty side down and baste with sauce. Leave this side down about 5 minutes or until brown. Turn meat-side-up. Again baste and broil 15 to 20 minutes more. Baste again. Turn over for 2 minutes.

Brandy Trawick
TSU Student
Kappa Delta Sorority

Steak Bake

4 - 6 eye round steaks
Meat tenderizer
Seasoned salt
Dale's steak sauce
2 packages brown gravy mix
3 - 4 medium potatoes, peeled and quartered

Sprinkle steaks with meat tenderizer and seasoned salt. Place in a dish with raised sides and cover with 1/2 inch of Dale's steak sauce. Refrigerate for 15 to 20 minutes. Mix gravy ingredients according to package directions but don't heat gravy. Place steaks in a 9 x 13-inch baking pan. Layer potatoes over steaks and pour gravy mix over potatoes. Cover with tin foil and bake in 350 degree oven for 1 1/2 to 2 hours.

Carrie Rogers
TSU Student

Main Dishes

Slow-Cooked Pepper Steak

After a long day in class, I appreciate coming home to this hearty beef dish. It's an easy entree for a family or casual company meal. A crock pot or slow cooker is needed.

1 1/2 - 2 pounds beef round steak
2 tablespoons cooking oil
1/4 cup soy sauce
1 cup chopped onion
1 garlic clove, minced
1 teaspoon sugar
1/2 teaspoon salt
1/4 teaspoon pepper
1/4 teaspoon ground ginger
1 (16 ounce) can tomatoes with liquid, cut up
2 large green peppers, cut into strips
1/2 cup cold water
1 tablespoon cornstarch
Cooked noodles or rice (enough for 4 - 6 servings)

Cut beef in to 3 x 1 inch strips; brown in oil in a skillet. Transfer to a crock pot. Combine soy sauce, onion, garlic, sugar, salt, pepper and ginger. Pour over beef. Cover and cook on low for 6 hours or until meat is tender. Add tomatoes and green peppers; cook on low for 1 hour longer. Combine the cold water and cornstarch to make a paste; stir into liquid in crock pot and cook on high until thickened. Serve over noodles or rice.

Jennifer Handke King
TSU Student

Winter-Style Barbecue Brisket

This recipe came from a 92-year-old woman in Texas. She said it was a great way to heat up the house in the winter and get a great meal. It works.

1 brisket of beef
1 can Coca-Cola (no substitutions)
1 package onion soup mix
1 jar chili sauce
*Glass pan with glass lid important

Place brisket in glass pan fat side up. Carefully mix coke, soup mix, and chili sauce. Pour mixture over brisket. Place glass lid on pan. Bake at 350 degrees for 3 hours. DO NOT OPEN until 3 hours is up. Serve with sauce. Great recipe.

Donna Morgan
TSU Student-Florida Region

Tastes and Traditions

Beef Stir-Fry

1 pound chuck roast
1 onion, chopped
1 green bell pepper, sliced
6 whole red peppers
1/4 cup oil
2 ounces Worcestershire sauce
4 ounces soy sauce
2 ounces honey
1 tablespoon pepper
6 cups cooked rice

Slice roast into thin strips. Stir fry with onion, bell pepper and red peppers in oil in large skillet until meat is tender. Add Worcestershire sauce, soy sauce, honey and pepper. Cook for 5 minutes, stirring constantly. Serve over rice.

Leigh Tranum
TSU Student
Phi Mu Sorority

Roast and Gravy

This is to be prepared in a crock pot.

1 small chuck roast
1 can cream of mushroom soup
1 can beef broth
salt and pepper

Place roast in crock pot. Add soup and broth. Cook 6 to 8 hours on medium. Add salt and pepper to taste.

Hope Hobdy
TSU Student
Kappa Delta Sorority

Biology professor Christi Magrath won a prestigious grant from the National Science Foundation in March 2000 to examine the workings of deoxyribonucleic acid, or DNA. The $400,000 grant was the largest research grant ever received by a TSU professor.

Main Dishes

Student Etiquette Luncheons

We have such wonderful students at T.S.U.! In the early 1990s, the Honors Leadership class requested an etiquette lesson so it would be better prepared for business luncheons. I have since given a version of this lesson to other campus groups and classes. The following are a few of the students' frequently asked questions, as well as some dining do's and don'ts we've discussed. We also talk about such topics as thank-you notes, R.S.V.P.'s, handshakes and proper dress. We have fun at these sessions and learn a lot. The food served at the luncheons has been delicious and different. We have served pâté, caviar and sorbet, so we can learn which utensils to use and experience new and different foods as well. We have included the recipe for Chicken Kiev, which was a favorite at our luncheons, along with Spinach Casserole, which is located in the vegetable section of this cookbook. The favorite dessert served is Oreo Ice Cream Pie, which can be found in the first edition of "Tastes and Traditions."

Janice Hawkins

Chicken Kiev

1/2 cup butter or margarine
1/2 teaspoon chopped fresh parsley
1 1/2 teaspoons chopped chives
1 tablespoon lemon juice
6 boneless chicken breasts
Salt and pepper to taste
3 tablespoons water
3 eggs, lightly beaten
2 cups fine dry bread crumbs
Oil for deep frying

In a small bowl, combine butter, parsley, chives and lemon juice. Blend all together and refrigerate. Place chicken breasts between two pieces of wax paper and pound well to flatten. Remove paper and season breasts with salt and pepper to taste. Remove seasoned butter from refrigerator and divide it into six portions. Place one portion in the center of each chicken breast. Fold the short ends of the breast into the center, then fold in the sides. Secure each breast with a wooden toothpick. Add the water to the eggs and beat together. Coat each breast with bread crumbs, dip into egg wash, then into bread crumbs again, coating well. Chill breasts for one hour. In a deep fryer, heat oil to 365 degrees. Carefully lower breasts into hot oil. Fry for 8 minutes or until golden brown. Drain on paper toweling and serve. Makes 6 servings.

Tastes and Traditions

Student Questions

Q. When is it appropriate to begin eating?
A. You may begin eating when everyone at your table is served or when your host suggests you begin.

Q. When you have finished eating, when is it appropriate to get up and leave the table?
A. You may leave when your host does, unless you excuse yourself.

Q. What do you do when someone asks a question and you have food in your mouth?
A. Chew - swallow - then talk.

Q. What if you don't like what is served?
A. It is polite to try everything that is served to you unless you are allergic to that food.

Q. What is the proper way to butter your bread during dinner?
A. Cut or break small pieces of your bread and butter as you eat them.

Q. What do you do with coffee cups, glasses, etc. that are not used?
A. You leave them where they are and a server will remove them.

Q. What is the most appropriate way to ask someone to pass food?
A. Ask the person the item is in front of, or if they are too far away, the person next to you. Say, "Please pass the rolls."

Q. Is it "OK" to rest your arm on the table?
A. Not during the meal; after the table is cleared, it is fine to rest your arms on the table.

Q. How do you know where to sit if there are no place cards?
A. Follow your host's lead; if he tells you to sit anywhere, then do so. Leave the chair to the host's right for the guest of honor.

Q. Which way do you pass food?
A. Always pass food to the right.

Q. When should you write a thank-you note?
A. It is never inappropriate to write a thank-you note or letter. If you know someone very well, a phone call will suffice but a note is always best.

Q. What does R.S.V.P. mean?
A. It is French for "please respond." This lack of response is the most common etiquette error. It is very impolite not to respond to an invitation.

Q. How do I know which fork to use?
A. If there is more than one fork, begin with the one farthest from your plate. If in doubt, follow the lead of your host.

Main Dishes

Some Dining "Do's and Don'ts"

If you wish to share food, use your bread plate.

Do: Wait until you have swallowed a bite of food before taking a sip of your beverage.

Soup should be spooned away from you. Tilt the bowl away from you. Don't crumble crackers into your soup, with the exception of oyster crackers. (Sorry! All of you who crunch up crackers in the cellophane and dump them in your soup have to stop. Do it at home -- alone.)

Do: Keep dinner conversation pleasant.

You may eat chicken and pizza with your fingers if you are at a barbecue or very informal setting. Otherwise use a knife and fork for chicken.

Keep your napkin in your lap until you leave the table. When you are finished dining, place your napkin in loose folds at the left side of your plate, never on top of the plate. Never use a napkin as a handkerchief.

Do: Put your napkin in your lap as soon as you are seated.

Don't: Wave cutlery when you talk.

When you are finished eating, don't push your plate away or stack your dishes. Place your knife and fork together in the "twenty past four" position, as if your plate were the face of the clock, with the knife on the outside and the fork on the inside. You may also place the utensils side by side in the middle of your plate, fork tines down, knife to the right, sharp blade turned inward toward the fork.

Initiate the passing of buns, butter and condiments even if you do not want any. Pass to the right.

Don't: Lean back in your chair.

Don't: Belch! Cover your mouth with your napkin. After it happens, say a quiet "pardon me" to no one in particular.

If you, yourself, or someone else spills on the table, discreetly use your napkin or ask the waiter for seltzer water. Do not dip your napkin into your water glass. Let victims of your indiscretion blot for themselves. Offer to cover any laundering or cleaning costs.

Don't: Use toothpicks, fingernails or napkins to dislodge food. If you're in agony, retire to the bathroom and take care of it.

Don't: Apply makeup or comb your hair at the table.

When you wish to use the washroom, excuse yourself and leave quietly. Don't ask people where they are going if they excuse themselves.

Tastes and Traditions

Chicken Breasts Florentine

8 boneless, skinless chicken breasts
1/3 cup flour
2 tablespoons olive oil
2 tablespoons light margarine
1 (10 ounce) package frozen chopped spinach
8 thin square slices part-skim mozzarella cheese
1/2 cup chicken broth
1/4 cup white wine
1/4 cup lemon juice

Dust chicken breasts with flour. In large skillet coated with nonstick spray, heat olive oil and margarine and sauté breasts until lightly browned, about 4 minutes on each side. Remove to a 3-quart oblong dish. Cook spinach according to directions on package, squeeze and drain well. Top each chicken breast with cooked spinach and a slice of cheese. Add chicken broth to the skillet. Next, add wine and lemon juice, scraping to remove drippings and stirring until heated. Pour sauce over chicken. Bake at 325 degrees for 25 minutes. Cheese should be melted and breasts heated thoroughly.

Vicki Schmidt
TSU

Lauren Patterson
TSU Student
Phi Mu Sorority

These Troy Normal students rehearse for a summer festival in the courtyard of Kilby Hall, circa 1927.

Main Dishes

Chicken Casserole

1 package egg noodles, cooked and drained
1 cup chicken broth
1 can cream of chicken soup
8 ounces sour cream
1 small chicken, cooked and cut in bite-size pieces
3 slices bread
1/4 stick butter or margarine

Mix egg noodles, chicken broth, soup and sour cream in bowl with chicken pieces. Pour into a baking dish and crumble bread on top. Do with butter and bake at 300 degrees for 45 minutes.

Edna Railey
TSU

Chicken Mornay

This is so good!

1/4 cup butter
5 tablespoons flour
2 cubes chicken bouillon
1/2 cup heavy cream
1/4 teaspoon salt
Dash pepper
1 teaspoon Worcestershire sauce
1 (10 ounce) can mushrooms, drained
1/4 cup sherry
1 (10 ounce) package frozen French-style green beans, cooked and drained
2 cups cooked chicken in small pieces
1/4 cup slivered almonds, toasted
1/3 cup grated Parmesan cheese

Melt butter in medium saucepan and blend in flour. In a separate bowl dissolve bouillon in 1/2 cup water or chicken broth. Gradually add bouillon and cream to flour. Cook on medium heat, stirring constantly, until smooth and thick. Stir in salt, pepper, Worcestershire sauce, mushrooms and sherry. Butter a 1 1/2-quart casserole dish. Arrange beans in bottom of dish, followed by chicken and almonds. Pour sauce over chicken. Top with cheese and bake at 375 degrees for 20 minutes until golden and bubbly.

Anita Hardin
TSU

Tastes and Traditions

Chicken Casserole

1 quart sour cream
2 (8 ounce) cans cream of chicken soup
1 pound boneless, skinless chicken or 6 - 8 chicken breasts, cooked and cut in bite-size pieces
Ritz crackers
1 stick butter or margarine
Poppy seeds, optional

Preheat oven to 350 degrees Combine the sour cream and cream of chicken soup in a bowl. Add chicken and stir well. Pour into a greased 9 x 13-inch glass casserole dish. Melt butter in bowl. Crush crackers and add to butter. Mix well. Spread cracker mixture over chicken. Sprinkle poppy seeds on top of crackers, if desired. Bake for 20 to 25 minutes or until brown on top. Let cool for 15 minutes, then enjoy!

Kate Duren *TSU Student* *Phi Mu Sorority*	*Elyse Toulmin* *TSU Student* *Alpha Gamma Delta Sorority*
Jade Smith *TSUD '98*	*Lindsay Rigdon Hutchisson* *TSU Student*
Stacy Gantt *TSU Student* *Alpha Gamma Delta Sorority*	

TSU benefactor Seymour Gitenstein honored his wife and beautified the campus when he funded creation of the Anna Green Gitenstein Memorial Rose Garden. Located in front of Smith Hall, the rose garden features a fountain, an arbor and several benches. Mr. Gitenstein has also funded several scholarships in honor of family members.

Main Dishes

Spinach-Stuffed Chicken Breast with Bearnaise Sauce

This recipe was prepared for the annual Alumni of the Year dinner hosted by Dr. and Mrs. Hawkins.

1 tablespoon butter
4 ounces mushrooms, finely chopped
1 (10 ounce) package frozen chopped spinach, thawed and squeezed dry
6 ounces cream cheese, room temperature
1/2 cup chopped fresh chives or green onion tops
6 chicken breasts, with skin
6 tablespoons Dijon mustard

Bearnaise Sauce:
1/4 cup white wine vinegar
1/4 dry white wine
1 tablespoon minced shallots
1 tablespoon dried tarragon
Salt and pepper
3 egg yolks
2 sticks unsalted butter, melted
2 tablespoons minced fresh tarragon

Preheat oven to 450 degrees. Melt butter in heavy medium skillet over medium heat. Add mushrooms and sauté until tender, about 5 minutes. Cool slightly. Blend spinach, cream cheese and chives in medium bowl. Mix in mushrooms and season with salt and pepper. Run fingers under the skin of each chicken breast to loosen, creating pocket. Spread a sixth of cheese mixture between skin and meat of each breast. Arrange chicken breasts on baking sheet. Spread 1 tablespoon Dijon mustard over each breast. Bake until golden brown and cooked through, about 20 minutes. Serve immediately.

For Sauce: In small saucepan combine vinegar, wine, shallots, and tarragon. Simmer over moderate heat until reduced to 2 tablespoons of liquid. Cool and strain through a fine sieve. In top of double boiler or a heatproof bowl whisk egg yolks until thick and sticky. Whisk in reduced vinegar mixture and pepper. Place the pan over a saucepan of simmering, not boiling, water. Whisk until mixture is warm, about 2 minutes. (If mixture becomes lumpy, dip pan immediately in a bowl of ice water to cool, whisk until smooth and then continue with recipe.) The yolk mixture has thickened enough when you can see the bottom of the pan between strokes and mixture forms a light cream on the wires of the whip. While whisking the yolk mixture, gradually pour in the melted butter, a tablespoon or so at a time, whisking thoroughly to incorporate before adding more butter. As the mixture begins to thicken and become creamy, the butter can be added more rapidly. Do not add the milk solids at the bottom of the melted butter. Season the sauce to taste with chopped tarragon, salt and pepper. To keep the sauce warm, set in lukewarm water or in a thermos. Drizzle sauce over chicken breast and around edges.

Sodexho-Marriott
TSU

Tastes and Traditions

Creamy Skillet Chicken

3 cups cubed, cooked chicken
1/2 teaspoon thyme
2 teaspoons oil
1 can cream of mushroom soup
1/2 cup milk
1 can green beans, drained
Hot buttered noodles

Heat chicken and thyme in oil in skillet, 3 minutes. Blend soup with milk; add to skillet with vegetables. Heat through. Serve over hot buttered noodles.

Bonnie, Kari Ann, Kendra and Missy
TSU Students
Kappa Delta Sorority

Members of Kappa Delta Sorority show their spirit at a 1999 pep rally.

Italian Baked Chicken

Boneless chicken breast
Italian dressing
Potato flakes

Preheat oven to 275 degrees Dip chicken breasts in a bowl of Italian dressing and roll in a plate of potato flakes. Place in a casserole dish. Repeat steps for all chicken breasts. Cover dish with foil and bake 30 to 40 minutes. Check to see that chicken is cooked all the way through. Remove foil and bake an additional 10 minutes, or until golden brown. Enjoy your moist, marinated chicken breasts.

Jessica Lewis
TSU Student
Kappa Delta Sorority

Main Dishes

Chicken Tetrazzini

1 can boneless white meat chicken, drained
1 can cream of mushroom soup
1 can cream of celery soup
1 package egg noodles, cooked and drained
Cheese slices

Mix chicken, soups and egg noodles together and put in a greased baking dish. Top with cheese slices and bake for 45 minutes at 350 degrees

Anna Senn
TSU Student
Phi Mu Sorority

Chicken and Broccoli Ring

This is a quick recipe to feed folks in a hurry. It looks like it took hours to fix when in reality it can be done in only a few minutes.

2 packages refrigerated crescent rolls
1/2 stick butter, melted
1 box frozen chopped broccoli (or fresh if you prefer)
1 (10 ounce) can white chicken breast or 3 cooked, deboned and finely chopped chicken breasts
1 can cream of chicken, mushroom or celery soup
1/2 cup chopped green, yellow and/or red bell pepper
1/4 cup finely diced onion or onion flakes
1 cup grated sharp cheese
Salt and pepper
1 egg white
Sesame seeds or poppy seeds, optional

Use a round pizza pan or baking stone. Unroll crescent rolls and separate into triangles. Arrange triangles in a circle with wide ends overlapping in center and points toward the outside. There should be at least a 5-inch opening in the center. Brush crust lightly with melted butter. If you use frozen chopped broccoli, microwave in bowl for about 3 to 5 minutes. Drain well. Place broccoli and chicken in a bowl. Add soup, bell pepper, onion and cheese and mix until well-blended. Salt and pepper to taste. Spoon mixture generously and equally onto crescent rolls (wide area). Bring outside points of triangles down over filling and tuck under wide ends of dough at center. Filling will not be completely covered. Brush over-lapped crust with egg white. Sprinkle with sesame or poppy seed, if desired. Bake at 375 degrees for 20 to 25 minutes or until golden brown. Serve hot. Reheats well in microwave.

Donna Reynolds
TSU '86

Tastes and Traditions

Mexican Chicken

This is a great dish to carry to a party or to take tailgating with the Trojans.

1 whole chicken, cooked and cut into bite-size pieces
1 onion, chopped
Garlic salt to taste
1/2 pound box processed cheese, sliced
1 bag Doritos
1 can cream of chicken soup
1 can cream of mushroom soup
1 can Rotel tomatoes

Arrange chicken in large casserole dish. Add onion and sprinkle garlic salt over chicken. Top with cheese. Crumble half of Doritos over chicken. Mix soups and Rotel tomatoes and pour over casserole. Top with remaining chips. Bake at 350 degrees for 45 minutes.

Judy Morgan
TSU

Three-Cheese Chicken Casserole

1/2 cup chopped green pepper
1/2 cup chopped onion
3 tablespoons melted butter
1 can cream of chicken soup
1/2 cup milk
1 cup sliced mushrooms
1/4 teaspoon black pepper
1 (5 ounce) package wide noodles, cooked and drained
1 (12 ounce) carton cottage cheese
3 cups cooked bite-size chicken pieces
1 (10 ounce) package mild Cheddar cheese, grated
1/2 cup grated Parmesan cheese
Paprika

Sauté green pepper and onion in butter until tender. Remove from heat. Stir in soup, milk, mushrooms, and pepper. Arrange half of noodles in ungreased 9 x 13-inch pan. Add half of soup mixture. Top with half of cottage cheese, half of chicken and half of Cheddar cheese. Repeat layers. Top with Parmesan cheese. Sprinkle with paprika. Bake at 350 degrees for 45 minutes.

Pat Hardin
TSU

Main Dishes

Chicken and Broccoli Casserole

4 chicken breasts, cooked and cut into bite-size pieces
2 packages frozen broccoli, thawed
1/2 cup mayonnaise
1 teaspoon curry powder
Juice of one lemon
1 can cream of mushroom soup
1/2 cup shredded Cheddar cheese
1/2 cup bread crumbs

Place chicken in casserole dish which has been coated with nonstick spray. Arrange broccoli over chicken. Combine mayonnaise, curry powder, lemon juice and soup. Pour over chicken and broccoli. Sprinkle with cheese and bread crumbs. Bake at 325 degrees for about 30 minutes.

Mrs. Mickey (Susan) Holmes
TSUM

Chicken Casserole

This dish is a favorite of Stan's, # 71, Trojan offensive line.

1 cup cooked rice
1/4 cup chopped onion
1/4 cup chopped celery
1/2 cup mayonnaise
3 hard-cooked eggs, chopped
1/2 teaspoon lemon juice
1 can cream of chicken soup
Salt and pepper to taste
1 stack Ritz crackers, crumbled
1 stick butter, melted

Mix all ingredients except crackers and butter and put in a greased casserole dish. Sprinkle cracker crumbs on top. Pour butter over crackers. Bake in a 350 degree oven about 30 minutes.

Linda Curington
TSU Parent

The Alabama Society of Certified Public Accountants renamed its annual Outstanding Professional Educator Award for Tom Ratcliffe, dean of the Sorrell College of Business, after he captured the award seven consecutive years from 1990-1996.

Tastes and Traditions

Chicken à la King

This is an excellent dish to serve at luncheons for ladies.

1/2 cup melted butter
3 tablespoons flour
1 can chicken broth
1 cup milk
1 teaspoon salt
2 cups diced cooked chicken
1 (3 ounce) can broiled sliced mushrooms, drained
1/4 cup chopped pimentos
Hot toast points

Blend butter with flour in a saucepan. Gradually stir in broth and milk. Cook over low heat, stirring constantly, until sauce is thick. Add salt, chicken, mushrooms and pimentos and heat thoroughly. Serve over hot toast points.

Eloise Thomason Kirk
TSU Friend

Grandma's Chicken and Dressing

First you have to prepare the bread that will be used later in the recipe:
2 cups self-rising corn meal
1 1/2 cups buttermilk
1 - 2 eggs
1 tablespoon oil

Mix all ingredients and add water, if needed, to make a soft batter. Pour into a greased 9-inch pie pan and bake at 450 degrees until golden brown, 25 to 30 minutes. Set aside to cool.

Step two:
Small bag of Pepperidge Farm bread crumbs
1 can cream of chicken soup
1/4 - 1/2 cup diced onion
3 - 4 tablespoons butter
3 - 4 chicken breasts, cooked and diced
2 eggs
1 cup milk
1 can chicken broth

Mix all ingredients together in a large bowl. Crumble the bread from step 1 and add to the bowl. Turn into a greased 9 x 13-inch baking pan and bake at 350 degrees for 35 to 45 minutes.

Carrie Rogers
TSU Student

Main Dishes

Chicken Pie

This is a dish for all chicken lovers. It tastes like you spent hours in the kitchen! If you don't have the time to boil the chicken you can easily substitute canned chicken instead.

1 fryer
2 cups chicken broth
1 can cream of chicken soup
1 can English peas and carrots, or 1 can mixed vegetables
4 hard-cooked eggs
1 cup self-rising flour
1 stick margarine
1 cup milk

Boil chicken until tender; remove meat from bone. Line dish with chicken. Mix chicken broth with soup and pour over chicken. Spread vegetables over soup mixture. Slice eggs over soup mixture. Mix together flour, margarine, and milk. Pour over casserole. Bake at 350 degrees for 1 hour.

Mrs. Mickey (Susan) Holmes
TSUM

Jean S. Helms
TSU Friend

Sara Jones
TSU Spouse

Classic Roast Chicken

1 roasting chicken (approximately 3 1/2 pounds)
1/2 teaspoon dried thyme
1/2 teaspoon salt
1 tablespoon butter, softened and divided
1 stalk celery, sliced
1 onion, quartered

Preheat oven to 425 degrees. Sprinkle inside cavity of chicken with thyme and salt. Add 1 teaspoon butter, celery and onion. Rub outside of chicken with remaining butter. Place chicken breast side down on rack in roasting pan. Add enough water to cover bottom of pan. Roast for 10 to 15 minutes. Reduce temperature to 375 degrees and roast for 20 minutes longer. Turn chicken breast side up and roast until chicken is brown, approximately 30 minutes longer.

Debbie Sanders
TSU

Tastes and Traditions

Mushroom Chicken

This recipe is delicious and incredibly easy to prepare! A perfect way to impress last-minute company.

4 boneless, skinless chicken breasts
1 can cream of chicken soup
1 large can of mushroom pieces, drained
1 onion, chopped, optional
1 teaspoon butter or margarine
1/2 cup milk
1/2 cup water
Cooked white rice

Coat large skillet with nonstick cooking spray. Add chicken breasts and cook on medium heat. Meanwhile, in small skillet sauté mushrooms and onions, if desired, in butter over low heat. When chicken is almost finished cooking (slightly pink in middle), add cream of chicken soup, milk, water, and sautéed vegetables. Cook until chicken is no longer pink. Serve over cooked white rice.

Erin Coates Whitehead
TSU Friend

Chicken Casserole

1 can cream of celery soup
1 medium onion, chopped
1 small can diced pimento, drained
1 can water chestnuts, drained and chopped
1 can French-style string beans, drained
1 cup mayonnaise
3 cups cooked chicken, chopped (I use frozen chicken tenderloin strips)
2 (6 ounce) packages wild rice, cooked according to directions
1/2 stick butter
1 cup grated Swiss cheese

Combine soup, onion, pimento, chestnuts, string beans and mayonnaise, mixing well. Stir in chicken and rice. Salt and pepper to taste. Melt butter in casserole. Spoon chicken mixture into casserole and sprinkle with cheese. Bake 25 to 30 minutes at 350 degrees, until casserole bubbles in middle and cheese melts.

Edna R. Beall Archibald
TSU '42

Main Dishes

Rotel Chicken Casserole

A good recipe to use if having company. Can be made ahead of time. A favorite of (Trojan quarterback) Brock Nutter and his football friends.

12 ounces egg noodles
1 pound processed cheese
1 large onion, chopped
2 tablespoons butter
1 can cream of chicken soup
1 can cream of mushroom soup
2/3 can Rotel tomatoes and green chiles
4 cups cooked chicken breast in bite-size pieces

Cook noodles, drain and layer in 9 x 12-inch Pyrex dish. Sauté onion in butter. Melt cheese and add to onions. Add soups, Rotel, and chicken and mix thoroughly. Pour over noodles. Bake at 350 degrees for 30 to 45 minutes.

Vicki Nutter
TSU Parent

Sour Cream Chicken Squares

2 cups Bisquik
1/2 cup cold water
1 cup cubed cooked chicken
1 (4 ounce) can mushrooms, drained
1 (2 ounce) jar diced pimentos, drained
1/3 cup thinly sliced green onions
1 cup shredded cheese
1 cup sour cream
1/3 cup mayonnaise
3 eggs
1 teaspoon garlic salt
1/8 teaspoon pepper

Heat oven to 425 degrees. Mix baking mix and water until soft dough forms; beat vigorously 20 strokes. Gently smooth dough into ball on floured cloth-covered board. Knead 5 times. Roll dough into rectangle. Place dough in a greased 9 x 13-inch baking dish so edges are 1/2 inch up sides. Mix remaining ingredients; pour evenly over dough. Bake until edges are golden brown and knife inserted in center comes out clean, about 25 minutes.

Elaine Thomas
TSU Student
Phi Mu Sorority

Tastes and Traditions

Garlic Mushroom Chicken Breast

4 skinless chicken breasts
1 package garlic and mushroom soup mix
1/4 cup grated Parmesan cheese
1/4 cup light mayonnaise
3 tablespoons bread crumbs

Preheat oven to 400 degrees. Wash and place skinless chicken breasts in casserole dish. Mix soup mix, cheese and mayonnaise. Spread mixture on chicken. Sprinkle with bread crumbs and bake for about 20 to 25 minutes.

Tracy Lee-Berry
TSU-New Orleans Student

Sesame Chicken

This is our family's favorite recipe. We got it on a United Air Lines flight to Hawaii in 1972.

6 tablespoons flour, divided
1/2 teaspoon salt
1/4 teaspoon pepper
4 boneless chicken breasts
2 eggs
1/4 cup milk
3 tablespoon sesame seeds

Supreme Sauce:
3 tablespoons butter
2 tablespoons flour
1 1/2 cups chicken broth
Salt and pepper
1 egg yolk

Combine 2 tablespoons flour, salt and pepper in a clean paper or plastic bag. Add chicken pieces and shake to coat. Beat eggs with milk. Mix the remaining 4 tablespoons flour and the sesame seeds. Dip each breast into egg mixture, then roll in sesame mixture to coat. Lower into deep oil for frying (350 degrees). Fry for 15 minutes or until golden and tender. Drain on crumpled paper towels. Serve with Supreme Sauce.

For Sauce: Melt butter in a saucepan. Stir in flour to make a smooth paste. Gradually add chicken broth, and cook, stirring, to make a smooth sauce. Season with salt and pepper. Beat egg yolk. Gradually whisk about 1/2 cup of the sauce into yolk. Gradually beat yolk mixture back into sauce and cook over low heat until thick.

Meg Crew
TSU Friend

Main Dishes

Barbecue Chicken Cubes

This is a quick way to have the old-fashioned taste of barbecue chicken. My mom used to prepare it for us after a long day at work.

1 tablespoon butter
6 boneless chicken breasts, cut in bite-size pieces
2 tablespoons creole seasoning
2 teaspoons soul seasoning
1 bottle barbecue sauce

Melt butter in frying pan, add chicken pieces and cook until meat turns white; sprinkle with seasonings. Drain. Pour barbecue sauce over meat and mix. Let simmer for about 3 to 4 minutes.

Connie Hawthorne
TSU Student

Sour Cream Chicken

Boneless, skinless chicken breasts
8 ounces sour cream
1/4 cup lemon juice
2 tablespoons Worcestershire sauce
2 teaspoons celery salt
2 teaspoons garlic salt
Dash of salt and pepper
Crushed Ritz and saltine crackers
1 cup melted butter, divided

Marinate chicken breasts in sour cream, lemon juice, Worcestershire sauce, celery salt, garlic salt and salt and pepper for 12 hours. Roll chicken in a mixture of crushed Ritz and saltine crackers. Place in casserole dish. Drizzle 1/2 cup melted butter over chicken. Cook at 350 degrees for 30 minutes. Drizzle remaining butter over chicken and cook an additional 30 minutes.

Brandi Baker
TSU Student
Phi Mu Sorority

TSU professors Ben Bateman and Ravinder Sandhu have participated in the NASA/JOVE project, a research and outreach project of NASA.

Tastes and Traditions

Chicken Pilaf

1 1/4 cups boiling water
1 can cream of mushroom soup
1/4 cup cooking sherry
1/2 envelope onion soup mix
1 1/3 cups minute rice
2 tablespoons chopped pimento
5 boneless chicken breasts
Salt and pepper to taste
Butter

Mix water, soup, sherry, soup mix, rice and pimento and spoon into a greased 1 1/2-quart casserole. Season chicken, place on top of mixture and dot with butter. Bake, uncovered, at 350 degrees for 1 1/2 hours.

Hope Hobdy
TSU Student
Kappa Delta Sorority

Pakistani Chicken Marsala

This is one of my favorite recipes from Pakistan.

4 medium onions, minced
1/2 cup vegetable oil
2 spring onions, chopped
10 cloves garlic, minced
1 tablespoon grated ginger root
6 medium tomatoes, chopped
1 1/2 teaspoons cumin
1/2 teaspoon curry powder
1 tablespoon coriander powder
1 teaspoon chili powder
1 teaspoon salt
2 1/2 pounds chicken breasts, cubed

Sauté onions in vegetable oil until tender. Add spring onions, garlic and ginger. Cook until brown, stirring frequently. Add 2 tablespoons water. Add spices and tomatoes to onion mixture and stir in 3 tablespoons water. Cover and simmer for 5 minutes on low heat. Stir until tomatoes come apart. Turn heat up and add chicken. Stir to cover with sauce. Cook for 25 minutes. Sauce will thicken. Add 1 cup water and stir. Lower heat, cover and simmer 5 minutes. Turn heat up and bring to boil. Stir, then lower heat and simmer for 15 minutes. Serve with pita bread.

Michael K. Armstrong
TSU '71

Main Dishes

Dahari Chicken

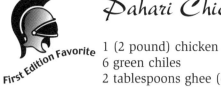

First Edition Favorite

1 (2 pound) chicken
6 green chiles
2 tablespoons ghee (clarified butter)
3 cardamom pods
1-inch piece ginger, minced
garlic
Salt
2 pints curd or yogurt
1 tablespoon chopped coriander leaves

Joint the chicken. Mince 2 green chiles and set aside. Slit the remaining chiles and fry in hot ghee with cardamom, ginger, and garlic. Add chicken pieces and fry till evenly browned. Whip curd and add to chicken; lower heat and simmer gently without stirring. Add salt to taste and cook until chicken is tender and a creamy thick gravy is produced. Garnish with coriander leaves and reserved green chiles. Serve with rice.

Sohail Agboatwala
TSU

Party Chicken

8 boneless chicken breasts
8 slices bacon
4 ounces dried beef
1 can cream of mushroom soup
1/2 pint sour cream

Wrap each chicken breast with slice of bacon. Line greased baking dish with dried beef. Place chicken breast over beef. Combine soup and sour cream. Pour over chicken and refrigerate. Bake at 275 degrees for 2 1/2 hours.

Ginger Armstrong
TSU Spouse

TSU has been rated one of the top 25 "best buys" in the nation among public colleges and universities by Money magazine and has been named one of the top southern regional universities by U.S. News & World Report.

Tastes and Traditions

Broccoli-Chicken-Ham Pizza

This recipe was an experiment. I love pizza but wanted to make one a little more healthy. Since broccoli is my favorite green veggie, I tried this and it was delicious.

1 ready-made pizza crust
1 can cream of chicken mushroom or celery soup
1 pound fresh, chopped broccoli
5 - 10 ounces chopped, thinly sliced ham or Canadian bacon
1 (10 ounce) can white chicken meat, drained
1/2 cup finely sliced or diced bell pepper
Chopped mushrooms, optional
1 cup grated sharp Cheddar or mozzarella cheese

Place prepared crust on baking stone, lightly greased pizza pan or cookie sheet. Spread a half to three-quarters can cream of chicken soup onto crust. Add broccoli, ham, chicken, bell pepper, and mushrooms, if desired. You can mix all together and spread evenly over crust or just sprinkle evenly over crust. Top with cheese. Bake for 20 to 25 minutes at 375 degrees until golden brown.

Donna Reynolds
TSU '86

College-Style Quesadillas

6 - 8 flour tortillas
2 cans cream of chicken soup
3 cups diced grilled chicken
Salsa
Grated Cheddar cheese

Arrange a layer of tortillas in a greased casserole dish. Alternate layers of soup, chicken and salsa. You should repeat 3 times. Place tortillas on top. Sprinkle with cheese and bake in a 450 degree oven for 30 to 45 minutes or until golden brown. Cool and serve.

Crystal Center
TSU Student

TSU has 21 honor societies recognizing student achievement and leadership.

Main Dishes

Szechwan Chicken

First Edition Favorite

2 large boneless chicken breasts
2 tablespoons soy sauce
2 tablespoons dry sherry
2 teaspoons cornstarch
1/4 teaspoon sugar
1/4 teaspoon ground ginger
1/4 teaspoon crushed red pepper
6 green onions
2 medium green peppers
Salad oil
1/2 cup dry-roasted peanuts

With knife held in slanted position almost parallel to the cutting surface, slice each breast half across width into 1/4-inch thick slices. In medium bowl, mix chicken, soy sauce, sherry, corn starch, sugar, ginger and red pepper; set aside. Cut green onions crosswise into 2-inch pieces; cut green peppers into bite-size pieces. Heat 2 tablespoons salad oil in 12-inch skillet or wok over medium-high heat. Cook green onions and peppers, stirring quickly and frequently, until vegetables are tender crisp (about 2 minutes). With slotted spoon, remove vegetables to small bowl. In same skillet over medium heat, in 3 more tablespoons hot salad oil, cook peanuts until lightly browned, stirring frequently. Remove peanuts to bowl with vegetables. In salad oil remaining in skillet over high heat, cook chicken mixture, stirring quickly and constantly, until chicken is tender (2 to 3 minutes). Return vegetables with any juices and peanuts to skillet. Heat thoroughly.

Gina Weinstein
TSU-Florida Region

The 1967 announcement that Troy State College had become Troy State University was well received by students at a rally in Sartain Hall.

Tastes and Traditions

Moroccan-Spiced Chicken with Rosemary Oil

This recipe was prepared for the luncheon honoring Howell Heflin in April 1999.

Rosemary Oil:
1 clove garlic, crushed
1/4 teaspoon freshly ground black pepper
Pinch dried red chile flakes
1 sprig fresh rosemary
1 bay leaf
1 cup extra-virgin olive oil

Spice Rub:
1/3 cup ground cumin
1/4 cup ground coriander
2 teaspoons ground cinnamon
2 teaspoons ground cloves
1 tablespoon hot chili powder
2 teaspoons paprika
1 teaspoon cayenne
1 teaspoon whole aniseed
1 tablespoon Herbes de Provence (or mixed dried fine herbes)
4 1/2 teaspoons kosher salt; more for serving
2 teaspoons freshly ground black pepper

Brochettes:
3 pounds boneless, skinless chicken breasts
1/4 cup olive oil
Lemon wedges for serving

To Make Rosemary Oil: In a medium saucepan, combine all ingredients. Heat on low until the oil just barely comes to a simmer and the garlic bubbles and floats to the surface, about 5 minutes. Immediately turn off the heat and allow the oil to infuse for 1 hour. When cool, strain through a fine sieve. The oil should be used the same day, or stored in refrigerator for a maximum of three days.

To Make Spice Rub: In a bowl, thoroughly blend all 12 spices; set aside.

To Make the Brochettes: Prepare the grill. Cut the chicken into equal 2 1/2-inch cubes. Put the chicken on a plate and sprinkle with enough spice rub to lightly coat, about 3 tablespoons. Store the remaining spice rub in an airtight container for future use. Drizzle the olive oil over the chicken and toss lightly. Thread the chicken onto skewers, folding when necessary to get round, even chunks, each a little bigger than a ping-pong ball. The

Main Dishes

chicken can be grilled immediately or held in the refrigerator for up to 1 hour. When the grill is at medium heat (you should be able to hold your hand just above the grate for 3 seconds), use tongs to clean the grate with a lightly oiled paper towel. Grill the brochettes for 4 minutes on one side, keeping the exposed skewer ends away from the hottest part of the fire if you're using bamboo. Turn and cook until the chicken is browned and firm, about 4 minutes more. You may need to turn and move the brochettes to keep the chicken from cooking at too high a heat, which will dry out the edges before the inside is done. If you're not sure that the chicken is completely cooked, pierce one piece to see that there's no pinkness. Remove the brochettes from the grill and drizzle with some of the rosemary oil. Serve with the oil, lemon wedges, and a bowl of kosher salt for extra seasoning.

Sodexho-Marriott
TSU

Longtime U.S. Senator Howell Heflin was the keynote speaker at the annual Helen Keller Lecture in April 1999.

Tastes and Traditions

Shrimp or Chicken Casserole

You can put this in two eight-inch square casserole dishes and have one to serve and one to freeze or share.

3/4 cup melted butter
1 medium onion, chopped
1 medium bell pepper, chopped
1 can French onion soup with beef stock
1 can cream of chicken soup
1 can Rotel tomatoes
3 tablespoons parsley
2 cups uncooked rice
1 teaspoon salt
Cleaned raw shrimp or cooked chicken

Mix all ingredients and place in a baking pan or large casserole dish. Cover with lid or foil. Bake at 350 degrees for 30 minutes. Remove from oven, stir, replace lid or foil and bake another 30 minutes.

Carla Musgrove Meadows
TSU Friend

Shrimp Pasta

Great for a summer patio party.

1 (16 ounce) package spaghetti
2 pounds fresh or frozen medium shrimp, cooked and peeled
3 tablespoons minced garlic
1 stalk celery, diced
1 (7 ounce) jar pimento, drained
1 (16 ounce) package frozen peas
1 - 1 1/4 cups mayonnaise
Seasoned salt to taste

Prepare spaghetti according to package directions, breaking pasta before cooking. Drain well. Add shrimp and garlic, tossing to mix thoroughly. Combine celery, pimento, peas, mayonnaise and seasoned salt. Add to spaghetti, mixing lightly, but well. Chill until ready to serve.

Debbie Fortune
TSU

Main Dishes

Shrimp Casserole

2 cups cooked wild and long grain rice
1/2 cup chopped bell pepper
1/2 cup chopped celery
1/2 cup chopped onion
1/2 cup slivered almonds
1/2 cup shredded Cheddar cheese
1 can sliced water chestnuts, drained
2 bags frozen, cooked shrimp, thawed
1 cup mayonnaise
1 cup Bloody Mary mix
Salt, pepper and paprika
Liberal shake of Creole seasoning

Mix all ingredients and pour into buttered 9 x 12-inch casserole dish. Bake at 350 degrees for 45 minutes.

Nancy Bradshaw
TSU Friend

Shrimp and Noodles

1 (12 ounce) package flat egg noodles
1/2 pound shrimp or scallops
2 tablespoons cooking oil
Blackened fish spices (no salt)
5 tablespoons butter or Morning Blend
Oregano, salt, pepper and granulated garlic
1 1/2 tablespoons lemon juice
Green onions, chopped
Parsley and lemon slices, optional

Cook egg noodles according to package directions, drain and set aside. In heavy skillet, heat cooking oil. Add shrimp; sprinkle with blackened fish spices and cook until pink. Remove from heat. Melt butter; add oregano, salt, pepper and granulated garlic to taste. Add lemon juice. Pour over shrimp and stir well. Run hot water over noodles to heat. Place in serving dish and add shrimp mixture. Sprinkle with green onions. Garnish with parsley and lemon slices if desired.

Larita Mitchell
TSU Friend

Tastes and Traditions

Salmon Croquettes

Traditional Recipe

1 can salmon, rinsed and drained
3 eggs
1 onion, finely chopped
Salt and pepper
3 - 4 crackers, crushed

Combine salmon, 2 eggs, onion and salt and pepper to taste. Mix well and form into egg-shaped patties. Dip in beaten egg and cracker crumbs and fry. Do not flatten out.

Lucy T. Nall
TSU '20

This Troy Normal School art class, circa 1888, paused from its studies to pose for this photograph. Second from left is "Collie" Gardner, a member of the school's first faculty who continued to teach at the college for nearly 50 years. When asked what she wanted for her 100th birthday, she replied, "A dress, and make sure it will last!" Miss Collie, who lived to be 105, is the namesake for Catherine Collins Gardner Hall, a female dormitory.

Main Dishes

Salmon Steaks with Caper Sauce

4 tablespoons butter, divided
1 small bulb fennel, trimmed and cut crosswise into 1/4-inch-thick slices
3/4 teaspoon salt, divided
1/2 teaspoon dried thyme, divided
4 salmon steaks, about 3/4 inch thick
1/2 teaspoon cracked pepper
1 cup cherry tomatoes, halved
1 tablespoon capers, drained and rinsed
garlic to taste
1/2 cup wine

In large nonstick skillet melt 1 tablespoon butter over medium-high heat. Add fennel, 1/4 teaspoon salt and 1/4 teaspoon thyme; cook, stirring occasionally, until lightly browned, 8 to 10 minutes. Remove from skillet and keep warm. Sprinkle both sides of salmon with pepper and remaining salt and thyme. In same skillet melt 1 tablespoon butter over medium-high heat. Add salmon; cook, turning once, until centers are opaque, 4 to 5 minutes per side. Remove from skillet and keep warm. In same skillet melt remaining butter over medium-high heat. Stir in tomatoes, capers, and garlic; cook 1 minute. Stir in wine; cook until mixture heats through and come to a boil, about 2 minutes. Serve sauce over salmon and fennel.

Carol Ann Ratcliffe
TSU Spouse

Low Country Boil

1/4 box salt
10 potatoes
Shrimp boil
2 teaspoons vinegar
1/2 bottle Tabasco sauce
2 teaspoons red pepper
2 teaspoons black pepper
2 1/2 pounds smoked sausage
4 onions
4 ears corn
2 1/2 pounds shrimp

Fill large pot 3/4 full of water and stir in salt to dissolve. Add potatoes, vinegar, Tabasco, red and black pepper. Boil for 5 minutes Add sausage, onions, and corn, one ingredient at a time, boiling for 5 minutes between each addition. Add shrimp and cook until they turn pink, about 3 minutes.

Michael K. Armstrong
TSU '71
Janey Adams
TSU Parent

Tastes and Traditions

Beef Stroganoff Casserole

After my husband Cecil stopped eating chicken, I changed a chicken casserole recipe to ground beef. It turned out very well.

1 pound lean ground beef
1 package egg noodles
1 cup beef broth
1 can cream of mushroom soup
8 ounces sour cream
3 slices bread
1/4 stick butter or margarine

Brown ground beef and drain off fat. Cook egg noodles until done and drain. Put egg noodles, beef broth, soup and sour cream into bowl with ground beef and mix well. Crumble bread on top and dot butter or margarine over bread crumbs Bake at 300 degrees for 45 minutes.

Edna Railey
TSU

Beef and Baked Bean Casserole

1 pound ground chuck
1 small bell pepper, chopped
1/2 cup onion, chopped
1 (16 ounce) can pork and beans
1/2 cup ketchup
2 tablespoons brown sugar
2 tablespoons vinegar
2 1/2 teaspoons chili powder
1/2 teaspoons salt
1/2 teaspoon pepper

Brown ground chuck and drain. Combine with remaining ingredients and turn into a greased casserole dish. Bake at 350 degrees for 30 to 45 minutes.

Mrs. Mickey (Susan) Holmes
TSUM

TSU has a beautiful, championship - caliber golf course right on campus.

Main Dishes

Hamburger Noodle Bake

1 1/2 pounds ground beef
1 can tomatoes and green chiles
1 can tomato sauce
1 teaspoon chili powder
1 package egg noodles
8 ounces cream cheese, softened
8 ounces sour cream
1 bunch green onions, chopped
Grated Cheddar cheese

Brown ground beef and drain. Add tomatoes and green chiles, tomato sauce and chili powder. Bring to a boil, reduce heat and simmer. Boil egg noodles, drain and set aside. Mix together cream cheese, sour cream and green onions. Coat 1 large or 2 small casserole dishes with nonstick cooking spray or butter. Layer noodles, sour cream mixture, and meat sauce. Repeat layers. Top with cheese. Bake at 350 degrees for 30 minutes. May be frozen before cooking.

Anne Schaeffer
TSUD '94

Mexican Casserole

1 1/2 - 2 pounds hamburger
1 package taco seasoning, optional
1 large package yellow rice
2 cans Rotel tomatoes
1/2 pound Velveeta cheese, cubed
Shredded cheese
Crushed Tostito chips
Sliced hot peppers, optional

Brown hamburger meat and drain. Stir in taco seasoning, if desired. As hamburger is browning, cook rice according to directions, leaving rice a little soupy. Combine cooked rice, hamburger and Rotel tomatoes and mix well. Season to taste. Add Velveeta cubes and mix well. Put in a casserole dish and sprinkle with shredded cheese and several handfuls of crushed chips. I like things hot so I layer sliced hot peppers on top of the cheese. Cook in a preheated 350 degree oven for 30 minutes. Enjoy.

Jami Wilks, Brandi Baker
TSU Students
Phi Mu Sorority

Tastes and Traditions

Mexican Mary

1 pound ground beef
1 package taco seasoning
1 jar salsa
1 package shredded mixed mozzarella and Cheddar cheese
1 can sliced black olives, drained
3 green onions, washed and chopped
Refried beans, green chiles, jalapeño peppers and guacamole, optional
2 tomatoes, diced
8 ounces sour cream
1 bag Doritos or Tostito chips

Brown ground beef, drain and crumble. Add taco seasoning and water as directed on package. When taco meat is ready, place in bottom of 9 x 13-inch dish. Top with layers of salsa, cheese, olives and onions. Add any optional ingredients desired. Bake in 350 degree oven for approximately 20 to 30 minutes or until cheese melts and mixture is bubbly around edges. Serve with tomatoes, sour cream and chips.

Mary Mitchell
TSU Friend

Hamburger Casserole

1 package tortilla chips
1 pound ground beef, browned and drained
1 can cream of chicken soup
1 can cream of mushroom soup
1 cup grated cheese

Line casserole dish with tortilla chips. Mix beef and soups. Spread over chips and sprinkle with cheese. Top with crumbled tortilla chips, if desired. Bake at 350 degrees about 20 minutes or until cheese melts.

Brandi Baker
TSU Student
Phi Mu Sorority

TSU's music education program has produced more than 300 high school bandmasters, more than any other program in the United States.

Main Dishes

Hamburger Pie

3 cups mashed potatoes
1 cup sour cream
1/4 cup milk
1/4 teaspoon garlic powder
1 pound hamburger, browned and drained
1 can corn, drained
2 cups grated cheese

Mix potatoes, sour cream, milk, and garlic powder. Spread half in an ungreased 9 x 13-inch baking dish. Sprinkle half of hamburger over potatoes. Spoon half of corn over beef. Sprinkle with half of cheese. Repeat steps. Bake at 350 degrees for 30 minutes. Serves 6 to 8.

Dori Patrias
TSU Student
Phi Mu Sorority

Built in the former location of Trojan Lanes in the Adams Student Center, the Trojan Fitness Center opened in September 1999. It offers quality exercise equipment and facilities for students, faculty and staff.

Tastes and Traditions

Marzetti

1 1/2 pounds ground beef
1 medium green pepper, chopped
1 medium onion, chopped
1 can tomato soup
1 can cream of mushroom soup
1 teaspoon chili powder
1/2 cup water
8 ounce package egg noodles
1/2 cup shredded mild Cheddar cheese
1/2 cup shredded mozzarella cheese
Salt and pepper to taste

Brown ground beef, bell pepper and onions until vegetables are tender. Drain and season with salt and pepper. Add soups, chili powder, and water. Bring to boil, reduce heat and simmer 10 to 15 minutes. Cook noodles according to directions and drain. Place in glass baking dish and top with meat mixture. Sprinkle with cheeses. Heat from the beef mixture should melt the cheese. If not, heat in oven or microwave just until cheese melts.

Helen Ricks
TSU

Spaghetti Carbonara

Quick, easy and absolutely fabulous! Serve with good wine and French bread.

2 cloves garlic, minced
1/2 cup butter
12 - 16 ounces spaghetti, cooked al dente
1 cup grated Parmesan cheese
2 cups heavy cream
1/2 teaspoon freshly ground pepper
12 - 15 strips bacon, fried crisp and drained

Sauté garlic in butter. Stir in cooked spaghetti, Parmesan cheese, cream and pepper. Simmer until thick. Add bacon, toss and serve immediately.

Elizabeth Bailey
TSU-Kadena AFB Okinawa

Main Dishes

Julie's Cajun Spaghetti

1 (12 ounce) package angel hair pasta or thin spaghetti
4 tablespoons butter, divided
1 cup chopped shrimp
1/2 cup white crab meat
3 green onions, chopped
1 to 2 cloves garlic, minced
1 tablespoon chopped parsley
1 cup sliced fresh mushrooms, optional
1/2 - 1 teaspoon cayenne pepper, to taste
1 teaspoon herbs or oregano
1 teaspoon blackened fish or Tony's seasoning
1 (14 ounce) can chicken broth
Grated Parmesan cheese

Cook pasta according to package directions. Drain and set aside. In a skillet combine 2 tablespoons butter, shrimp, and crab meat or chicken. Sauté for 1 to 2 minutes. Add green onions, garlic, parsley, mushrooms, if desired, pepper, oregano and seasonings. Sauté for 5 minutes over medium heat. Add chicken broth and cook until bubbly. Add remaining butter. (For low fat, substitute 2 teaspoons cornstarch dissolved in a small amount of water.) Serve over spaghetti and garnish with grated Parmesan cheese. Variation: Substitute 1 to 1 1/2 cups cubed chicken breast for seafood.

Janice Blakeney
TSU Spouse

Chicken Spaghetti

6 cups cooked chicken
1 can chicken broth
1/2 cup chopped bell pepper
4 teaspoons celery salt
1 small jar pimentos, drained
2 cans cream of mushroom soup
8 ounces spaghetti, cooked and drained
1 onion, grated
Salt and pepper to taste
1 package grated Cheddar cheese, divided

Mix all ingredients except half of cheese. Place in a greased casserole dish and top with reserved cheese. Bake at 350 degrees until heated and cheese is melted, about 35 minutes.

Beverly Weeks
TSU '97

Vicki Browder
TSU Friend

Tastes and Traditions

Rotel Chicken Spaghetti

1 (12 ounce) package spaghetti
1 large green pepper, chopped
1 large onion, chopped
1 stick margarine
1 can Rotel tomatoes and green chiles
1 pound Velveeta cheese
2 tablespoons Worcestershire sauce
Salt to taste
1/2 teaspoon crushed red pepper
1 large can English peas, drained
1 jar mushrooms, drained and sliced
3 cans boned chicken, drained and chopped

Cook spaghetti according to package directions. Drain and set aside. Sauté green pepper and onion in margarine until tender. Add tomatoes and stir until slightly thickened. Cut cheese into one-half inch cubes and add to tomato mixture. Cook, stirring, until cheese melts. Stir well to prevent sticking. Add Worcestershire sauce, salt and red pepper. Remove from heat; blend well. Stir in spaghetti, peas, mushrooms and chicken. Pour mixture into a buttered casserole dish and bake at 350 degrees for 30 minutes.

Loretta Sykes
TSU Friend

Twenty-Minute Spaghetti

1 pound hamburger meat
2 tablespoons dry minced onion
2 (6 ounce) cans tomato paste
1 1/2 cups chopped tomatoes with juice
1 1/2 cups water
1 tablespoon sugar
1/2 teaspoon basil
1/2 teaspoon oregano
1/2 teaspoon salt
1/8 teaspoon granulated garlic
1/8 teaspoon pepper
1 beef bouillon cube
1 pound spaghetti, cooked and drained

Brown meat and onions in skillet. Drain fat. Stir in remaining ingredients except spaghetti, bring to a boil and reduce heat. Cover and simmer 20 minutes, stirring occasionally. Serve over hot spaghetti.

Kelly Miller
TSU Student
Phi Mu Sorority

Main Dishes

Spaghetti Pie Casserole

A cross between spaghetti and lasagna. Delicious and a great way to use leftover spaghetti sauce.

8 ounces angel hair pasta
2 tablespoons margarine or butter, melted
2 eggs, beaten
1/3 cup grated Parmesan cheese
1 cup cottage cheese
Spaghetti sauce with meat.

Cook pasta for 3 minutes and drain. (Don't overcook). In bowl, mix butter, eggs and Parmesan cheese. Add pasta. Place this mixture into a greased 10-inch pie plate. Spread cottage cheese on top of the pasta mixture and top with spaghetti sauce. Bake at 350 degrees for 20 minutes, uncovered.

Donna Stevens
TSU Friend

Spaghetti Arrabiatta

My brother is an artist and lived in Italy for three years. He came home and taught my family to cook this recipe. Since we began eating this, no one cooks spaghetti with meat sauce anymore. Over the years I have added things but I just cook it to taste. I think the real key to this spaghetti is the fresh parsley. Experiment and enjoy.

Olive oil
1 medium onion, chopped
4 cloves garlic, sliced lengthwise
Chopped fresh Italian parsley
Salt
1 large can stewed tomatoes
Crushed red pepper
White wine
Spaghetti noodles

Cover skillet bottom with about 1 inch of good olive oil. Add onions and garlic and sauté until done. Add parsley and salt well. Do not let parsley or garlic burn. Add white wine and stewed tomatoes and cook hard while spaghetti is cooking. Cook spaghetti al dente. Drain and add to sauce and finish cooking in the sauce.

Jane Ward Hawk
TSU

Tastes and Traditions

TSU students (from left) Matt Owen, Christy Bedingfield and Michael Bonner help Charlie Spivey catch a few fish at the 1999 Catfish Roundup, sponsored by Wheelin' Sportsmen. TSU students play an active part in community and volunteer activities.

Zucchini Lasagna

A dieter's recipe. This has 164 calories per serving, no cholesterol, 13 grams of fat and 48 milligrams of salt.

1 pound ground round
Garlic powder, salt, and pepper to taste
1 can tomato paste
4 tomatoes, chopped, or 1 can water-packed whole tomatoes, chopped
Basil
Oregano
3 eggs, beaten
2 zucchini, sliced and lightly steamed
1 pound low-fat cottage cheese

Brown beef and season to taste with garlic powder, salt and pepper. Add tomato paste and tomatoes, season with basil and oregano. Let simmer over low heat about 45 minutes. If sauce becomes too thick, add water. Beat eggs well and season with basil and oregano. Combine eggs and cottage cheese. Mix well. In 9 x 13-inch pan, layer meat sauce, zucchini, and cottage cheese; repeat layers, ending with sauce. Bake in preheated oven 350 degrees for 1 hour. Let stand 10 to 15 minutes before serving.

Mary Beth Green
TSU Friend

Main Dishes

Low-Fat Lasagna

2 medium jars spaghetti sauce
3 egg whites
1 large carton fat-free cottage cheese
1 (8 ounce) package fat-free cream cheese, softened
1 box lasagna, cooked and drained
1 large package shredded low-fat mozzarella cheese

In a 9 x 13-inch pan, pour a small amount of sauce to cover bottom of pan. In a mixing bowl, combine egg whites, cottage cheese and cream cheese. Mix well. Layer in the pan: noodles, sauce, noodles, cheese mix, noodles, sauce, continuing until all ingredients are used. Top with mozzarella cheese. Cover with foil and bake at 350 degrees for 1 hour. Let stand 15 minutes before serving.

Kappa Delta Sorority

Julie Neher
TSU Student
Phi Mu Sorority

Slow-Cooker Lasagna

This recipe is so easy, you may never go back to the conventional method with boiled noodles and complicated assembly.

1 pound ground chuck
1 teaspoon dried Italian seasoning
1 (28 ounce) jar spaghetti sauce
1/3 cup water
8 lasagna noodles, uncooked
1 (4 1/2 ounce) jar mushrooms, drained
1 (15 ounce) carton ricotta cheese
1 cup shredded part-skim mozzarella cheese, divided

Cook beef and Italian seasoning in a large skillet over medium-high heat, stirring until beef crumbles; drain. Combine spaghetti sauce and water in a small bowl. Place 4 uncooked noodles in bottom of a lightly greased 5-quart slow cooker. Layer with half each of beef mixture, spaghetti sauce mixture and mushrooms. Spread ricotta cheese over mushrooms. Sprinkle with 1 cup mozzarella cheese. Layer with remaining noodles, meat, sauce mixture, mushrooms, and mozzarella cheese. Cover and cook on high setting 1 hour; reduce and cook on low setting 5 hours. (I have cooked on low setting all day and it turns out fine).

Debra Grant
TSU

Tastes and Traditions

Vegetarian Lasagna

I found this basic recipe in a magazine and I have experimented with it in many different ways. I have used different kinds of vegetables and even combined two or more vegetables. I really like grated zucchini best. You will not miss the meat -- I think the grated carrots give it the texture of the meat. I have also used Monterey jack cheese with jalapeño peppers for a spicier dish.

10 lasagna noodles
2 packages frozen chopped spinach
1/2 cup chopped onion
1 tablespoon oil
1 cup grated raw carrots
2 cups sliced fresh mushrooms
1 (15 ounce) can tomato cause
1 (6 ounce) can tomato paste
1/2 cup chopped pitted ripe olives
1 1/2 teaspoons dried oregano
2 cups cream-style cottage cheese
1 pound sliced monterey jack cheese
1/4 cup grated Parmesan cheese

Place noodles in a pot of boiling, salted water and cook for 8 to 10 minutes. Drain. Prepare spinach according to package directions or simply defrost. Meanwhile, sauté onion in oil until soft. Add carrots and mushrooms and cook until crisp-tender. Stir in tomato sauce, pasta, olives, and oregano. Butter or grease a 9 x 13-inch casserole or pan. Layer half each of noodles, cottage cheese, spinach, sauce mix and 1/3 of cheese slices. Repeat, placing remaining third of monterey jack on top. Sprinkle with Parmesan cheese. Bake in preheated 375 degree oven for 30 minutes. Serves 8.

Jane Ward Hawk
TSU

TSU's Larry Blakeney was named Southland Football League (SFL) Coach of the Year in 1999. Also that year, Al Lucas won the Buck Buchanan Award as the nation's top defensive player in Division I-AA, and Anthony Rabb was named SFL Defensive Player of the Year.

Main Dishes

Turkey Lasagna

This is Mike's favorite!

1 box firm tofu
1 egg, beaten
1 pound ground turkey
2 (16 ounce) cans Mushroom Spaghetti Sauce
1 (8 ounce) box Oven Ready Lasagna
1 package shredded low-moisture mozzarella and Parmesan cheese

Heat oven to 350 degrees. Hand mix drained tofu and egg in a bowl until the consistency of cottage cheese. Brown turkey and drain. Add spaghetti sauce to turkey and simmer about 5 minutes. Set aside. In a 9 x 13-inch greased casserole dish, layer the ingredients, beginning with meat sauce. Sprinkle with cheese. Top with three noodles, spread lightly with tofu mixture. Repeat meat sauce, cheese, pasta and tofu. End layering with meat sauce and cheese on top. Cover with foil and bake 30 minutes or until bubbly.

Janice Malone
TSUD First Lady

Dr. Michael Malone (right), pictured here with Trojan football coach Larry Blakeney, has served as president of Troy State University Dothan since April 1996. He has directed the institution's efforts to become a premier community university, including the construction of the Library/Technology Building in 2000-01.

Tastes and Traditions

Crock Pot Stew

1 pound beef stew meat, cut into smaller pieces
4 potatoes, peeled and chopped
6 carrots, peeled and chopped
1 (16 ounce) can crushed tomatoes
1 can cream of mushroom soup
1 tablespoon Dale's sauce
4 ounces water
Salt and pepper to taste

Combine all ingredients in a crock pot. Cook on low for 6 to 8 hours.

Barbara Findley Harrington
TSU '77

Easy-Do Veggie Stew

With time being a precious commodity today, this recipe fits right in. It's quick, easy to make and tastes great. It freezes well too. I love to fix it and serve in crock pot or chafing dish at large gatherings or when tailgating in cool weather.

1 can barbecue beef
1 can barbecue pork
1 can barbecue chicken
1 pound Polish sausage, sliced
1 large can stewed tomatoes
2 cans sliced potatoes, drained
1 large can mixed vegetables, drained
1 can butter peas, drained
1 can chopped tomatoes with okra
2 cans sliced carrots, drained
1 can whole kernel corn, drained
1/2 cup barbecue sauce
Salt and pepper to taste
1 heaping teaspoon Cavender's seasoning

Dump all ingredients into a 5 quart Dutch oven. Mix well. Heat for about an hour on medium heat on the stove top, stirring occasionally. Serve with Mexican cornbread, with a variety of crackers or just plain.

Donna Reynolds
TSU '86

Main Dishes

New initiates of Alpha Kappa Alpha enjoy their "coming out" on the Bibb Graves Quad.

Brunswick Stew

4 pounds fresh pork roast
1 (4 pound) fryer
5 pounds potatoes, peeled and cubed
5 cans tiny garden peas, drained
1 (32 ounce) bottle ketchup
3 tablespoons salt
1 tablespoon black pepper
1 tablespoon red pepper
1 tablespoon hot sauce
1/2 cup sugar
4 cans cream-style corn

Cook pork and chicken in water until well done. Remove all fat and save broth. Peel meat off in small strips. Cook potatoes, drain and set aside. (Don't overcook potatoes.) Put meat, peas, catsup, salt, pepper, hot sauce and sugar in pork broth and cook as long as desired. When almost done, add cooked potatoes and corn. Simmer until flavor is cooked in. If stew is too thin, add cornstarch. If too thick, add chicken broth, water or tomato juice.

Bobby Ross Phillips
TSU '59

Rhudolph Armstrong
TSU Parent

Sandy Gouge
TSUM

Tastes and Traditions

Sandra's Easy Brunswick Stew

1 large onion, chopped
Butter
2 cups canned diced potatoes
1(14 1/2 ounce) can diced tomatoes, undrained (I like mine with a little
  "kick" so I use tomatoes and chiles.)
1 (15 ounce) can tomato sauce
1 (15 1/2 ounce) can whole kernel corn, drained
1 (15 1/2 ounce) can lima beans, drained
3/4 pound barbecue pork, chopped
1 cup chopped chicken
2 cups canned chicken broth
1/2 teaspoon salt
1/2 teaspoon pepper
1/2 teaspoon Worcestershire sauce

Sauté onion in a little butter in a Dutch oven until tender. Add remaining
ingredients, bring to a boil, reduce heat and cook, covered, for about an
hour or so since all ingredients are already cooked.

Sandra Sims DeGraffenreid
Alabama Association of School Boards
TSU Friend

Chili Chicken Stew

6 boneless, skinless chicken breasts, cut into 1-inch cubes
1 medium onion, chopped
1 medium bell pepper, chopped
2 cloves garlic, minced
1 tablespoon vegetable oil
2 (14 ounce) cans stewed tomatoes, undrained and chopped
1 (15 ounce) can pinto beans, drained
2/3 cup picante sauce
1 teaspoon chili powder
1 teaspoon cumin
1/2 teaspoon salt
Shredded cheddar cheese, sour cream, diced avocado and chopped green
  onion, optional

Cook chicken, onions, bell pepper and garlic in hot oil in a large heavy
saucepan until lightly browned. Add tomatoes, beans, picante sauce, chili
powder, cumin and salt. Cover, reduce heat and simmer 20 minutes. Top
individual servings with optional ingredients, if desired.

Sara Jones
TSU Spouse

Main Dishes

Venison Stew

3 pounds of venison, cut in 1-inch cubes
3 large cans tomatoes
1 (12 ounce) can V-8 juice
Several stalks celery, chopped
2 - 3 onions, chopped
5 - 10 tablespoons Worcestershire sauce
Tabasco to taste
3 bay leaves
1 tablespoon celery salt
Pepper
1 bag frozen chopped okra
2 bags frozen mixed vegetables
1 bag frozen small lima beans
1 bag frozen shoe peg corn

Place venison, tomatoes, juice, celery, onion, Worcestershire, Tabasco, bay leaves, celery salt and pepper in stock pot. Cover with water, bring to a boil, reduce heat and simmer 3 to 3 1/2 hours. Add remaining ingredients along with more Worcestershire sauce and cook until heated through. Serve.

Helen McKinley
TSU Friend

Tailgate Chili

This recipe has evolved over the years and can be changed to suit the occasion, or the taste. Great for that cool fall tailgating.

4 pounds hamburger
2 cans diced tomatoes
2 (12 ounce) cans tomato sauce
4 packages chili seasoning
2 cans mexibeans or pinto beans
1 large onion, chopped
1 can sliced green chiles, optional
16 ounces shredded Cheddar cheese
1 pint sour cream

Brown meat, drain fat and rinse meat. Place meat in a 5-quart crock pot. Add remaining ingredients except cheese and sour cream. Mix well and cook at least 6 hours. Serve in bowls or large mugs garnished with cheese and sour cream.

Kathy Kallman
TSU-Western Region

Tastes and Traditions ─────────

Mickey's Chili

This dish is perfect for those cold evenings in front of the fire. Really great served with cornbread!

1 large onion, chopped
1 pound ground beef
1 can kidney beans, drained
1 can tomatoes with green chiles
1 (8 ounce) can tomato sauce
1/4 cup ketchup
2 cups water
1 tablespoon chili powder
Salt and pepper to taste

In skillet brown the onions and ground beef. In a large saucepan, combine beans, tomatoes, tomato sauce, ketchup, water, and chili powder. Add meat and onions. Season with salt and pepper. Bring to a boil, reduce heat and simmer for a least one hour.

Mrs. Mickey (Susan) Holmes
TSU Friend

An enduring TSU tradition is the Chancellor's Reception for graduating seniors. On the morning of commencement exercises, graduates visit the Chancellor's Home for breakfast and special congratulations from the Chancellor. Here, Dr. Hawkins greets visitors prior to a commencement in 2000.

Main Dishes

Cajun Jambalaya

This is a meal in itself served with a green salad. Dessert is optional.

2 pounds sausage
2 medium chicken breasts, cubed
2 tablespoons flour
2 medium onions, chopped
1 bunch green onions, chopped
2 tablespoons chopped parsley
2 cloves garlic, minced
2 1/2 cups water
2 cups regular rice
2 teaspoons salt
3/4 teaspoon red pepper

Brown sausage in a skillet and remove. Brown chicken in skillet and remove. Add flour to skillet drippings and brown. Add onions, green onions, parsley and garlic. Cook until soft. Add water, rice, salt, red pepper, sausage and chicken. When mixture comes to a boil, lower heat to lowest setting. Cover tightly with lid and cook 1 hour. When rice is done, remove lid and let rice sit until mixture thickens. Do not stir rice, just shake the pot.

Evelyn W. Anderson
TSU Friend

Henry Hughes
TSU Friend

When a high school band takes the field or the stage anywhere in the United States, it could well be playing music arranged by Robert Smith, director of bands at TSU. Smith has arranged more than 40 percent of the music played by high school bands across the country.

Tastes and Traditions

Lamar's Jambalaya

1 pound package Conecuh sausage
1 small package fresh sliced mushrooms
1 bunch baby Vidalia green onions, chopped
2 green bell peppers, chopped
Accent Seasoning
Chef's Magic vegetable seasoning
3/4 cup uncooked rice

Cut sausage into very small slices and cook in a large skillet over low heat for about 5 minutes. Add vegetables; season liberally with Accent and Chef's Magic. Simmer vegetables and sausage for about 10 minutes or until mushrooms are fully cooked. Add rice and 1/2 cup, or less, of water to the sausage mixture. Mix thoroughly. Cover and simmer,stirring often, until rice is fully cooked.

Lamar Higgins
TSU Board of Trustees

When Kim Davis was voted Homecoming queen in 1979, she became the first African-American student to wear the queen's crown at TSU. Another milestone was reached that year, when Lamar Higgins became the first African-American student elected as president of the SGA. Higgins later served on the TSU Board of Trustees.

Main Dishes

Barras Cajun Gumbo

Dr. Donald Barras closely guarded his authentic Cajun Gumbo recipe for many years, but in his older mellower days, he shared it with a few people. I was honored to be given personal instruction in the secrets of his gumbo technique. This recipe is the result of several years of my own attempts. The TSU debut of this recipe was the first annual Don Barras Memorial Gumbo Festival held in December 1999 in the Barras Anatomy and Physiology Lab. The faculty and staff of the College of Arts and Sciences and many guests enjoyed Dr. Barras' gumbo and remembered him fondly.

1 pound hot link sausage
2 cups chopped green onions
1 bell pepper, diced
1 chicken, cut into pieces
1/2 pound okra
1 quart can of tomatoes, chopped
Salt and pepper to taste
1/2 - 3/4 cup cooking oil
1 cup all-purpose flour, approximately
Seafood of choice (see below)

Cut sausage into thin slices, boil in water, skim grease and reserve water. Cover onions, bell pepper, and chicken with water and smother until tender. Reserve stock. Remove chicken from bones and return chicken to stock. Add one quarter of water from sausage boiling. In a separate pot cook okra in the tomatoes, mashing okra into small pieces. Transfer to a 2-gallon pot and add chicken mixture. Salt and pepper to taste. Prepare roux: Mix 1/2 to 3/4 cup cooking oil and approximately 1 cup flour. You want the roux to be soupy. Heat to a boil in a well-seasoned cast iron skillet on medium to medium low heat and cook slowly for about 30 minutes, stirring constantly, until the roux is dark brown and glittery. Do not scorch (see note below). The darker the roux the richer the gumbo. Leftover roux can be frozen for later use. Prepared roux can be purchased. Add roux to taste (I use 4 to 6 tablespoons) and cook gumbo 1 hour. Add water if it needs thinning.
During last 30 minutes add peeled raw shrimp (1 to 2 pounds) and 2 cans crab meat. Simmer. Salt and pepper to taste. Oysters, crayfish, fish, or other types of seafood can be added during this last step if desired. Serve with rice.
Notes from Dr. Barras: Creole gumbo is spicy but Cajun gumbo is not, so you can taste the seafood. Do not use celery because it kills the seafood taste. Don't scorch the roux or you will have to throw out the whole pot of gumbo. Add Tabasco or pepper sauce if you want it hotter.

Robert Pullen
TSU

Tastes and Traditions

Last-Minute Supper

I am submitting this recipe in memory of my daughter, Lisa Kay Kelly Williams (TSU Class of '89), who died in June 1997. This very tasty and easy-to-prepare dish was one of her favorites. Busy college students living on a tight budget should find it especially appealing.

1 (12 ounce) can Spam, sliced and cut into strips
1 medium onion, thinly sliced
1 tablespoon butter or margarine
1 (10 1/2 ounce) can cream of mushroom soup
1/2 cup milk
2 cups cooked, cubed potatoes (about 4 medium)
2 tablespoons chopped parsley, optional
Dash pepper

Lightly brown meat and onion in butter until onion is tender. Blend soup and milk and stir into meat. Add remaining ingredients and gently stir. Cook over low heat 10 minutes or until flavors are blended, stirring often.

Thelia Whigham Kelly
TSU '62

Tagliarini

This dish is great prepared ahead.

1 large onion, chopped
1 clove garlic, minced
1 green pepper, chopped
Vegetable oil
1 pound ground round steak
1 can tomato sauce
2 cans water
1 can cream of mushroom soup
1/4 cup parsley flakes
1 teaspoon basil
1 teaspoon oregano
1 can cream-style corn
1/2 cup chopped ripe olives
4 ounces egg noodles
1 cup grated Parmesan cheese

Brown onion, garlic, and pepper in oil. Add meat and sear well. Add tomato sauce, water, soup, seasonings, corn and olives. Add uncooked noodles and pour into a greased casserole dish. Sprinkle with cheese and bake at 350 degrees for 1 hour.

Mrs. Mickey (Susan) Holmes
TSU Friend

Main Dishes

Cabbage Rolls

First Edition Favorite

This is my mother's recipe for cabbage rolls. They are out of this world!

1 large or 2 medium cabbages
1 pound ground beef
1/2 pound pork sausage
1 onion, chopped
1 cup uncooked rice
3 teaspoons salt
1/4 teaspoon black pepper
2 cans tomato soup

Wilt outside cabbage leaves that are large enough to make good-sized rolls in very hot water with a small amount of salt added. Reserve rest of cabbage for other uses. Mix together the meats, onion, rice, salt and pepper. Shape into balls and roll up in cabbage leaves; secure with toothpicks. Place rolls in large cooking pot (an iron Dutch oven is ideal). Add water to about halfway up pot. Bring to a boil, reduce heat, cover and steam for 1 1/2 hours. Remove rolls from pot and transfer to large casserole dish. Mix soup with 1 can of water and pour over the rolls. Bake in a 350 degree oven about 30 minutes longer.

NOTE: Pork may be omitted if beef alone is desired. You may use inside of cabbage to make slaw to go along with the rolls.

Bob Howell
TSU '71

A TSU tradition, the Miss TSU pageant continues to be a campus highlight each year. At left, the finalists from the 1980 pageant are pictured with winner Becky Redd, while Miss TSU 2000 Heather Moran is crowned by Dr. Hawkins, at right.

Tastes and Traditions

Mandarin Pork Stir-Fry

While I was in the Far East, Win-Won taught me this recipe.

1 pound lean pork, cut in strips
1/4 pound mushrooms, halved or quartered
1 medium green pepper, cut in strips
1 small onion, chopped
1 cup water, divided
2 teaspoons cornstarch
1 tablespoon soy sauce
1 chicken bouillon cube
1/2 teaspoon dry mustard
1/8 teaspoon garlic powder
1 (8 ounce) can water chestnuts, drained and sliced
1 orange, sectioned
Salt and pepper

Coat a large skillet or wok with nonstick cooking spray. Place over medium heat and cook and stir half the pork at a time until lightly browned. Remove to a plate. Reduce heat to low; add mushrooms, green peppers and onion. Cook and stir 3 minutes. Stir together 1/4 cup water and cornstarch until smooth. Mix in remaining water, soy sauce, bouillon cube, mustard and garlic powder. Add to skillet. Cook and stir until mixture thickens and boils. Add meat and water chestnuts and simmer 3 minutes. Gently stir in orange sections. Heat to serving temperature. Season to taste.

Todd MacArthur
TSU '80, '82

The "Trojan Drop" has become a Homecoming tradition and a key fund-raising event for women's athletics. Here, TSU student David Stroud parachutes to the floor of Memorial Stadium, landing on a grid and making a lucky ticket holder a $2,500 winner. But the real winners are TSU's female athletes. From 1996-1999, The Drop raised more than $100,000 for women's athletics.

Main Dishes

Taco Rice

This Oriental twist on an American favorite was popular in Okinawa. We cook this about once a week. It's so quick and easy.

1 pound ground beef
1 package taco mix
1 cup cooked rice
Shredded lettuce
Chopped tomato
Salsa
Chopped onion
Tortilla Chips

Prepare beef and taco mix according to package directions. Put rice in a large bowl. Add meat mixture and other ingredients.

Sue and Jeff Danielson
TSU Students
Air Force ROTC

L.A. (Lower Alabama) Pheasant

Great for impressing those Yankee friends.

2 dressed pheasant
1 large bottle Zesty Italian dressing
1 cup red wine
1 tablespoon Creole seasoning
1 tablespoon lemon pepper
1 ounce Moore's or Dale's sauce
1 ounce chopped chives

Place pheasant in saucepan with a cover. Mix remaining ingredients together and heat. Pour over pheasant, bring to a boil, reduce heat and cover. Bake in 300 degree oven for approximately 2 hours. Check routinely and do not let birds dry out.

Ken Gardner
TSU '68

Studies done by the Alabama Commission on Higher Education in 1998 and 1999 showed that TSU does the best job in Alabama of replacing outdated academic programs with new, relevant ones.

Tastes and Traditions

Marinated Pork Tenderloin with Jezebel Sauce

1/4 cup lite soy sauce
1/4 cup dry sherry or Madeira wine
2 tablespoons olive oil
1 tablespoon dry mustard
1 teaspoon ground ginger
1 teaspoon sesame oil
8 drops hot sauce
2 cloves garlic, minced
2 3/4 pounds pork tenderloin
1/2 cup apple cider vinegar
3 dozen party rolls

Jezebel Sauce:
1 cup apple jelly
1 cup pineapple-orange marmalade or pineapple preserves
1 (6 ounce) jar prepared mustard
1 (5 ounce) jar prepared horseradish
1/4 teaspoon pepper

Combine soy sauce, wine, olive oil, dry mustard, ginger, sesame oil, hot sauce and garlic in a shallow dish or heavy-duty, zip-top plastic bag; add tenderloin. Cover or seal, and chill 8 hours, turning tenderloins occasionally. Remove tenderloins from marinade, reserving 1/2 cup marinade; combine reserved marinade and apple cider vinegar. Cook tenderloins, covered with grill lid, over medium-hot coals, (350 to 400 degrees) about 20 minutes or until meat thermometer inserted into thickest portion registers 160 degrees, turning occasionally and basting with marinade mixture during first 15 minutes of cooking time. Remove from heat, slice and serve warm or chilled with party rolls and Jezebel Sauce. 10 to 12 appetizer servings.

For Jezebel Sauce: Beat apple jelly in a mixing bowl at medium speed until smooth. Add marmalade and remaining ingredients, beat until blended. Cover and chill. Makes 3 cups.

Doug and Rachel Hawkins
TSU Board of Trustees

You never breathe the same air twice in the state-of-the-art TSU Science Center, also known as McCall Hall, which was renovated in 1998-99. Giant air scrubbers continuously recirculate and clean the air to ensure maximum air quality and safety.

Main Dishes

Seafood Alfredo

Absolutely mouth-watering! It is my husband's and daughter's favorite recipe and the most requested recipe at office parties. Actually it tastes best if refrigerated overnight, then rewarmed–more time to blend the flavors.

1 stick margarine
6 - 8 green onions, chopped
3 - 4 cloves garlic, chopped
1 (10 ounce) can cream of mushroom soup
1 (8 ounce) package shredded mild Mexican Velveeta cheese
1/2 pint whipping cream
1 pound seafood of your choice or a combination of several
1 (16 ounce) package egg noodles or fettuccine, cooked and drained

Melt margarine in a 4-quart pot. Sauté onions and garlic. Add soup, cheese, whipping cream and seafood consecutively, waiting 5 minutes between each ingredient. Make sure cheese melts thoroughly before adding any more ingredients. Cook mixture on medium to medium-low temperature for about 25 minutes, stirring often. Serve over pasta.

Donna Puhr
TSU Parent

Trojan athletic teams have claimed a number of national championships – Football: 1968, 1984, 1987; Baseball: 1986, 1987; Men's Golf: 1976, 1977, 1984; Women's Golf: 1984, 1986, 1989. Pictured here are Coach Chase Riddle and the 1987 baseball champions.

Tastes and Traditions

Veal Roll-Ups

This recipe is excellent for dinner parties. The veal rolls may be prepared ahead of time. All you have to do is pop them into the oven and enjoy your company.

4 boneless veal cutlets
1 (3 ounce) can deviled ham
1 tablespoon chopped onion
1 (3 ounce) package cream cheese
1 egg, beaten
1/2 cup fine dry bread crumbs
2 tablespoons margarine
3/4 cup water
1 envelope dry mushroom gravy mix
1/4 cup dry sherry

With meat mallet, pound cutlets very thin. Mix deviled ham with onion. Spread on cutlets just to edge. Slice cream cheese into 12 narrow strips. Place 3 strips on each cutlet. Roll cutlet jelly-roll style; fasten with wooden toothpicks. Dip rolls in beaten egg, then roll in crumbs. Melt margarine in skillet. Add veal rolls and brown on all sides. Arrange browned rolls in 10 x 6 x 1 1/2-inch baking dish. Remove picks. Pour water into skillet. Add gravy mix and sherry. Cook and stir until mixture is bubbly. Pour over veal rolls. Bake, covered, at 350 degrees for 45 minutes or until tender.

Dianne L. Barron
TSU

Pizza Italiano

Two packets self-rising pizza crust
1 cup hot water
1 tablespoon vegetable oil
1 cup pizza sauce
1/2 pound mozzarella cheese, shredded
1/2 pound Cheddar cheese, grated

Combine packets of pizza crust with hot water. Whip and let sit in heated area for 5 minutes. Add vegetable oil. Cover pizza pan with additional vegetable oil and spread crust evenly. Spread pizza sauce over crust. Sprinkle cheeses over sauce. Bake at 450 degrees until cheese is melted and crust is golden brown.

Erica Merrill
TSU Student
Phi Mu Sorority

Main Dishes

Homemade Pizza

Crust:
1 cup self-rising flour
2 eggs
2/3 cup milk
1 teaspoon garlic
1 teaspoon Italian seasoning
1/8 teaspoon pepper

Toppings:
Pizza sauce
Shredded Cheddar cheese
Shredded mozzarella cheese
Optional Toppings: Sliced pepperoni, browned hamburger, cooked sausage, sliced mushrooms, chopped onions, sliced peppers

Place all crust ingredients in a jar and shake until smooth. Pour onto greased pan. Bake at 350 degrees until cooked thoroughly. Spread with pizza sauce and sprinkle with cheeses. Add desired optional toppings and bake until cheese melts.

Brandi Baker
TSU Student
Phi Mu Sorority

Linguine Primavera

This is a favorite among men, especially visiting coaches.

Sweet or Italian Sausage
1 tablespoon cooking oil
1/4 pound mushrooms, washed and sliced
1 red pepper, sliced
1 sweet onion, sliced
1/4 pound green beans, washed, trimmed and sliced diagonally
1 head broccoli, chopped
1 zucchini, chopped
1 yellow squash, chopped
1 pound linguine, cooked and drained
2 tablespoons butter
Grated Parmesan cheese

Cover sausage in salt water and cook 20 minutes. Remove, drain and slice. Heat 1 tablespoon oil in a skillet and add mushrooms, red pepper and onion. Cook, stirring, 2 minutes. Add sausage, green beans, broccoli, zucchini, squash and 1/2 cup water to skillet. Cover and simmer for 5 minutes. Toss linguine with butter and top with vegetable mixture. Serve with Parmesan cheese.

Sherry J. Dye
TSU Spouse

Tastes and Traditions

Tortilla Rolls

First Edition Favorite

This recipe is a hit with tailgaters. Plates and napkins are not needed; just grab one and eat as you visit from group to group.

2 packages flour tortillas (larger are better)
2 pounds thinly sliced smoked turkey and ham
1 head lettuce, finely chopped
2 cups grated cheese
Mayonnaise
Large jar thick salsa
Salt and pepper

This recipe will go much faster if two prepare. Lay tortilla on paper towel. Spread a thin layer of mayonnaise on tortilla, covering it evenly. Layer with meat next, starting on one edge and going to the middle of the tortilla. Add layer of lettuce, layer of cheese, and salt and pepper to taste. Drizzle about a tablespoon of salsa down the tortilla. Roll tortilla as tightly as you can and secure with a toothpick. Lay them into 9 x 13-inch pan and you're ready to go.

Kenneth Odom
TSU '76

Stuffed Peppers

6 bell peppers
1 pound ground beef
1/3 cup chopped onion
1/2 teaspoon salt
Dash pepper
1 (16 ounce) can tomatoes
1/2 cup water
1/2 cup uncooked rice
1 teaspoon Worcestershire sauce
4 ounces cheese, grated

Boil peppers in salted water until tender. Remove from water, drain and cut in half lengthwise. Sprinkle with salt. Cook ground beef and onion until lightly browned; season with salt and pepper. Add tomatoes, water, rice, and Worcestershire sauce. Cover and simmer until rice is tender, about 15 minutes. Stir in cheese and heat until cheese is melted. Spoon mixture in peppers and place in a baking dish. Bake uncovered at 350 degrees for 20 to 30 minutes.

Mrs. Mickey (Susan) Holmes
TSUM

Main Dishes

Spatzle (Noodles)

This is a good side dish for beef, pork or chicken. While we were in Germany with TSU, I was taught to make spatzle by Frau Weiss, who, with her husband, owned the Idyll Restaurant near Kaiserslautern.

3 eggs
1 cup flour
Dash of salt
1/4 teaspoon nutmeg
1 tablespoon butter

Blend eggs with flour, salt, and nutmeg. Hold bowl over pot of boiling water. As dough comes to edge of bowl, cut off small bits with a knife. (Dip knife into water frequently to prevent sticking.) As spatzle rises to top of water, remove with slotted spoon and put in pan of cold water. After cooking is finished, drain in colander. May be refrigerated for 2 to 3 days. To reheat, put into hot water for about 5 minutes. Drain. Toss with butter. Serves 4 to 6.

Willetta Hatcher
TSU Friend

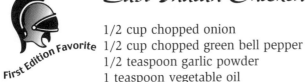

East Indian Chicken

1/2 cup chopped onion
1/2 cup chopped green bell pepper
1/2 teaspoon garlic powder
1 teaspoon vegetable oil
2 cups skinless, cooked, diced chicken
1/2 teaspoon salt
1/2 teaspoon pepper
1 1/2 teaspoons curry powder
1 (28 ounce) can whole tomatoes
1 tablespoon Worcestershire sauce
1/4 cup raisins, optional
2 cups cooked brown rice

Sauté onion, pepper, and garlic powder in oil until tender, about 3 minutes. Add remaining ingredients except the rice, and cook over low heat for about 30 minutes. Serve over rice. Serves 4.

Mary R. Taylor
TSU

Tastes and Traditions

Goulash

This is a recipe I learned from my mother when I was first learning to cook. It is fast and easy to make when you're in a hurry.

1 pound ground beef
1 cup chopped onion
1/2 green bell pepper, chopped
1 (14 ounce) can diced tomatoes, with juice
1 can cream of mushroom soup
Salt and pepper to taste
1 (8 ounce) package medium egg noodles, cooked and drained
6 slices American cheese

In a large skillet, brown ground beef with onions and peppers. Drain off fat from skillet. Add the tomatoes, mushroom soup, salt and pepper. Simmer, uncovered, for 10 minutes, until heated through and bubbling. In a 9 x 13-inch casserole dish combine meat mixture with cooked noodles. Stir until well mixed. Top with sliced cheese. Place in 350 degree oven for 10 minutes or until cheese is melted.

Jan Cooper
TSU Spouse

"Nutter for Heisman" was a popular cheer during the 1999 football season. This one was led by Alpha Gamma Delta sorority members.

Main Dishes

Sour Cream Enchiladas

Sauce:
1 can cream of chicken soup
1/4 cup sour cream
1/4 teaspoon salt
1 can cream of mushroom soup

Filling:
1 cup boned, cooked shredded chicken
1/2 can diced green chili peppers
1/4 cup finely chopped onion
1 cup grated cheese
2 cups cottage cheese

6 tortillas
1/2 cup oil

For Sauce: Heat all ingredients until smooth; do not boil.
For Filling: Mix ingredients together.
Dip tortillas in hot oil just to soften. Spread filling on tortilla and roll up, seam down. Place in baking dish. Pour warm sauce over top. Bake at 350 degrees for 30 minutes.

Mary Nall Hollis
TSU Friend
Mother of Nall Hollis

Shackelford Hall was the center of campus activities before and after World War II. This student social took place in 1946.

Tastes and Traditions

Pork Tenderloin Elizabeth

This may be the best tenderloin you have ever tried. If you like blue cheese, you'll love it.

1/2 cup honey
1/4 cup hosen (oriental market)
1/4 cup soy sauce
1 tablespoon elephant garlic
fresh ginger
2 whole, small pork tenderloins
2 tablespoons butter

Combine honey, hosen, soy and garlic and ginger. Marinate in zip lock bag overnight in refrigerator or for 2 to 3 hours at room temperature. Pork may be grilled on hot grill for 15 minutes or until meat thermometer registers 170 degrees. In oven; preheat to 450 degrees. Put tenderloins on broiler pan in hot oven for 10 minutes and then turn down to 300 degrees for remaining time; 20 minutes per pound (I always use a meat thermometer so I won't overcook.)

Sauce:
1 cup heavy cream
1/4 cup blue cheese

Heat cream and cheese until blended and hot. Cheese will begin to melt; do not boil. Serve slices of tenderloin with 2 tablespoons sauce spooned over meat.

Janice Hawkins
TSU First Lady

Jimmy Lunsford, mayor of Troy, has been integral to the development of a strong "town and gown" relationship between the Troy community and TSU. Under Lunsford's leadership, the City of Troy committed $4.5 million in 1998 to help upgrade TSU's athletic facilities. Mayor Lunsford, a TSU alumnus, is considered by his alma mater to be the best mayor in America.

Main Dishes

Italian Sausage and Peppers

If you like Italian food, you will love this! There is just something wonderful about the way these flavors blend. Try it.

4 large bell peppers, green, red or yellow or combination, sliced
2 large banana peppers, sliced
2 sweet onions, sliced
4 cloves garlic, minced
1 pound fresh mushrooms
2 pounds Italian sausage links, sweet or hot
4 tablespoons olive oil
2 cups spaghetti sauce, homemade or bottled
salt and pepper to taste

Sauté peppers, onions and garlic in olive oil until tender. Remove and add sausage to pan and brown. Put peppers, sausage and mushrooms in 9 x 13 inch pyrex dish; pour spaghetti sauce over this mixture and bake on 350 degrees uncovered for 45 minutes. You may add meatballs, homemade or bought or chicken pieces to this casserole if you like. Serve over pasta with additional spaghetti sauce and fresh grated parmesan cheese.

Rita Higdon
TSU Friend

Shrimp Newburg

Simply the best!

2 pounds fresh shrimp
1 1/2 pounds fresh mushrooms, sliced
6 tablespoons butter
1/2 teaspoon salt
6 tablespoons flour
3 teaspoons Dijon mustard
1/4 cup white wine

Cook and peel shrimp. Do not overcook. Sauté mushrooms in 2 tablespoons butter until soft, add white wine and continue to simmer for 5 minutes. In a sperate pan, melt 4 tablespoons butter until bubbly and add flour and whisk until smooth. Add cream and continue to whisk until slightly thick and creamy. Remove from heat, add salt, mustard, shrimp and mushrooms. Put in buttered casserole dish and bake at 375 degrees for 20 minutes Serve with rice or angel hair pasta with a crisp salad and white wine.

Mamie Mason
TSU Friend

Tastes and Traditions

Shrimp & Broccoli

Delicious served with a salad and crusty bread.

1 tablespoon butter
3 tablespoons shallots, chopped
1 clove garlic, minced
2 tablespoons cognac or brandy
2 ripe tomatoes, peeled and chopped or 1 small can, drained
1 cup heavy cream
1/4 cup bottled clam juice
1/4 cup white wine
1 tablespoon tarragon
1/8 tablespoon red pepper
Dash black pepper
1 bunch broccoli, broken in florets
24 shrimp, peeled and cleaned
4 (12 inch) squares foil

Sauté garlic and shallots in butter for 2 minutes. Pour in brandy, warm, and ignite, shake pan until flame subsides. Stir in the remaining ingredients except broccoli and shrimp. Spread foil on counter. Spoon 2 tablespoons sauce in center of each piece. Place broccoli and shrimp on top, dividing equally. Spoon more sauce over and fold packets. Place on cookie sheet and bake 15 minutes on 450°. Serve over rice or angle hair pasta. Serves 4

Dick Pridgen
TSU Friend

White Bean Turkey Chili

1 package ground turkey breast
1 cup onion, chopped
1 medium green bell pepper, seeded and chopped
1 can (14.5 ounce) diced tomatoes in juice
2 cans (15.5 ounces) Great Northern beans, drained
2 cans (11.5 ounces) cocktail vegetable juice
1 tablespoon chili powder
1/2 teaspoon ground cumin, optional
1/4 teaspoon salt

Spray large saucepan or dutch oven with nonstick cooking spray. Add turkey, onion and green pepper. Cook over medium heat, stirring to break up turkey, until turkey is no longer pink, about 8 minutes. Add remaining ingredients and bring to a boil Reduce heat and simmer covered 15 minutes.

Dot Helms
TSU

Main Dishes

Roy's Tacos

1 envelope taco seasoning
1 box Velveeta shells & cheese
2 pounds ground chuck
1 (4 ounce) can green chilies
16 ounces sour cream
2 tomatoes, chopped
1 cup water

Brown meat and drain. Add taco seasoning and 1 cup water to meat. Cook shells according to package directions on box. Drain shells; add green chilies and cheese seasoning packet from shells. Put shell mixture in 2 quart casserole dish, then add meat mixture. Bake at 350 degrees for 20 minutes. Top with sour cream and tomatoes.

Roy H. Drinkard
TSU Board of Trustees

Cullman businessman Roy Drinkard, who was appointed to the TSU Board of Trustees in May 2000, presented a special gift – a marionette of himself – to Chancellor Jack Hawkins, Jr., prior to a board of trustees meeting on May 12, 2000. Joining Mr. Drinkard was Karen Drinkard, his daughter.

Tastes and Traditions

White Chili

My mom created this chili recipe for me since I don't like beef. It is really good.

12 ounces dried navy beans
12 ounces dried great northern beans
12 ounce dried yellow-eyed or black-eyed peas
1 small fryer, cooked and cut up
6 cups chicken broth
1 (4 ounce) can green chilies, chopped
1 large onion, diced
1 package chili seasoning
additional salt, cumin, chili powder and red pepper to taste.

Soak beans overnight. Sauté onion with 2 tablespoons olive oil. Add spices to onion. Cook beans according to package directions until almost tender. Add beans to chicken broth, onion and spice mixture, cook on medium/low heat for 2 hours. Add chicken and green chilies and cook for 30 minutes more. Taste for salt and spices before serving. Serve over crushed tortilla chips and sprinkle your favorite cheese on top. Enjoy.

Kelly Hawkins
TSU Student

Major League baseball Hall of Fame member and home-run king Henry Aaron was a guest speaker at TSU in spring 1998. Here, "Hammerin' Hank" greets a young fan.

Vegetables & Side Dishes

Eggplant and Cheese Casserole

1 medium eggplant
1 cup onion and garlic croutons
1 cup shredded Cheddar cheese, divided
1 tablespoon flour
1/2 cup milk
1/2 teaspoon salt
1/2 teaspoon pepper
1/4 teaspoon oregano
Butter

Peel eggplant and cut into 3/4-inch cubes. Cook, covered in boiling salted water, for 3 minutes and drain. Combine eggplant, croutons and 1/2 cup cheese. Spoon into lightly greased 1-quart casserole. Combine flour, milk, salt, pepper and oregano and pour over eggplant mixture. Dot with butter and top with remaining cheese. Bake covered at 350 degrees for 20 minutes. Remove cover and continue baking 5 to 10 minutes until lightly browned.

Lucy Baxley
TSU Friend
Alabama State Treasurer

Lucy T. Nall
TSU '20

Alabama State Treasurer Lucy Baxley was a featured speaker when Girls State was held at TSU in June 2000.

Tastes and Traditions

Mushroom-Stuffed Mushrooms

3 dozen medium mushrooms
1 tablespoon flour
1/2 cup light cream or milk
1 teaspoon lemon juice
1/4 cup butter or margarine
1/2 teaspoon salt
2 teaspoons minced chives

Wipe mushrooms with damp cloth; remove stems and reserve caps. Chop stems finely and sauté in butter in a large skillet. Stir in flour and salt; add cream and cook, stirring until thick. Stir in chives and lemon juice. Sprinkle mushroom caps lightly with salt, stuff with filling and place on cookie sheet. NOTE: may be covered and refrigerated for several hours at this point. Bake in a hot oven (400 degrees) for 8 minutes until the filling begins to bubble and mushrooms are just crisp tender.

Edna S. Railey
TSU

Broccoli and Rice Casserole

1/2 cup finely chopped bell pepper
1/2 cup finely chopped onion
1/2 stick margarine
2 packages frozen chopped broccoli
1 1/2 cups uncooked rice
1 (8 ounce) jar Cheez Whiz
1/2 cup milk
1 can cream of chicken soup
Grated cheddar cheese

Sauté bell pepper and onion in margarine. Cook broccoli and rice according to package directions. Drain broccoli and mix with sautéed vegetables and remaining ingredients except cheese. Pour into a 9 x 13-inch baking dish. Top with lots of cheese. Bake at 350 degrees for 30 minutes.

Amy Shiverly
TSU Student

Vegetables & Side Dishes

Broccoli Casserole

This recipe has been passed from one Troy State generation (my mother) to another! This is my favorite dish to take to Alpha Gam potluck dinners.

1 box Uncle Ben's Long Grain Wild Rice (Original Recipe)
1 large bag frozen broccoli
1 can cream of chicken soup
1 large jar Cheez Whiz

Cook rice according to package directions. Cook broccoli in microwave. Stir soup and Cheez Whiz together in large bowl. Place broccoli in greased 9 x 13-inch casserole dish. Spoon rice over broccoli and top with Cheez Whiz mixture. Bake at 350 degrees for 30 minutes.

Hillary Hart
TSU Student
Alpha Gamma Delta Sorority

Stephanie Behrens
TSU Student
Phi Mu Sorority

Leon's Broccoli and Spaghetti Casserole

The Minsky family of Louisiana rarely had a Thanksgiving or any other holiday meal without including this recipe. It can be prepared a day early and kept in the refrigerator.

1 (16 ounce) package regular or thin spaghetti
5 (10 ounce) packages frozen broccoli spears
5 bunches green onions, chopped
Salt and pepper to taste
2 sticks butter
32 slices American cheese
1/2 pint whipping cream

Cook spaghetti according to package directions, rinse and set aside. Sauté broccoli, green onions, salt and pepper in butter. Do not overcook; broccoli should be slightly firm. Spread half of spaghetti in large Pyrex dish which has been coated with nonstick spray. Spoon half of broccoli mixture over spaghetti. Top with 16 slices of cheese. Repeat layers. Pour whipping cream over casserole. Bake at 350 degrees until bubbly, around 15 to 20 minutes or longer, if it's been refrigerated.

Leon Minsky
TSUD

Tastes and Traditions

Corn Casserole

1 can whole kernel corn, drained
1 can creamed corn
6 ounces sour cream
1 box Jiffy Corn Muffin Mix
Chopped jalapeño peppers, optional
1/2 cup grated Cheddar cheese, optional

Preheat oven to 325 degrees. In medium bowl, mix whole corn, creamed corn, sour cream, Jiffy mix and jalapeños, if desired. Pour into casserole dish. Bake for 25-30 minutes. If desired top with cheese and bake an additional 10 minutes.

Bonnie, Kari Ann, Kendra, and Missy
TSU Students
Kappa Delta Sorority

Karen (Coad) Woods
TSU '83
Paige Myers
TSU

Corn Fritters

This recipe and others contributed by Dejerilyn King-Henderson, a member of the TSU class of 1993, have been submitted as a tribute to her late mother, Mrs. Essie Mae King. For more than 30 years, "Miss Essie" prepared meals for the Leo and Elizabeth Bashinsky family of Troy, gaining high regard for her craft. She passed her art of cooking – and her recipes – to her children. Many of the recipes have also been collected by Elizabeth Bashinsky and compiled in a book. Look for Miss Essie's special recipes throughout "The Tastes and Traditions."

1 can corn
1 egg
1/3 cup sugar
1/4 cup all-purpose flour sifted with 1 teaspoon baking powder
2 teaspoons butter
Salt to taste

Heat corn and strain. When cold, add other ingredients in order given. Drop by spoonfuls into very hot grease and fry.

Dejerilyn King-Henderson
TSU '93

Vegetables & Side Dishes

Corn Pudding

A delicious, old-fashioned corn pudding that is a must at Thanksgiving and Christmas dinner. Our family loves it!

4 cups frozen shoepeg corn, thawed
4 large eggs
1 cup whipping cream
1/2 cup whole milk
3 tablespoons sugar
1/4 cup butter, room temperature
2 tablespoons all-purpose flour
2 teaspoons baking powder
1 teaspoon salt

Preheat oven to 350 degrees. Butter an 8-inch square glass baking dish. Blend all ingredients until almost smooth. Pour into prepared dish and bake until brown and center is just set, about 45 minutes. Cool 10 minutes and serve.

Julia Wilson
TSUM

Mexican Corn Casserole

1 package yellow rice
1/2 stick butter
1 can mexicorn
1 can cream of chicken soup
Grated cheese

Preheat oven to 350 degrees. Cook rice according to package directions. Melt butter and stir in corn and soup. Cook, stirring, until mixed well. Stir in rice. Pour mixture into a greased baking dish and cover with cheese. Bake approximately 20 minutes, until cheese is melted well.

Beth Wilson
TSU Student
Alpha Gamma Delta Sorority

TSU accounting graduates consistently attain the top pass rate in Alabama on the CPA exam.

Tastes and Traditions

Pasta and Vegetable Toss

1/2 cup chopped onion
1 clove garlic, finely chopped
1 teaspoon Italian seasoning
1 tablespoon olive oil
1/2 cup water
2 teaspoons beef-flavored instant bouillon
2 cups broccoli florets
2 cups sliced zucchini
1 medium red bell pepper, cut into strips
8 ounces fresh mushrooms, sliced
8 ounces fettuccine, cooked according to package directions and drained

In large skillet, cook and stir onion, garlic and Italian seasoning in oil until onion is tender. Add water, bouillon and vegetables. Cover and simmer 5 to 7 minutes, until vegetables are tender-crisp. Toss with hot fettuccine. Serve immediately. Refrigerate leftovers.

Sherri Musgrove Wenick
TSU '87

Green Bean Casserole

2 cans green beans, drained
1 can cream of mushroom soup
1/2 cup milk
1 can fried onion rings

Combine green beans, soup and milk and pour into a greased casserole dish. Cook at 400 degrees for 30 minutes. Top with onion rings on top and bake for 5 more minutes.

Hilary West
TSU Student
Alpha Gamma Delta Sorority

TSU has the most racially diverse student body of all of Alabama's colleges and universities.

Vegetables & Side Dishes

Red Wine Vinegar Green Beans

1 large can cut green beans, drained
Garlic powder to taste
Regina red wine vinegar to taste
4 - 5 pieces bacon, chopped

Combine all ingredients together, place in a casserole dish and bake at 350 degrees until warm.

Blake Cooper
TSU Student
Alpha Gamma Delta Sorority

Marinated Vegetable Salad

1/2 to 3/4 cup sugar
1/2 cup vinegar
1/4 cup salad oil
1 teaspoon salt
1/2 teaspoon pepper
1 pound can French-style green beans
1 pound can petite English peas
1 can white shoe peg corn
1 cup finely chopped green pepper
1 cup chopped celery
1 small jar chopped pimento

Mix sugar, vinegar, oil, salt and pepper in a saucepan and bring to boil. Drain canned vegetables and combine with vinegar mixture. Refrigerate, stirring occasionally.

Lucy Baxley
TSU Friend
Alabama State Treasurer

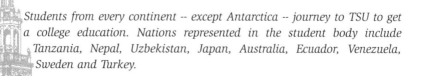

Students from every continent -- except Antarctica -- journey to TSU to get a college education. Nations represented in the student body include Tanzania, Nepal, Uzbekistan, Japan, Australia, Ecuador, Venezuela, Sweden and Turkey.

Tastes and Traditions

Cheese Potato Casserole

7 large potatoes, peeled and thinly sliced
2 tablespoons salt
2 cans cream of chicken soup
1 can Cheddar cheese soup
2/3 cup milk
1 cup grated sharp cheese, divided
1 medium onion, grated
Paprika

Cover potatoes with water and add salt. Boil until tender, about 5 minutes, and drain. Heat soups and milk, stirring until smooth. Add 1/2 cup cheese and onion. Layer potatoes and soup mixture alternately in a greased 2-quart casserole dish, starting with potatoes. Sprinkle with remaining cheese and a dusting of paprika. Bake at 375 degrees for 30 to 40 minutes.

Brandi Baker
TSU Student
Phi Mu Sorority

Potato Casserole

4 - 5 potatoes, diced
2 tablespoons cooking oil
1 package Lipton's onion soup mix
3/4 cup water

Arrange potatoes in a baking dish. Pour oil and soup mix over potatoes and mix together with fingers. Add water. Cover with foil and bake at 350 degrees for 1 hour.

Candi Phillips
TSU Student
Kappa Delta Sorority

In February 1997, TSU acquired the 12-acre site of the former Alabama Baptist Children's Home near campus. The property is now home to the Southeast Alabama Inservice Center and Sorority Hill.

Vegetables & Side Dishes

Hashbrown Casserole

1 (2 pound) bag frozen hashbrowns
1 stick butter
1 cup sour cream
1 can cream of mushroom, chicken soup or potato soup
2 cups grated cheese
1/2 cup chopped onion, optional
2 cups crushed corn flakes
1/4 cup melted butter

Mix all ingredients together except corn flakes and 1/4 cup butter. Place in 9 x 13-inch greased casserole dish and cook at 350 degrees for approximately 45 minutes. Mix corn flakes and butter and sprinkle on casserole. Cook for another 5 minutes.

Kristen Nelson, Kate Duren, Stephanie Jenkins
TSU Students
Phi Mu Sorority

Eve Julian
TSU Student
Alpha Gamma Delta Sorority

Janel Corliss
TSU Student
Kappa Delta Sorority

TSU students are also active members of the local community and lend their support to a number of organizations, including Troy-Pike Habitat for Humanity. Students have helped build several Habitat houses.

Tastes and Traditions

Twice Stuffed Baked Potatoes

During my college career I found that my mother had taught me way too much about the kitchen. I began to cook for some of my fraternity brothers who were less skilled in the culinary arts. I quickly found out they could eat a lot. My twice stuffed baked potatoes filled them up. No matter what I chose as my main course they always wanted my twice stuffed baked potatoes. It didn't matter if we had fish or steaks I would always prepare the potatoes. Now whenever I eat one of my popular potatoes, I remember my days at TSU and the great times that I had those evenings at dinner with my brothers and best friends.

6 potatoes
1 bag of shredded cheddar cheese
1 (8 ounce) sour cream
1 stick of butter
1 pound bacon
salt and pepper

Bake the potatoes until they are soft. While the potatoes are baking, fry the bacon in a skillet. Once the bacon is fried and slightly cooled, break it into small pieces and put it in a large mixing bowl. Add butter, half of the cheese, sour cream, and salt and pepper to taste. When the potatoes have been baked, cut a top off of each potato and clean the contents out of the skin. (This should be done carefully as not to break the shell). Place the inside of the potato in the mixing bowl with the other ingredients and mix. The hot potato will melt the cheese, butter and sour cream. Carefully stuff potato mixture in potato shell. Sprinkle the remaining cheddar cheese on top of the potato and replace the lid of the potato. Put all of the twice stuffed baked potatoes on a cookie sheet and place in the oven at 425 degrees for 10-15 minutes or until the cheese is melted and serve.

Phillip Burk
TSU Student
Lambda Chi Alpha Fraternity

The Collegiate Singers, TSU's principal concert choir, traveled to New York City in May 2000 to perform in one of the world's premier music arenas, Carnegie Hall. Under the direction of Dr. Terre Johnson, the Collegiate Singers gave two concerts and became the first TSU choral group to perform in New York.

Vegetables & Side Dishes

Aunt Aileen's Stuffed Baked Potatoes

This recipe was given to me by my aunt Aileen Wilson (Wilson's Bar-B-Q House) when Wiley and I first married. Those of you who remember Aunt Aileen know what a wonderful cook and person she was.

4 medium baking potatoes
1 egg, beaten
1/2 - 3/4 cup finely chopped onions
Mayonnaise, to taste
Salt and pepper

Bake potatoes until done. Cut in half end to end and scoop out pulp, reserving shells. While pulp is still hot, add egg and mash. Add onions, mayonnaise and salt and pepper to taste. Stir mixture until consistency of mashed potatoes. Put mixture into reserved shells. Bake at 300 degrees for about 30 minutes, until egg has had time to cook.

Glenda Locklar
TSU

Sweet Potato Casserole

Thanksgiving is not the same without it. TSU Athletics has come to expect it at the traditional Christmas dinner. Can be doubled to serve a crowd.

3 cups canned mashed sweet potatoes
3/4 cup sugar
2 eggs
1 teaspoon vanilla
1/2 cup milk
1/2 cup butter

Topping:
1 cup brown sugar
1/3 cup flour
1/3 cup butter
1 cup chopped nuts

Mix casserole ingredients well and pour into a greased casserole dish. Mix topping ingredients and sprinkle over sweet potato mixture. Bake at 350 degrees 30 minutes or until piping hot.

Sherry J. Dye
TSU Spouse

Ann Hart
TSU

Paige Myers
TSU

Joyce F. Gardner
TSU '53

Tastes and Traditions

Candied Sweet Potatoes

My niece, Belinda Starks Wright, is the queen in our family of making these candied sweet potatoes. She also learned how to cook from my mother, her grandmother.

4 - 5 medium sweet potatoes
1 cup sugar
1/2 cup butter

Boil potatoes until almost done. Peel, cut into quarters, and arrange in baking dish. Combine 2 cups water, sugar and butter. Boil together for a few minutes. Pour over potatoes and brown in oven, basting from time to time. If syrup is not thick enough when removed from oven, set on back of stove to candy.

Dejerilyn King-Henderson
TSU '93

When construction began on the Chancellor's Home in 1961, Troy State College was the only college in Alabama without a permanent residence for its chief official. The Southern colonial mansion, situated among pine trees and azaleas on McKinley Drive, is also the focal point for receptions for graduation, honor students, visiting dignitaries and others.

Vegetables & Side Dishes

Vegetable Casserole

1 can Veg-all, drained
2 tablespoons mayonnaise
1 cup grated cheese
5 Ritz crackers
1 tablespoon melted butter

Preheat oven 350 degrees. Mix Veg-all, mayonnaise and grated cheese in large bowl and put in casserole dish. Crush crackers in melted butter and sprinkle over casserole. Cook at 350 degrees for 20 to 25 minutes.

Blair Coker
TSU Student
Alpha Gamma Delta Sorority

Green Bean and Corn Casserole

1 can French-style string beans, drained
1 can whole kernel corn, drained
1 can cream of celery soup
1/2 cup grated cheese
1/3 cup sour cream
1/4 teaspoon salt
1 tablespoon minced onion
1 stick margarine, melted
1 sleeve Town House crackers, crumbled
1/2 cup almonds, optional

Mix beans, corn, soup, cheese, sour cream, salt and onion and put in baking dish. Combine crackers and margarine and sprinkle over vegetables. Sprinkle with almonds, if desired. Bake at 325 degrees for about 45 minutes.

Susan M. Thompson
TSU Student
Phi Mu Sorority

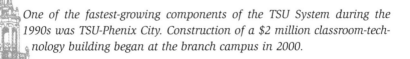

One of the fastest-growing components of the TSU System during the 1990s was TSU-Phenix City. Construction of a $2 million classroom-technology building began at the branch campus in 2000.

Tastes and Traditions

Asparagus Casserole

1 can asparagus, drained
1 can cream of mushroom soup
Cracker crumbs
Cheddar cheese

Mix asparagus and soup and put in a greased casserole. Bake at 350 degrees for about 45 minutes. Cover with cracker crumbs; grate cheese over the top and return to oven to brown.

Lanie Steube
TSU Student
Alpha Gamma Delta Sorority

Squash Casserole

3 cups sliced cooked squash
3/4 stick butter or margarine
1 teaspoon salt
1/2 teaspoon black pepper
1 cup evaporated milk
2 eggs, lightly beated
3/4 cup chopped onion
1 cup grated cheese
2 cups cracker crumbs

Combine squash with butter, salt, pepper and milk. Mix well and then add eggs and onion. Add cheese and cracker crumbs, reserving some for topping. Pour into well-greased casserole dish and sprinkle top with reserved cheese and cracker crumbs. Bake for 40 minutes at 375 degrees.

Amy Jones
TSU Student
Alpha Gamma Delta Sorority

TSU is a leading force in the Higher Education Partnership, an advocacy group for Alabama's public colleges and universities. By July 1999, more than 700 faculty, staff and students had joined TSU's chapter, making it the largest chapter in the Partnership.

Vegetables & Side Dishes

Fighting Bob La Follette's Acorn Squash

This dish was served at family holiday dinners by the Wisconsin governor, U.S. senator and presidential candidate Robert M. "Fighting Bob" La Follette.

3 acorn squash
1 cup brandy
1 stick low-fat margarine or 3 strips thick bacon
1 cup dark brown sugar
3/4 cup maple syrup
1 1/2 teaspoons ground cloves, nutmeg and cinnamon

Cut a plug out around the stem of squash. Remove all inside of squash, retaining the plug, including the stem. Place a third of brandy, margarine, brown sugar and syrup in each squash. Add a half teaspoon each of spices. Replace plug in each squash and bake upright at 300 degrees for 2 hours or until done. Cut squash in half lengthwise and top with brandied sauce.

Don Gaetz
TSU '00

When Don Gaetz, far left, gave the commencement address at the TSU-Florida Region graduation ceremony in June 2000, he was the first TSU student to give the keynote talk at his or her own graduation. Gaetz is pictured with, from left, Dr. Hawkins; Dr. Micky Crews, associate director for academic affairs, TSU-Florida Region; and Dr. Manfred Meine, director of TSU-Florida Region.

Tastes and Traditions

Squash Fritters

2 medium yellow squash, chopped
1/4 cup diced onion
2 tablespoons diced green bell pepper
1 teaspoon brown sugar
1 teaspoon salt
1 tablespoon all-purpose flour
1 large egg, lightly beaten
2 teaspoons butter, melted
1/2 cup olive oil

Stir together all ingredients except oil. Heat oil in a large skillet. Drop mixture by tablespoonfuls into hot oil, frying in batches. Cook until golden, turning once. Drain on paper towels. Serve immediately.

Elaine Dutton
TSU Student
Kappa Delta Sorority

Vidalia Onion Pie

When the Vidalia onions come into season, this is a great way to put them to good use.

2 cups chopped Vidalia onions
1/2 stick margarine, divided
1 sleeve Ritz crackers, crushed
2 eggs
3/4 cup milk
Salt and pepper to taste
Cheddar cheese, grated

Sauté onions in 1/4 stick margarine until translucent. Melt remaining margarine and mix with crackers crumbs. Spread crumbs in 9 x 13-inch casserole dish. Spoon onions over cracker mixture. Beat eggs and add milk, salt and pepper to taste. Pour over onions. Cover with grated cheese. Bake at 350 degrees for 30 to 40 minutes.

Randy Head
TSU

Vegetables & Side Dishes

Spinach and Artichokes

2 (10 ounce) packages frozen chopped spinach
1/2 cup melted butter
1 (8 ounce) package cream cheese, softened
1 large can artichoke hearts, drained
1 teaspoon lemon juice
Buttered cracker crumbs

Cook spinach and drain. Add butter, lemon juice and cream cheese to spinach, stirring over low heat until cheese is melted. Place artichoke hearts in bottom of greased casserole. Top with spinach mixture. Sprinkle buttered crackers crumbs over spinach. Bake at 350 degrees for 25 minutes.

Dodie Pridgen
TSU Friend

Spinach Casserole

This recipe has been served at many of our student etiquette luncheons.

2 (10 ounce) packages frozen chopped spinach or equivalent amount of
   fresh
1 (10 1/2 ounce) can cream of mushroom soup
1 (8 ounce) package cream cheese, cubed
1 medium onion, chopped
2 tablespoons margarine
1 small can french-fried onion rings

Cook spinach according to directions and drain well. Sauté onion in margarine and add the soup and cream cheese. Stir over low heat until the cheese in melted. Mix together with spinach. Turn into a greased casserole and top with onion rings. Bake at 350 degrees for 30 to 35 minutes.

Sodexho-Marriott
TSU

The women's basketball team experienced "March Madness" for the first time in 1997, when it made its initial appearance in the NCAA Division I championship tournament.

Tastes and Traditions

Spinach Madeline

2 packages frozen chopped spinach
4 tablespoons butter
2 tablespoons chopped onion
3 tablespoons flour
1/2 cup evaporated milk
1 (6 ounce) roll jalapeño cheese, sliced
1/2 teaspoon salt
1/2 teaspoon pepper
3/4 teaspoon celery salt
3/4 teaspoon garlic salt
1 teaspoon Worcestershire sauce

Cook spinach and drain, reserving 1/2 cup broth. Melt butter and cook onion. Stir in flour, then reserved broth and milk. Cook over low heat, stirring constantly, and add cheese. Stir until cheese is melted. Add seasonings to spinach mixture. Place in buttered 1 1/2-quart casserole. Bake at 350 degrees for 30 minutes.

Lise Patterson
TSU Spouse

Brussels Sprouts

Even people who don't like brussels sprouts will like these.

1 pound brussels sprouts
2 tablespoons butter
1/4 cup honey
1 clove garlic, crushed
Salt and pepper to taste

Wash brussels sprouts and trim ends. Remove damaged leaves. Place brussels sprouts in pan of salted water. Bring to a boil and boil for 10 minutes. Drain. In frying pan melt butter and honey and add garlic. Add brussels sprouts and stir 5 to 10 minutes until tender and coated with honey mixture. Add salt and pepper as needed.

Dodie Pridgen
TSU Friend

Vegetables & Side Dishes

Leek Casserole

This is a delicious and different way to fix vegetables.

2 pound leeks
2 carrots
2/3 cup olive oil
1 tablespoon salt
1 1/2 tablespoons sugar
1/4 cup uncooked rice

Wash leeks well and cut into 1-inch slices. Cut carrots into 1/4-inch slices. Cook in oil until tender and barely brown. Add 1 cup water, salt and sugar. Simmer 1/2 hour. Add rice and 1/2 cup water. Cover and simmer for 30 minutes. Serve hot or cold.

Anita Hardin
TSU

Baked Ziti

1 green pepper, seeded and chopped
1 onion, chopped
1/2 pound mushrooms
Pepper, garlic powder and oregano to taste
1 (16 ounce) box ziti noodles, cooked
1 (26 ounce) jar pasta sauce
1/2 pound mozzarella cheese, shredded

Lightly coat a nonstick skillet with cooking spray. Sauté green pepper, onion and mushrooms over medium-high heat until tender. Add seasonings to taste. Mix cooked ziti noodles with pasta sauce. Add mozzarella cheese and sautéed vegetables and mix well. Place in a casserole dish which has been lightly coated with cooking spray. Cover with aluminum foil, and bake in a preheated 350 degrees oven for 30 minutes. Uncover and bake 15 minutes more to brown.

Bonnie, Kari Ann, Kendra and Missy
TSU Students
Kappa Delta Sorority

Every year, the nation's elite accounting firms – Pricewaterhousecoopers, Ernst and Young, KPMG Peat Marwick – recruit students from the Sorrell College of Business' award-winning accounting program.

Tastes and Traditions

Macaroni and Cheese

1 (8 ounce) package elbow macaroni, cooked by package directions and
   drained
1 can cream of mushroom soup
1/2 cup mayonnaise
1 small onion, chopped
1 small jar sliced mushrooms, drained
1 small jar diced pimento, drained
2 cups grated Cheddar cheese, divided
1/2 stick butter

Mix all ingredients except 1 cup grated cheese and butter. Melt butter in
casserole. Add macaroni mixture to buttered casserole and sprinkle with
remaining cheese. Bake 25 to 30 minutes at 350 degrees or until casserole
bubbles.

Mrs. Charles M. Archilbald
TSU '42

Baked Cheesy Macaroni Casserole

*In my family macaroni-and-cheese has been a favorite for many years, with
each generation adding its own individual spices or seasoning to the recipe.
My interpretation is as follows.*

6 ounces elbow macaroni
4 tablespoons butter or margarine
3 tablespoons self-rising flour
1 1/2 cups milk
Salt and pepper to taste
1 tablespoon grated onion
12 ounce mild Cheddar cheese, divided

Preheat oven to 350 degrees. Bring to boil 6 cups water. Add macaroni and
cook until tender. In saucepan melt butter over medium heat. Add flour,
stirring constantly until smooth. Slowly pour in milk, stirring frequently,
until mixture is smooth and bubbly. Add salt, pepper, onion, and 4 ounces
of the cheese, evenly sliced. Do not allow to stick. Repeat with remaining
cheese, stirring occasionally until cheese is melted. Mix cheese sauce and
macaroni in a lightly greased casserole dish. Bake for 20 minutes.

Laurence McDade
TSUM '98

Vegetables & Side Dishes

Layered Macaroni and Cheese

I encourage my mom to make this every time I come home.

1 (8 ounce) box macaroni
2 cups shredded sharp cheese
1/2 stick butter or margarine, melted
2 eggs, lightly beaten
1/4 cup cream or half and half
2 cups milk
Salt and pepper to taste
Paprika

Preheat oven to 350 degrees. Boil macaroni as directed on package. Mix melted butter, eggs, cream and milk. In a 2-quart greased baking dish, spread half of macaroni on bottom. Salt and pepper and sprinkle with half of cheese. Repeat with remaining macaroni, seasoning and cheese. Pour milk mixture over macaroni and cheese and sprinkle with paprika. Bake 35 to 40 minutes.

Micki Sims
TSU '00

Pineapple Soufflé

You can serve this as a side dish for pork chops or at a ladies luncheon or even for dessert.

1 cup butter, softened
1 cup sugar
4 egg yolks
1 (15 ounce) can crushed pineapple, drained
6 slices bread, remove crust and cube
4 egg whites, beaten until frothy

Cream butter and sugar. Beat one egg yolk at a time and add to butter and sugar. Add pineapple and fold in bread crumbs and egg whites. Put in ungreased casserole dish. Bake at 350 degrees for 20 minutes.

Ginny Faulk
TSU Student
Alpha Gamma Delta Sorority

Emma Hollon
TSU Student
Phi Mu Sorority

Tastes and Traditions

Mama's Stuffing

1 box Jiffy cornbread mix, prepared according to package directions
Buttermilk
1 cup all-purpose flour
1 cup yellow corn meal
3/4 cup chopped celery
3/4 chopped onion
1 egg, lightly beaten
1/4 cup oil
1/2 package Pepperidge Farm stuffing mix
Salt and pepper to taste
2 (8 ounce) cans chicken broth

Mix cooked cornbread and buttermilk until moist. Combine flour, corn meal, celery, onion and egg. Stir in oil. Film bottom of a skillet with oil and heat until smoking. Pour batter into smoking skillet and bake in a 425 degree oven about 30 minutes, until lightly brown on top. Cool. Crumble and combine with cornbread and buttermilk mixture. Add stuffing mix, salt and pepper. Stir in broth. Bake at 350 degrees for 30 minutes. Makes a lot!!

Mary Toulmin
TSU Student
Alpha Gamma Delta Sorority

Cheese and Tomato Casserole

2 packages sliced mozzarella cheese
2 packages Swiss cheese
1 large can tomatoes (or sliced fresh tomatoes)
Grated Parmesan cheese
Chopped fresh basil
Buttered bread crumbs

Put layer of mozzarella cheese on bottom of dish. Lay Swiss cheese on top. Drain tomatoes and put on top of cheese. Sprinkle with Parmesan cheese and fresh chopped basil. Repeat layers. Put buttered bread crumbs on top and bake 350 degrees, 25 to 30 minutes. Let stand 5 minutes before serving.

Dodie Pridgen
TSU Friend

TSU -- then known as the "Red Wave" – won its first football national championship in 1968, under the direction of head coach Billy Atkins.

Vegetables & Side Dishes

Risotto with Gold

This recipe serves four people.

1 large onion, chopped
Butter
1 cup uncooked rice
1 bouquet garni (bay leaf, thyme, parsley and basil)
2 tablespoons pureed tomato paste
3 cups boiling hot broth
Saffron powder
Grated Parmesan
Gold leaf

In a stew pan, brown onion in butter. Add rice and stir with a wooden spoon until it becomes translucent. Add the bouquet garni, two tablespoons of tomato puree, salt, pepper, and broth. Cover and simmer. Add the saffron powder. Stir and check that the liquid has been absorbed. Sprinkle with cheese and place the gold leaf in the middle when served.

Tuscia and Nall Hollis
TSU Friends

Renowned artist and Troy native Nall Hollis visited TSU in April 1999, when his work was displayed in the Malone Gallery of Art. Joining Nall at the show's opening were Alabama First Lady Lori Siegelman, left, and his wife, Tuscia.

Tastes and Traditions

Five-Vegetable Stir-Fry

This recipe was served at the luncheon honoring W.E.B. Griffin, following his commencement address in June 1999.

1 tablespoon plus 1 teaspoon vegetable oil
4 medium carrots, peeled, cut diagonally into 1/4-inch thick slices
1 large onion, cut into 1-inch pieces
1 bell pepper, cut into 1-inch pieces
3 cups small broccoli florets
3 cups sliced red cabbage
1/2 cups canned low-salt chicken broth
3 tablespoons chopped fresh mint
Salt and pepper to taste

Coat a large nonstick skillet with vegetable oil spray. Heat 1 tablespoon oil in skillet over medium-high heat. Add carrots, onion and bell pepper. Sauté 6 minutes. Add 1 teaspoon oil, broccoli and cabbage. Add broth; stir-fry until cabbage wilts and vegetables are crisp-tender, about 8 minutes. Stir in mint. Season with salt and pepper. Makes 6 servings

Sodexho-Marriott
TSU

Best-selling author W.E.B. Griffin gave the keynote speech at the spring commencement ceremony in June 1999. Griffin, author of the popular "Brotherhood of War" series, returned to TSU as a visiting lecturer later that year. He is pictured here in a TSU captain's chair, which was presented to him following his commencement address.

Vegetables & Side Dishes

Rice Ring with Creamed Mushrooms

This special dish is served at holiday dinners at our house. For a large crowd, double the recipe. It just makes a larger ring.

1 cup wild rice, cooked
1 cup white rice, cooked
4 tablespoons butter, melted
1/2 cup chicken broth
1 1/2 teaspoons corn starch

Cook rice according to package directions. When rice is cooked, add melted butter and salt and pepper to taste. Heat chicken broth and add cornstarch, cook on low heat and stir until it makes a smooth paste. Add to rice mixture. Pour into well greased ring mold. Place ring mold in shallow pan of water and bake at 350° for 25 minutes. Let stand at room temperature for 15 minutes before unmolding. Place on large plate or platter and fill with creamed mushrooms just before serving.

Mushroom Filling:

1 pound fresh mushrooms, sliced
2 tablespoons butter or olive oil
1/2 tablespoon fresh chives, chopped
1/2 teaspoon salt
1 teaspoon soy sauce
dash cayenne pepper
3 tablespoons butter
3 tablespoons flour
2 cups half and half cream
salt and pepper to taste
2 egg yolks

Saute mushrooms in oil, add chives, salt and cayenne pepper. Set aside. Melt 2 tablespoons butter until bubbly and whisk in flour until it becomes a smooth paste. Beat egg yolks and add to cream. Whisk in cream and egg mixture to flour and butter mixture. Cook over medium heat and whisk until thickened. Mix with mushroom mixture and pour into rice ring. Sprinkle fresh, chopped parsley over top before serving.

Janice Hawkins
TSU First Lady

Tastes and Traditions

Apples, Onions, and Red Cabbage Sauté

6 tablespoons butter or bacon fat
4 Golden Delicious apples, peeled, cored, and thinly sliced
2 onions, cut in half lengthwise and slivered
1/2 head red cabbage, thinly shredded
1/4 cup apple cider vinegar
salt and freshly ground black pepper

Melt 2 tablespoons of butter in a pan over medium heat and sauté apples, stirring frequently, until just tender. Set aside. Repeat process with onions. Set aside. Melt remaining butter in a pan, add cabbage, and sauté until just cooked through. Add cider vinegar, stir, and cook until mixture turns pink. Toss apples, onions, and cabbage together in a bowl. Season with salt and pepper to taste. Place mixture in a baking pan. Cover loosely with aluminum foil and bake in a preheated 350° oven for 45 minutes. Serve warm with roast pork.

Debbie Sanders
TSU

Holiday Spinach Mold

This recipe can be doubled if you are serving a crowd. It is so good and very pretty.

2 (10 ounce) packages frozen, chopped spinach
2 tablespoons grated onion
1 red bell pepper, finely diced
2 tablespoons butter
1 cup sour cream
3 eggs, beaten
1/4 cup sherry
1/4 teaspoon nutmeg
salt and pepper to taste
pinch of cayenne pepper

Cook and squeeze dry spinach. Sauté onion and bell pepper in butter until tender. Add spices to onion mixture. Mix all ingredients and place into thoroughly greased ring mold. Place mold in a shallow pan of water and bake at 350° for 45 to 50 minutes. Let stand at room temperature for at least 15 minutes then unmold on pretty serving platter. Fill center with cooked, buttered carrots (or whatever you like).

Dian Mahone
TSU Parent

Vegetables & Side Dishes

Asparagus Bread Pudding

This recipe is bidding to become a new family favorite for the holidays.

2 tablespoons unsalted butter
1 tablespoon water
Pinch salt
1 pound (2 small) leeks, cleaned and cut into 1/2 inch thick slices (white and light green parts only)
5 eggs
2 1/2 cups milk
1 cup heavy cream
1 pound asparagus, trimmed and cut on the diagonal into 1-inch pieces
1 pound dry bread, cut into 1-inch cubes (if fresh, toast lightly)
1/4 pound Fontina cheese, shredded
1/4 pound Gruyére or Cantal cheese, shredded
1/2 cup mixed chopped fresh herbs (chives, parsley, tarragon, chervil)
1/2 teaspoon grated lemon peel
Pinch cayenne
1 teaspoon salt
Freshly ground black pepper to taste

Heat the oven to 375 degrees. In a medium skillet over medium heat, melt the butter with the water and a pinch of salt. Add the leeks and cook until tender, about ten minutes. Set aside to cool. In a large bowl, whisk together the eggs and milk. Add the remaining ingredients, including the leeks, and gently toss them. The mixture should be well coated and somewhat soupy. Spread the mixture into a 4-quart soufflé dish, a 13x9-inch baking dish, or another ovenproof dish that's at least 2 inches deep and big enough to hold the mixture. Put the dish on a baking sheet and bake until the top is crusty brown and a knife inserted in the middle comes out clean, 45 to 60 minutes. If the pudding looks too dark before it's finished, cover with foil. Let cool slightly before serving.

Steve Knockemus
TSU

TSU's fine arts students have displayed their talents in some of the United States' premier arenas, including the Kennedy Center in Washington, D.C. and Carnegie Hall in New York.

Tastes and Traditions

Herbed Mushrooms & Artichokes

This is so good with baked chicken or roast beef. It can be prepared in the microwave or on the stove.

1 (9 ounce) package frozen or canned artichoke hearts
1 pound fresh mushrooms, halved
1/4 cup sliced green onion or chives
2 tablespoons butter or olive oil
2 tablespoons all-purpose flour
1 teaspoon instant chicken bouillon granules
1/4 teaspoon dried thyme, crushed
Dash ground nutmeg
1/2 cup shredded Swiss cheese
1/3 cup sour cream
1/2 cup coarsely chopped pecans, toasted.

Defrost artichokes and drain thoroughly. Melt oil in large pan and sauté onions and mushrooms for 3 to 5 minutes. Add drained artichokes and toss with mushrooms until tender. Remove mixture and place in a 2 quart casserole dish. Add 2 tablespoons butter to pan and put flour in when butter is bubbly to make white sauce. Add bouillon, thyme, and nutmeg; stir until smooth and add 2/3 cup water. Cook on medium until mixture is thickened and bubbly. Remove from heat and stir in cheese until melted; add sour cream. Stir this mixture into mushrooms and artichokes in casserole dish. Bake uncovered at 350 degrees for 20 to 30 minutes until heated through. Put toasted pecans on top the last ten minutes of baking.

Mildred Finlay
TSU

Alumnus McDowell Lee, '50, was the recipient of the first Distinguished Leadership Award in April 2000. The longtime secretary of the Alabama Senate, Lee (right) was recognized for his service to TSU by Chancellor Jack Hawkins, Jr.

Vegetables & Side Dishes

Apple Cheese Casserole

This is good for just about any meal as a side dish. Try it with roast pork and gravy.

16 ounce processed cheese loaf
1 1/2 sticks butter, melted
1 1/2 cups sugar
1 cup plain flour
2 (20 ounce) cans unsweetened apples (packed in water)

Drain apples, combine other ingredients and mix well. Place apples in 8" x 12" glass dish and spread cheese mixture over apples. Bake at 375 degrees for 30 minutes or until light brown. Serves 12. For smaller crowd, half the ingredients.

Sisters Restaurant
TSU Friend
Troy, Alabama

Lisa Henderson
TSU Student
Phi Mu Sorority

Eggplant Creole

1 pound eggplant
2 tablespoons margarine or butter
1/2 cup onion, chopped
1 stalk celery, chopped
1 large tomato, chopped
2 tablespoons flour
1 teaspoon salt
1/2 teaspoon pepper
1/2 teaspoon sugar
1 cup buttered bread crumbs
1/2 cup shredded cheddar cheese

Peel and cut eggplant. Cook till tender, drain and chop. Melt butter in skillet and sauté onion and celery for 2-3 minutes. Add tomato, sprinkle with flour and stir well; cook and additional 2-3 minutes. Season with salt, pepper, and sugar. Mix eggplant and tomato mixture and spoon into buttered casserole. Combine buttered bread crumbs and shredded cheese and sprinkle over casserole. Bake at 350 degrees for 25-30 minutes.

Sue McCrimmon
TSU Friend

Tastes and Traditions

Cheese Soufflé

First Edition Favorite

This is one of my favorite recipes. Our devoted domestic technician, Johnson (Dee) Bailey, baked this "never-fail" cheese soufflé for us for 40 faithful years.

3 tablespoons butter
3 tablespoons flour
1 cup milk
1 cup grated cheese
3 eggs, separated
Salt and pepper to taste

Make cream sauce with butter, flour and milk. Add grated cheese while sauce is hot. Beat in egg yolks. Beat whites stiff and fold cooled cheese mixture into the whites. Place in buttered baking dish. Bake at 325 degrees for 35 minutes or until firm.

Eunice Davis-McNeill
TSU Friend

Baked Fruit

Traditional Recipe

This is the recipe of Martha Smith Dubois, the daughter of former Troy State president Dr. C. B. Smith.

1 (20 ounce) can Comstock unsweetened pie apples
1 large banana, sliced
1/2 cup raisins
1/2 cup chopped nuts
2 tablespoons lemon juice
3/4 cup light brown sugar
2 tablespoons flour
1/4 teaspoon salt
3/4 teaspoon apple pie spice
2 teaspoons butter

Mix apples, banana, raisins and nuts. Sprinkle with lemon juice. Mix together brown sugar, flour, salt and apple pie spice. Add to fruit and mix. Spoon into a baking dish and dot with butter. Bake at 400 degrees for 30 to 40 minutes. Cover for 15 minutes.

Margaret Pace Farmer
TSU '32

Finishing Touches

Desserts

Photo by Monica Morgan Photography
Rosa Parks

A dessert, a "finishing touch," is a meal's sweet and pleasant conclusion, the fitting complement to a main course. Of course, a finishing touch can be more than the final act in a culinary play. It can be a show unto itself, a cornerstone upon which memories are built, a beginning point for new traditions.

For one of its finishing touches, "The Tastes and Traditions" turns to TSU friend Rosa Louise Parks, whose singular act of courage in 1955 brought about both an end and a beginning. Mrs. Parks was working as a seamstress when she defied a Montgomery busdriver and refused to give up her bus seat on December 1, 1955. Her action sparked the Montgomery Bus Boycott, signaling the end of codified racial segregation and heralding the beginning of the modern Civil Rights movement.

Mrs. Parks duly gained a key place in American history and has since become an important part of the Troy State University System, as she is the namesake for the Rosa Louise Parks Library and Museum at Troy State University Montgomery. The facility, which is built near the historic bus stop and contains the same city bus Mrs. Parks tried to ride that day, is home to a Civil Rights museum, a 21st-century library and high-tech classrooms and meeting facilities. It promises to offer a beginning point -- of study and understanding -- for many people.

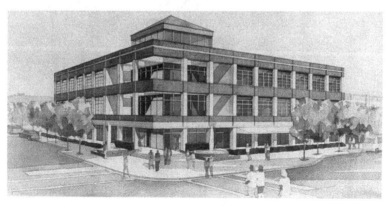

The Rosa Parks Library and Museum at Troy State University Montgomery

Desserts

Desserts

Bread Pudding

1 stick butter or margarine
6 slices white bread, toasted
4 eggs
1 1/2 cups sugar
3 cups milk
Nutmeg and cinnamon to taste
Raisins and pecans, optional

Rum Sauce:
1 stick butter
1 cup packed brown sugar
1 cup milk or cream
1/4 cup rum (brandy or bourbon may be substituted)

For Pudding: Melt butter in 6 x 12-inch baking dish. Break bread in large pieces and add to butter. Beat eggs and sugar together. Add milk and mix. Stir some spices into mixture and sprinkle some on top. Add raisins and pecans, if desired. Pour over bread. Let set until bread is soft or can make and refrigerate overnight. Bake at 325 to 350 degrees until set. If you want it less stiff do not cook as long.
For Sauce: Combine all ingredients in a heavy saucepan and cook over low heat until the mixture boils, stirring frequently. Pour sauce over pudding just before serving, making sure sauce and pudding are warm.

Rosa Parks
TSU Friend

Orange Blossoms

1 package yellow cake mix

Glaze:
Rind and juice of 2 oranges
Rind and juice of 1 lemon
1 pound powdered sugar, sifted

Prepare cake mix according to package directions. Fill greased and floured mini-muffin pans with 1 teaspoon batter each. Watch blossoms carefully. Do not let them get too brown. Begin checking at 5 minutes. Remove them from the oven and top each with glaze. For glaze, combine all ingredients and beat until smooth and sugar is dissolved.

Margaret Pace Farmer
TSU '32

Tastes and Traditions

Aunt Claudia's Tea Cakes

Aunt Claudia makes the best tea cakes. We always look forward to her visits to Troy and her famous tea cakes.

3/4 cup shortening
1 cup sugar
2 cups self-rising flour
2 eggs
1 teaspoon vanilla

Blend sugar and shortening. Add flour, eggs and vanilla. Spoon onto cookie sheet. Bake at 350 degrees for 10 to 12 minutes

Marilyn Ash
TSU '79

Brown Sugar Shortbread

This recipe was given to me recently by a neighbor who was a former TSU employee, Melton Carter. It's so easy and oh so good.

1 cup butter, softened (do not substitute)
1/2 cup packed brown sugar
2 1/4 cups all-purpose flour

In mixing bowl cream butter and sugar. Gradually stir in the flour. Turn onto a lightly floured surface and knead until smooth. Pat into a 1/3 inch thick rectangle measuring 11 x 8 inches. Cut into 2 x 1-inch strips. Prick with a fork. Bake at 300 degrees for 25 minutes or until bottoms begin to brown. Cool 5 minutes.

Mary Beth Green
TSU Friend

TSU's roots as a normal school are still strong: The University guarantees the performance of its graduates as teachers, and more than 100 of Alabama's school systems employ TSU-trained teachers.

Desserts

Potato Chip Cookies

1 cup butter, softened (do not substitute)
1 teaspoon vanilla
1 1/2 cups sifted all-purpose flour
1/2 cup crushed potato chips

Cream butter and sugar. Add vanilla, flour and potato chip crumbs. Drop by 1/2 teaspoonfuls on ungreased cookie sheet. Bake 10 to 12 minutes at 350 degrees. Makes about 4 dozen cookies.

Helen McKinley
TSU Friend

Vergil Parks McKinley (insert photo), a graduate and professor at Troy Normal School during the first decade of the 20th century, was instrumental in the development of the school's athletic program. His son, former Texaco CEO John McKinley, honored his memory in 1997 when he created the Vergil Parks McKinley Outstanding Employee Award. The monthly award salutes TSU's top staff members with a keepsake clock and cash award. Helen McKinley, far left, and John McKinley are pictured here with Mildred Finlay, one of the recipients of the McKinley Award.

Tastes and Traditions

Gingerbread Cookies

1/3 cup shortening
1 cup packed brown sugar
1 1/2 cups molasses
7 cups all-purpose flour
1 teaspoon cinnamon
1 teaspoon allspice
1 teaspoon ginger
1 teaspoon cloves
1 teaspoon salt
1/2 cup plus 3 tablespoons cold water, divided
2 teaspoons baking soda

Cream shortening and brown sugar in mixing bowl. Blend in molasses. Sift flour with spices and salt. Stir dry ingredients into molasses mixture alternating with 1/2 cup water. Dissolve baking soda in 3 tablespoons of water and add to mixture. Chill dough, then roll about 1/2-inch thick. Place cookies on greased cookie sheet. Bake at 350 degrees for 15 to 18 minutes.

Loretta Sykes
TSU Friend

Pound Cake Cookies

These are my favorite cookies. The taste of them reminds me of buttered toast made in the oven with the bread lightly brown and the butter just melted. The recipe makes about six dozen small cookies: three dozen for me and three dozen for my family!

3 sticks butter at room temperature (do not substitute)
1 cup sugar
2 egg yolks
3 cups all-purpose flour, sifted
1 teaspoon vanilla
Strawberry jam or pecan halves

Cream butter and sugar. Add egg yolks. Blend flour into butter mixture. Add flavoring. Refrigerate dough until thoroughly chilled. Pinch off a small piece of dough, about the size of a quarter, and press onto ungreased cookie sheet. Using thumb, press indentation in top of each cookie and fill with small amount of strawberry jam or press a pecan half on top of cookies. Bake 12 minutes at 300 degrees, until lightly browned. Cool several minutes, then slide cookies off pan, using a spatula. Keep stored in an airtight container for a crisp, delightful treat.

Helen Ricks
TSU

Desserts

Refrigerator Nut Cookies

1 stick margarine, softened
1 cup sugar
2 teaspoons vanilla
1 egg
1 3/4 cups all-purpose flour
1/2 teaspoon soda
1/2 teaspoon salt
1/2 cup chopped nuts

Cream margarine and sugar. Beat in vanilla and egg. Sift dry ingredients together. Gradually add to sugar mixture. Shape in long rolls in wax paper and chill in refrigerator several hours. Slice 1/8 to 1/4-inch thick. Bake on ungreased cookie sheet in 400 degree oven about 7 to 8 minutes.

Charlotte Hall
TSU '69

"Killer" Chocolate Chip Cookies

These are the best chocolate chip cookies I have ever made. My sister gave me this recipe but I claim it as my own. When asked to bring dessert, I always bring my "Killers."

1 cup shortening
1 cup sugar
1/2 cup brown sugar
2 eggs
2 teaspoons vanilla
2 cups all-purpose flour
1 1/2 teaspoons salt
1 teaspoon baking soda
1 (12 ounce) package chocolate chips
1 cup chopped nuts, optional

Beat shortening, sugars, eggs and vanilla until light and fluffy. Stir in remaining ingredients, stirring only until flour is blended. Drop by rounded tablespoonfuls onto ungreased baking sheets. Bake at 375 degrees for 10 minutes. Allow to cool on bakers rack or wax paper.

Jenni James Clark
TSU '89

Four of every five TSU science graduates who apply to professional schools – medical, dental, optometry, veterinary -- are accepted.

Tastes and Traditions

Awesome Chocolate Chip Cookies

1 cup butter, softened
1/2 cup shortening
1 1/3 cups granulated sugar
1 cup packed brown sugar
4 eggs
1 tablespoon vanilla extract
1 teaspoon lemon juice
3 cups all-purpose flour
2 teaspoons baking soda
1 1/2 teaspoons salt
1 teaspoon cinnamon
1/2 cup oats
2 (12 ounce) packages semisweet chocolate chips
2 cups chopped nuts

In large bowl, beat butter, shortening, and sugars on high speed until light and fluffy, about 5 minutes. Add eggs, one at a time, beating well after each addition. Beat in vanilla and lemon juice. In another bowl, stir together flour, baking soda, salt, cinnamon and oats. Gradually add to butter mixture, blending thoroughly. Stir in chips and nuts. Use a scant 1/4 cup of dough for each cookie. Drop dough onto lightly greased cookie sheet, spacing cookies 3 inches apart. For soft cookies, bake in a 325 degree oven for 17 to 19 minutes, until light golden brown; for crisp cookies bake at 350 degrees for 16 to 18 minutes, until golden brown. Makes 3 dozen very large cookies or 8 to 9 dozen if you use a teaspoon of dough for each cookie.

Sara Jones
TSU Spouse

Strawberry or Peach Pavlova

My son, L.T. (Lawrence Tynes #10 on the Trojan football team), loves this dessert.

5 egg white
1 1/2 cups granulated sugar
1 teaspoon white vinegar
2 teaspoons cornstarch
1/2 teaspoon vanilla

Preheat oven to 275 degrees. Draw a nine inch circle on non-stick baking paper. Place on a baking sheet. Beat egg whites until stiff; gradually beat in sugar until mixture is thick and glossy. Beat in vinegar, cornstarch and vanilla. Spoon mixture on to circle on paper, swirl with knife to make pavlova. Cook on bottom shelf for 2 hours. Peel off paper, place on plate, fill with whipped cream and strawberries or peaches.

Margaret Tynes
TSU Parent

Desserts

Chocolate Chip Treasure Cookies

This was a favorite of my boys, Chris and Michael, when they were young.

1 1/2 cups graham cracker crumbs
1/2 cup all-purpose flour
2 teaspoons baking powder
1 (14 ounce) can sweetened condensed milk
1 stick margarine, softened
1 (3 1/2 ounce) can coconut
1 (12 ounce package) semisweet chocolate chips
1 cup chopped nuts

Heat oven to 325 degrees. In small bowl mix graham cracker crumbs, flour and baking powder. Set aside. In large mixing bowl, beat milk and margarine until smooth. Add crumb mixture. Mix well. Stir in coconut, chocolate chips and nuts. Drop by rounded tablespoonfuls onto ungreased cookie sheet. Bake 9 to 10 minutes or until lightly browned. Makes about 3 dozen cookies.

Judy Morgan
TSU

Vanishing Oatmeal Raisin Cookies

1 cup (2 sticks) margarine, softened
1 cup firmly packed brown sugar
1/2 cup granulated sugar
2 eggs
1 teaspoon vanilla
1 1/2 cups all-purpose flour
1 teaspoon baking soda
1 teaspoon cinnamon
1/2 teaspoon salt, optional
3 cup Quaker oats
1 cup raisins

Heat oven to 350 degrees. Beat together margarine and sugars until creamy. Add eggs and vanilla; beat well. Combine flour, baking soda, cinnamon and salt; add to creamed mixture. Stir in oats and raisins and mix well. Drop by rounded tablespoonfuls onto ungreased cookie sheet. Bake 10 to 12 minutes, until golden brown. Cool 1 minute on cookie sheet; remove to wire rack.

Nikki Phipps
TSU Student
Chi Omega Sorority

Tastes and Traditions

Old-Fashioned Oatmeal Cookies

1 spice cake mix
2 cups uncooked oats
2 eggs
3/4 cup cooking oil
1/2 cup milk
2 cup raisins
1 cup chopped nuts
1/4 cup brown sugar

Combine all ingredients and mix well. Drop by teaspoonfuls onto an ungreased cookie sheet. Bake at 350 degrees for twelve minutes.

Emily Withus
TSU Student
Alpha Gamma Delta Sorority

Giant Cashew White Chocolate Cookies

2/3 cup butter or margarine, softened
2/3 cup packed brown sugar
1 egg
1 teaspoon vanilla
2 1/2 cups all-purpose flour
1 teaspoon baking soda
1 (12 ounce) package vanilla baking chips, divided
1 1/2 cups coarsely chopped salted cashews, divided
1/3 cup semisweet chocolate chips, melted

Preheat oven to 325 degrees. In large bowl cream butter and sugar. Stir in egg and vanilla; mix until well blended. Stir in flour and soda. Add three-quarters of vanilla chips and 1 cup cashews; mix well. Shape dough into 2-inch balls. Place 2 inches apart on ungreased cookie sheet; flatten slightly. Bake 15 to 18 minutes, until golden brown. Cool 10 minutes. Melt remaining vanilla chips. Dip an edge of each cookie into melted chips and decorate with remaining chopped cashews. If desired, drizzle with melted chocolate.

Bonnie, Kari Ann, Kendra, Missy
TSU Students
Kappa Delta Sorority

Desserts

Snicker Doodle Cookies

1/2 cup butter, softened
1/2 cup shortening
1 1/2 cups sugar
2 eggs
2 3/4 cups all-purpose flour
2 teaspoons cream of tartar
1 teaspoon baking soda
Cinnamon-sugar mixture

Mix butter, shortening, sugar and eggs. Blend in flour, cream of tartar and baking soda. Shape into balls. Roll balls in cinnamon-sugar mixture and place on an ungreased baking sheet. Bake 5 to 7 minutes at 400 degrees. Immediately remove from cookie sheet. Makes 6 dozen.

Christy Symes
TSU Student
Kappa Delta Sorority

Easy Peanut Butter Cookies

This is perfect for those of us who haven't mastered our cooking skills!

1 cup peanut butter
1 cup sugar
1 large egg

Preheat oven to 350 degrees. Mix ingredients. Roll into 1 inch balls. Place on cookie sheet. Bake for 10 minutes. Remove to wire racks to cool. Yields about 3 dozen cookies.

Heather Hines
TSU Student
Alpha Gamma Delta Sorority

The Hall School of Journalism offers the only broadcast program in Alabama in which students produce and air a live noon and evening news report each weekday while school is in session.

Tastes and Traditions

Congo Bars

A favorite after band practice with the Sound of the South from 1971 to 1975. Made in minutes! Eaten as fast!

2 3/4 cups all-purpose flour
1 tablespoon baking powder
1/2 teaspoon salt
2/3 cup butter, softened
1 teaspoon vanilla
1 package light brown sugar
3 eggs
1 cup chopped nuts, optional
1 (6 ounce) package chocolate chips

Preheat oven to 350 degrees. Sift dry ingredients together. Melt shortening in a large saucepan. Stir in brown sugar and vanilla. Cool. Add eggs one at a time, beating well after each addition. Add dry ingredients slowly. Fold in nuts and chocolate chips. Spread in greased 15 x 10 x 1-inch pan. Bake 25 to 30 minutes. Cut in bars.

Debbie Bradley
TSU '75, '77 and '99

Faith Weathington
TSU

Claxton Fruitcake Cookies

1 pound Claxton Fruit Cake
1 package yellow cake mix
2 eggs
1/3 cup oil
1/2 teaspoon rum flavoring
1 1/2 cups chopped pecans

Crumble fruit cake into dry cake mix. Add eggs and oil and mix. Add flavoring. Mix in pecans with your hands. Drop by teaspoonfuls onto greased cookie sheet, about one inch apart. Bake at 350 degrees for 10 to 12 minutes; do not cook longer than 12 minutes. Yields approximately 75 to 100 cookies. Store in airtight container.

Susan Thompson
TSU Student
Phi Mu Sorority

Desserts

Date Nut Balls

This is a favorite of some very special TSU alumni. The Blakeney girls find it a real treat! Good especially at festive times.

2 sticks butter
1 cup sugar
1 box chopped dates
1 cup chopped pecans
2 cups Rice Krispies cereal
Powdered sugar

Melt together butter and sugar over medium heat. Add dates and cook until tender and butter is absorbed. Remove from heat. Add pecans and cereal. Mix well. When mixture is cool enough to handle, form into balls. Roll balls in powdered sugar and store in an airtight container.

Sherry J. Dye
TSU Spouse

Janel Corliss
Kappa Delta Sorority
TSU Student

Easy Cookie Bars

1 box butter cake mix
1 cup chocolate chips
1/2 cup oil
2 teaspoons water
2 eggs
3/4 cup chopped pecans

Combine all ingredients and mix well, adding pecans last. Pour into a greased 9 x 13-inch glass baking dish. Bake for 30 minutes. Let cool and cut into bars.

Allison Houston
TSU '95

TSU is one of the safest college campuses in the United States, according to studies done by USA Today and The Chronicle of Higher Education.

Tastes and Traditions

Imitation Reese Peanut Butter Bars

My mom can't make enough of these for me.

1 1/2 cups graham cracker crumbs
1 pound powdered sugar
2 sticks margarine, divided
1 1/2 cups smooth or crunchy peanut butter
1 cup chocolate chips

Mix cracker crumbs and powdered sugar. Melt 1 1/2 sticks margarine and peanut butter. Add to powdered sugar mixture. Mix well. Press firmly with back of spoon into 9 x 13-inch pan. Melt chocolate chips and remaining margarine. Spread over the top of the peanut butter mixture. Cool. Cut into squares. Eat to full.

Scott Erb
TSU Student
Sound of the South

Peanut Butter Brownies

1 package yellow cake mix
2 large eggs, lightly beaten
1 cup chunky peanut butter
1 stick butter, melted
1 (10 ounce) package peanut butter chips
1 (14 ounce) can sweetened condensed milk

Preheat oven to 350 degrees. Combine cake mix, eggs, peanut butter and butter in a large bowl. Mix well. Press half into bottom of an ungreased 9 x 13-inch pan and reserve rest. Bake 10 minutes. Remove from oven. Top with chips and drizzle with milk. Crumble reserved mixture over top. Bake 25 to 30 minutes or until golden. Cool and cut into bars.

Elaine Thomas
TSU Student
Phi Mu Sorority

Faculty members of TSU's Department of Biological Sciences joined forces in summer 2000 to win a prestigious grant from the Alabama Department of Public Health's ALERT (Alabama Legacy for Environmental Research Trust) program. With the help of the ALERT grant, the biology faculty will examine the nature of -- and seek solutions to -- a variety of environmental problems affecting Alabama.

Desserts

Cream Cheese Blond Brownies

This is my boyfriend's favorite snack after playing baseball for TSU.

1 large package nonfat cream cheese, softened
1/2 cup sugar
2 large egg whites
1/4 cup nonfat sour cream
3 teaspoons vanilla, divided
1 1/4 cups plus 1 tablespoon all-purpose flour, divided
1 teaspoon baking powder
1/4 cup chopped walnuts
1/3 cup pure maple syrup
1/3 cup brown sugar
1/3 cup butter
1 large egg

In a small bowl, combine cream cheese, sugar, egg whites, sour cream, 1 tablespoon flour and 1 teaspoon vanilla. Beat until smooth; set aside. In another small bowl, stir together remaining flour, baking powder and walnuts; set aside. In a large bowl, combine syrup, brown sugar, butter, egg, and remaining vanilla. Beat until smooth. Add flour mixture; beat until dry ingredients are evenly moistened. Pour two-thirds of batter into a lightly greased 8-inch square baking pan; spread to make level. Pour cheese mixture evenly over batter. Drop remaining batter by spoonfuls over cheese mixture; swirl with knife to blend batter slightly with cheese mixture. Bake in a 350 degree oven until a wooden pick inserted comes out clean, about 25 minutes. Let cool in pan, then cut into 2-inch squares.

Sarah Gilchrist
TSU Student
Alpha Gamma Delta

The Southeast Alabama Technology Network – also known as the SEAL Network – went into operation in August 2000. Designed and administered by TSU, the SEAL Network uses distance-learning technology to provide unique academic opportunities to students at rural high schools in southeast Alabama.

Tastes and Traditions

Craig's Favorite Brownies

This is my son's favorite dessert. I would bake them, cool, cut into squares, place on wax paper on a cookie sheet and freeze. Then I would put them in a plastic bag and put them in the freezer. When Craig got home from school, he would go to the freezer and get three or four out of the bag and enjoy. I couldn't hide them. They were his birthday cake too!

4 (1 ounce) squares unsweetened chocolate
2/3 cup shortening
2 cups sugar
4 large eggs
1 1/4 cups self-rising flour
1 teaspoon vanilla
1 cup chopped nuts

Heat oven to 350 degrees. Grease a 9 x 13 x 2-inch pan. In a medium saucepan, melt chocolate and shortening over low heat. Remove from heat. Mix in sugar and let mixture cool. Add eggs alternately with flour, starting with eggs. Add vanilla, stir in nuts. Spread in prepared pan and bake at 350 degrees for 30 minutes, until brownies pull away from sides of pan. Do not overbake. Cool slightly and cut into bars about 2 x 2 1/2-inches. Makes 32.

Edna S. Railey
TSU

Chocolate Caramel Brownies

2/3 cup evaporated milk
1 bag caramels
1 german chocolate cake mix
1 1/2 sticks margarine
1 (6 ounce) bag chocolate chips
1 cup pecan pieces

Melt caramels in 1/3 cup evaporated milk on low heat. Set aside. Mix 1/3 cup evaporated milk, cake mix and melted butter. Beat with mixer. Spread 1/2 cake mixture into ungreased 9 x 13-inch pan and bake at 350° for 6 minutes. Remove from oven and put caramel mixture, chocolate chips and pecans on top of cake mixture. Put all this in freezer for 30 minutes. Take out of freezer and pour the remaining cake mixture on top. Bake at 350 degrees for about 10 minutes more. You must watch to see when cake is done and do not overcook. Cool and cut into brownie squares. Wonderful!

Eloise Hood
TSU Friend

Desserts

Mint Brownies

Wonderfully rich and different brownies. Great for a party.

2 cups sugar
4 eggs, beaten
1 cup sifted flour
1 1/2 cups chopped nuts
1 cup butter
4 (1 ounce) squares unsweetened chocolate
1/2 teaspoon peppermint extract

Mint Frosting:
3 cups powdered sugar
4 tablespoons butter
3 to 4 tablespoons cream
2 teaspoons peppermint extract
Few drops green food coloring

Chocolate Icing:
4 tablespoons butter
4 (1 ounce) squares semisweet baking chocolate

For Brownies: Mix sugar, eggs, flour and nuts together. Melt butter and chocolate; add to flour mixture. Add peppermint extract, blending well. Pour into greased jelly-roll pan. Bake at 350 degrees for 20 to 25 minutes. Cool and frost.

For Mint Icing: Mix powdered sugar, 4 tablespoons butter, cream, peppermint extract and green food coloring together. Beat until creamy and spread over cooled bars. Cover with chocolate icing.

For Chocolate Icing: Melt butter and chocolate together; stir until smooth; cool slightly. Spread over mint frosting.

Janice Hawkins
TSU First Lady

The "kissing rock" continues to be a distinctive TSU landmark, as it remains a popular site for students to propose marriage. Quick quiz: Where is the kissing rock located?

Tastes and Traditions

Brownie Bonbons

This is a recipe I made for the folks in the Library on the main campus, on the premise that a candy bar can be too much of a good thing, but that there is never too much of a good cookie.

5 (1.9 ounce) Mounds bars, the double kind
2 ounces unsweetened chocolate
1/2 cup butter
1 cup sugar
2 eggs
1 teaspoon vanilla
3/4 cup all-purpose flour

Chocolate Glaze:
1 ounce unsweetened chocolate
1 tablespoon butter
2 teaspoons light corn syrup
3/4 cup powdered sugar, or as needed
1 - 2 tablespoons water, to desired consistency

Grease 5 mini-muffin tins, the kind with 12 muffin cups, and set aside. If you don't have this many, divide the batter into 5 equal parts and bake in succession. The batter won't suffer from waiting. Heat oven to 375 degrees Cut each Mounds bar section into 6 pieces to make 60 pieces Set aside. Melt butter and chocolate together over low heat, stirring to prevent scorching. Remove from heat and stir in sugar. Beat in eggs, one at a time. Beat in vanilla. Stir in flour. Put a little batter into each muffin cup. Drop piece of Mounds bar on top. Cover with remaining batter. Bake at 375 degrees for 12 to 15 minutes; if you prefer brownies moist, be sure not to overcook. Remove from oven and let cool completely in pans. Remove from pans, using point of paring knife, if necessary. Turn upside down, that is, with large part on the bottom, and glaze. To make glaze, melt chocolate and butter together, stirring to avoid scorching. Stir in corn syrup. Stir in sugar and add water, a teaspoon at a time, to desired consistency, for either a glaze or frosting effect.
These may be frozen before or after glazing. If frozen after, the glaze may streak. This is easily cured by heating slightly in microwave or conventional oven, or leaving in a hot car.
If you're in a hurry and appearance isn't critical, just mix the candy pieces into the batter, pour it in a greased 8-inch square pan, separating the candy pieces fairly evenly, and bake it at 350 degrees for 20 to 25 minutes. Cool and frost with glaze.

Tuny Jennings
TSU-Florida Region

Desserts

Peanut Butter Nut Chews

This recipe came from a friend at a church social many years ago. It has always gotten many compliments and I have shared it many times. It recently won a blue ribbon at the Peanut Butter Festival Recipe Contest.

1/3 cup margarine, softened
1 box butter recipe cake mix
1 egg
1 small package miniature marshmallows
2/3 cup corn syrup
1/2 cup peanut butter chips
2 cups Rice Krispies
1 small can salty cocktail peanuts

Mix margarine, cake mix and egg together. Press in 9 x 13-inch pan that has been coated with nonstick spray. Bake 14 minutes at 375 degrees. Remove from oven, cover with miniature marshmallows and return to oven for 2 additional minutes. Remove and cool. Melt syrup and peanut butter chips on low heat, stirring constantly as it scorches easily. Stir in cereal and peanuts. Spread over marshmallows. Cool. Cut into squares. Serve in paper muffin cups.

Mary G. Taylor
TSU

Peanut Butter Cookies

I like to prepare this recipe in my Bennington bowls, which I got from my mother. She liked to keep milk in them and wait for the cream to rise.

3 cups all-purpose flour
1/2 teaspoon salt
1 teaspoon baking soda
1 cup brown sugar
1 cup sugar
1 cup shortening
2 eggs
1 cup peanut butter
1 teaspoon vanilla

Sift flour, salt, and soda together. Cream sugars and shortening. Add eggs, peanut butter and vanilla. Add flour mixture and mix until well blended. Form into small balls and arrange on baking sheet. Flatten with fork tines. Cook at 350 degrees.

Margaret Pace Farmer
TSU '32

Tastes and Traditions

Neiman Marcus Bars

While this recipe won't win any beauty contest, as the name suggests it is rich enough to be sinful.

2 sticks butter or margarine, divided
2 eggs
1 box German chocolate cake mix
1 cup pecans
1 cup coconut
8 ounces cream cheese, softened
1 box powdered sugar

Cream 1 stick butter and 2 eggs. Add cake mix, pecans and coconut. Mix and pour in 9 x 12-inch pan. Bake in a 300 degree oven just until firm. Do not overcook. Mix cream cheese, remaining butter and powdered sugar. Spread over cake and cook just until top is golden brown. Let cool completely before cutting.

Helen Ricks
TSU

Lemon Squares

Crust:
1 cup flour
1/4 cup powdered sugar
1/2 cup butter, softened

Topping:
2 eggs
1 cup sugar
Dash of salt
1/2 teaspoon baking powder
2 1/2 tablespoons lemon juice

For Crust: Sift flour and sugar into mixing bowl. Blend in butter until well mixed. Pat evenly into bottom of an 8-inch square pan. Bake at 350 degrees for 20 minutes.
While crust is baking blend together all topping ingredients. Pour over baked crust and return to oven for 20 to 25 minutes. You can sprinkle with powdered sugar if you prefer.

Mary Mitchell
TSU Friend

Desserts

Chess Cake Squares

1 box yellow cake mix
1 stick butter or margarine, divided
4 eggs, divided
1 cup chopped pecans
8 ounces cream cheese, softened
16 ounces powdered sugar

Preheat oven to 350 degrees. Melt half of margarine and stir into cake mix. Add one egg. Mix and press evenly into a lightly greased 9 x 13 x 2-inch pan. Sprinkle with pecans. Melt remaining margarine and add to cream cheese and powdered sugar. Beat in 3 eggs. Pour over cake mixture. Bake 40 minutes or until golden brown. Cool and cut into squares to serve.

Faith West Ward
TSU

Kacie Wells
TSU Student
Alpha Gamma Delta Sorority

Jane Segar's Coconut Pound Cake

The TSU football coaches enjoy eating this on Sundays after game day. This is also a favorite at the Blakeney's annual fish fry before the season opener.

3 cups sugar
3/4 cup shortening
2 sticks butter, softened (do not substitute)
3 cups sifted cake flour
1 teaspoon baking powder
5 eggs
1 cup milk
1 1/2 teaspoons coconut flavoring
1 large can flaked coconut

Cream sugar, shortening and butter. Combine flour and baking powder. Add flour, eggs and milk alternately to creamed mixture. Beat well. Add coconut flavoring and mix well. Stir in flaked coconut. Pour in greased and floured pan. Bake at 325 degrees for 1 1/2 hours.

Sherry J. Dye
TSU Spouse

Tastes and Traditions

Five-Flavor Pound Cake

1/2 pound butter, softened
1/2 cup lard
3 cups sugar
5 eggs
3 cups cake flour
1 cup milk
1/2 teaspoon salt
1/2 teaspoon baking powder
1 teaspoon each vanilla, coconut, rum, and lemon flavoring

Glaze:
1 cup sugar
2/3 cup water
1 teaspoon almond flavoring

For Cake: Cream butter, lard and sugar together. Add eggs one at a time. Sift flour, salt and baking powder together. Add flour and milk. Mix flavorings. Add to cake mixture. Bake in greased tube pan at 325 degrees for 1 hour and 20 minutes.
For Glaze: Bring water and sugar to a rolling boil. Add almond flavoring. Spoon hot glaze over cake.

Pat Hardin
TSU

No Trojan football game would be complete without a few key elements: Tailgating; the Sound of the South; and Ann Williams. A longtime supporter of the University and TSU athletics, Mrs. Williams can be found at the front of the crowd at each game, urging the Trojans to victory. Her late husband, Frank "Red" Williams, served on the TSU Alumni Association Board and as interim athletic director.

Desserts

Brown Sugar Pound Cake

This is a wonderful and different version of pound cake. The lemon glaze adds nicely to the brown sugar but you can use your favorite icing.

1 1/2 cups butter or margarine (preferably unsalted butter), softened
1 box dark brown sugar
1 cup sugar
5 large eggs
3 cups all-purpose flour
1/4 teaspoon baking soda
1/2 teaspoon salt
1 cup buttermilk
2 teaspoons vanilla

Lemon Glaze:
Lemon juice
2 cups powdered sugar

For Cake: Cream butter with sugars until light and fluffy, about 3 to 4 minutes. Add eggs, one at a time, beating well after each addition. Sift flour with baking soda and salt. Add dry ingredients alternately with buttermilk to the batter. Stir in vanilla. Spoon batter into a greased and floured 10-inch tube pan and bake at 325 degrees for 1 hour 15 to 20 minutes or until a wooden pick inserted in center comes out clean. Cool cake in pan 10 to 15 minutes; then remove from pan. Glaze while warm. For Glaze: Add lemon juice to sugar a little at a time until you have a smooth, runny glaze. Drizzle over cake a little at a time, going back several time to ensure glaze adheres to top of cake.

Marsha Johnson
TSU Friend

Twelve-Minute Pound Cake

2 cups all-purpose flour
1 3/4 cups sugar
5 eggs
2 sticks butter
1 teaspoon vanilla flavoring
Juice of 1 lemon

Mix all ingredients in large bowl and beat 12 minutes. Put into greased tube pan. Bake at 350 degrees for 1 hour.

Ginny Taylor
TSU Student
Phi Mu Sorority

Tastes and Traditions

Lemon-Orange Pound Cake

I got this recipe from my mother-in-law. This cake is very light and delicious – you can't imagine how good it is until you try it.

2 sticks margarine, softened
1/2 cup shortening
3 cups sugar
5 eggs
1 teaspoon orange flavor
2 teaspoons lemon flavor
1 cup milk
3 cups all-purpose flour
1/4 teaspoon salt

Cream margarine, shortening and sugar. Add eggs one at a time. Add flavorings. Mix dry ingredients together and add to creamed mixture alternately with milk. Mix well. Pour batter into a greased and floured tube pan. PUT IN COLD OVEN. Turn oven on to 350 degrees and bake until a tester inserted in center comes out clean, about 1 hour and 15 minutes.

Mary G. Taylor
TSU

Pecan Pound Cake

My grandmother was a very good cook. She made everything from scratch and never wrote down her recipes. A couple of years ago my aunt and I were talking about the good things she could cook and we thought about her pecan pound cake. My aunt decided she could remember what she put in the cake, so she wrote down the recipe and tried it and it is almost as good as I remember as a little girl. Thanks, Aunt Edna.

2 sticks butter, softened
1 2/3 cups sugar
5 eggs
2 cups all-purpose flour
1 teaspoon vanilla
1 quart pecans, chopped

Beat butter and sugar. Add eggs and beat well. Add flour and vanilla. Fold in pecans. Bake at 275 degrees in a greased and floured tube cake pan for 1 1/2 hours.

Bonnie Money
TSU

Desserts

Cherry Pound Cake

This recipe was handed down from my maternal grandmother. She said "if you bake a pound cake in the morning, it will rise with the sun," which meant you get a taller cake.

3 cups sugar
1 1/2 cups shortening
6 eggs
3 3/4 cups all-purpose flour
3/4 cup milk
1/2 (10 ounce) jar maraschino cherries, with juice, chopped
1 teaspoon almond flavoring
1 teaspoon vanilla

Frosting:
3 cups powdered sugar, sifted
2 tablespoons butter
Remaining cherries
1/2 cup pecans, optional

For Cake: Cream sugar and shortening. Add eggs, one at a time. Alternately add flour and milk to mixture until well blended. Add chopped cherries with juice and flavorings. Pour into a greased and floured tube cake pan. Bake at 275 degrees for 2 hours. Cool, then frost.
For Frosting: Mix all ingredients together.

Mary Pinckard
TSU Friend

Chocolate Chip Pound Cake

1 box deluxe yellow cake mix
1 small box instant vanilla pudding
1/2 bar semisweet chocolate, grated
1 cup milk
4 eggs, beaten
2/3 cup vegetable oil
1 (6 ounce) package chocolate chips

Mix cake mix, pudding and grated chocolate. Add milk, eggs and oil and beat with mixer until blended. Stir in chocolate chips. Pour into a greased and floured tube or Bundt pan. Bake at 350 degrees until done, 50 minutes to 1 hour.

Jane Hughes
TSU '65, '89

Ann Parish
TSU '61

Tastes and Traditions

Pound Cake

1/2 pound butter or margarine, softened
1/2 cup shortening
3 cups sugar
5 eggs
3 cups self-rising flour
1 cup milk
1 tablespoon vanilla

Preheat oven to 325 degrees. Grease and flour large tube pan. Cream butter and shortening. Add eggs one at a time. Add sugar. Sift flour and add to mixture. Cream together. Add milk and vanilla. Pour into prepared pan. Bake at 325 degrees for 1 hour and 20 minutes.

Elfriede B. Marsh
TSUD '92

Chocolate Pound Cake

2 sticks margarine, softened
1/2 cup shortening
3 cups sugar
5 large eggs
4 tablespoons cocoa
3 cups all-purpose flour
1/2 teaspoon baking powder
1 cup milk

Chocolate Frosting:
4 tablespoons butter or margarine
4 ounces unsweetened baking chocolate
1/3 cup hot milk
3 cups sifted powdered sugar
1/8 teaspoon salt
1 teaspoon vanilla

For Cake: Preheat oven to 350 degrees. Grease and flour 10-inch tube pan. Cream margarine and shortening. Add sugar. Add eggs one at a time and beat well; add cocoa. Mix flour and baking powder. Add flour mixture to creamed mixture alternately with milk. Spoon batter into prepared pan and bake for 1 hour and 20 minutes.

For Icing: Melt butter and chocolate in top of double boiler, stirring until blended. Stir hot milk into sugar and beat until smooth. Stir in vanilla, salt and chocolate mixture. Beat until smooth and thickened, about 5 minutes. Enough frosting for filling and top of two 9-inch layers or one pound cake.

Edna S. Railey
TSU

Desserts

Chocolate Pound Cake

My daughter's co-workers are excited when she comes to my house for the weekend. They know they will be sharing this cake on Monday.

2 cups milk chocolate chips
1/2 cup butter or margarine, softened
2 cups sugar
4 eggs
2 teaspoons vanilla extract
1 cup buttermilk
2 tablespoons water
2 1/2 cups sifted cake flour
1/2 teaspoon salt
1/4 teaspoon baking soda
1/2 cup chopped pecans, optional
Powdered sugar, optional

In a saucepan over low heat, melt chocolate. Remove from the heat. In a mixing bowl, cream butter and sugar until light and fluffy. Add eggs one at a time, beating well after each addition. Blend in melted chocolate and vanilla. Combine buttermilk and water. Combine flour, salt and baking soda; add to batter alternately with the buttermilk mixture. Fold in nuts if desired. Pour into a greased and floured 10-inch tube or fluted tube pan. Bake at 325 degrees for 1 1/2 hours, until a toothpick inserted near the center comes out clean. Cool for 10 minutes; remove from pan to a wire rack. Dust with powdered sugar, if desired.

Mary Mitchell
TSU Friend

Cream Cheese Pound Cake

8 ounces cream cheese, softened
3 sticks margarine, softened
3 cups sugar
3 cups all-purpose flour, sifted
6 eggs
1 teaspoon vanilla

Cream together cream cheese, margarine and sugar. Add flour and eggs alternately to creamed mixture. Add vanilla. Pour mixture in a greased and floured tube pan. Bake 1 1/2 hours at 325 degrees. DO NOT preheat oven.

Linda Curington
TSU Parent

Tastes and Traditions

Three-Layer Banana Cake

This recipe was created by the late Rev. Robert Atkins, my father-in-law.

2 cups sugar
2 eggs
1 cup shortening or 2 sticks margarine
3/4 cup buttermilk
3 cups all-purpose flour
2 teaspoons baking soda
2 teaspoons vanilla extract
2 cups mashed ripe bananas

Frosting:
1 (8 ounce) package cream cheese, softened
1 box powdered sugar
1 cup chopped pecans

For Cake: Mix sugar, eggs, and shortening; add buttermilk, flour, soda, and vanilla. Add mashed bananas and mix well. Divide batter among three greased and floured 8-inch cake pans. Bake at 350 degrees for 30 to 35 minutes.
For Frosting: Beat cream cheese until smooth. Add powdered sugar and blend well. Stir in chopped nuts. Spread over cooled cake.

Kathy Atkins
TSUD

Miss Callie's Christmas Cake

As a child I remember my older siblings' friends coming to our home to eat some of "Miss Callie's" desserts. My mother, Callie Hudson Thomason of Birmingham, Alabama, was known affectionately as "Miss Callie." They especially liked these Christmas goodies.

Use your favorite devil's food cake recipe. Bake in 2 rectangular pans.

Icing:
1 tablespoon baking soda
1 cup buttermilk
2 cups sugar
1 box raisins
1 1/2 cups ground or chopped pecans
Pecan halves for garnish

Stir soda into buttermilk until it foams and streaks brown. Put sugar into a large saucepan. Stir buttermilk mixture into sugar and cook until thick. Stir in raisins and chopped pecans. Spread thin layer over 1 cake layer. Top with second layer and cover top and sides well. Place 4 rows of pecan halves on top of cake.

Eloise Thomas Kirk
TSU Friend

Desserts

Sour Cream Poppy Seed Cake

This recipe is a favorite of my sister, who lives in California. It's also a favorite dessert during holidays or social gatherings.

1 (2-layer size) package yellow cake mix, any variety
1 (4-serving size) package vanilla instant pudding and pie mix
4 eggs
1 cup sour cream
1/2 cup oil
1/2 cup orange juice
1/4 cup poppy seed
Powdered sugar, optional

Beat cake mix, pudding mix, eggs, sour cream, oil and juice in large bowl with electric mixer on low speed just to moisten, scraping sides of bowl often. Beat on medium speed 2 minutes. Stir in poppy seeds. Spoon into greased and floured 12-cup fluted tube pan or 10-inch tube pan. Bake at 350 degrees until toothpick inserted near center comes out clean, 50 to 55 minutes. Cool 15 minutes; remove from pan and cool completely on wire rack. Sprinkle with powder sugar, if desired.

Angie Westberg
TSU

Coconut Cake

This is one of my favorite recipes to prepare ahead of time. It tastes just as great when prepared one day and served the next. Keep refrigerated.

1 package yellow butter cake mix
1 can Eagle Brand sweetened, condensed milk
1 (8 ounce) container frozen whipped topping, thawed
1 can coconut

Prepare cake mix according to directions and bake in a rectangular baking pan. When done, remove from oven, leaving the cake in its pan. Punch holes in the cake with a fork. Pour condensed milk over it while cake is still hot. Let cake cool completely and spread with whipped topping. Sprinkle with the coconut.

Susan Holmes
TSU Friend

TSU changed from a two-year to a four-year school in 1934.

Tastes and Traditions

Mandarin Orange Cake

This cake is very light, so there is always room for this dessert. Keep cake in refrigerator.

1 package Duncan Hines butter cake mix
4 eggs
1/2 cup vegetable oil
1 can mandarin oranges with juice

Icing:
1 large instant vanilla pudding mix
1 large crushed pineapple, drained and juice reserved
1 (16 ounce) container frozen whipped topping, thawed

For Cake: Mix all ingredients well. Pour into three greased 9-inch cake pans. Bake at 350 degrees for 25 to 30 minutes. Remove from oven and cool completely.
For Icing: Sprinkle pudding mix over pineapple. Fold in whipped topping. Mix thoroughly, adding enough reserved juice to reach desired consistency. Ice cooled cake.

Mrs. Mickey (Susan) Holmes
TSUM

Strawberry Cake

1 box pudding in a mix, yellow cake mix
8 ounces sour cream
4 eggs
1/4 cup sugar
1 stick butter, softened

Icing:
1 large container frozen whipped topping, thawed
8 ounces cream cheese, softened
1 box powdered sugar
Fresh strawberries

For Cake: Mix all ingredients and divide between two greased 9-inch cake pans. Bake at 325 degrees until a tester inserted in center comes out clean, 25 to 30 minutes. Let layers cool.

For Icing: Mix whipped topping, cream cheese and powdered sugar until smooth. Spread icing between each layer and top with sliced strawberries. Cover top and sides of cake with icing. Top with whole strawberries.

Kacie Ross
TSU Student
Phi Mu Sorority

Desserts

Chocolate Sheath Cake

Cake:
2 cups all-purpose flour
2 cups sugar
1 teaspoon baking soda
1 cup water
1 cup margarine
1/2 cup buttermilk
1/4 cup cocoa
2 eggs
1 teaspoon vanilla

Icing:
1/2 cup margarine
1/4 cup plus 2 tablespoons evaporated milk
1/4 cup cocoa
1 box powdered sugar
1 teaspoon vanilla
1 cup chopped pecans

For Cake: Combine flour, sugar, and soda in a mixing bowl. In a saucepan, combine water, margarine, buttermilk, and cocoa. Heat until margarine melts. Do not boil. Pour melted margarine combination over flour mixture. Mix well. When cool, add eggs and vanilla. Mixture will be very thin. Pour in 2 greased and floured 9 x 13-inch baking pans. Bake at 350 degrees for 20 to 30 minutes. Do not overcook.

For Icing: Heat margarine, milk, and cocoa until margarine melts. Add powdered sugar, vanilla, and pecans. Stir well. Pour over cake while still warm.

Montgomery Chapter
TSU Alumni Association

TSU's longest-serving president is Dr. Edward M. Shackelford, who led the institution from 1899 to 1936. Under his leadership, the campus moved from downtown Troy to its current location; Kilby, Shackelford and Bibb Graves halls were constructed; and the institution changed from a two-year to a four-year school.

Tastes and Traditions

Heath Bar / Butterfinger Cake

Quick and easy for last-minute company.

1 box German chocolate cake mix
1 can sweetened condensed milk
1 large container whipped topping, thawed
2 Heath candy bars or 6 Butterfingers

Cook cake according to directions in a greased 9 x 13-inch pan. Punch holes in cake with knife and pour condensed milk over the top of cake. Refrigerate for 4 to 6 hours. Top with whipped topping; crush candy bars and sprinkle on top.

Paige Myers
TSU

Mary Mitchell
TSU Friend

Crystal Center
TSU Student
Chi Omega

Fresh Apple Cake

2 eggs
1 1/3 cups oil
2 teaspoons vanilla
2 cups sugar
1 teaspoon salt
1 1/2 teaspoons baking soda
1 teaspoon cinnamon
3 cups cubed fresh apples
1 cup chopped pecans
1 teaspoon allspice
3 cups flour

Mix eggs, oil, vanilla and sugar well. Add salt, baking soda, cinnamon, apples, pecans and allspice. Mix well. Add flour and mix well. Pour into a grease and sugared tube cake pan. Bake at 350 degrees about 1 hour and 10 minutes.

Heather Moran
TSU Student
Phi Mu Sorority

Desserts

Do-ee Goo-ee Cake

1 stick butter
1 box yellow cake mix
3 eggs
1 cup chopped pecans
8 ounces cream cheese, softened
1 box powdered sugar

Melt butter. Add to cake mix; then add one egg. Mix by hand until smooth. Add pecans. Press mixture in the bottom of a 9 x 13-inch baking dish. Combine remaining eggs, cream cheese and powdered sugar. Beat until smooth and pour over batter. Bake at 350 degrees for 45 minutes.

Jennifer Delaney
TSU Student
Alpha Gamma Delta Sorority

The record for stuffing the authentic English phone booth, located on the Bibb Graves Quad, is nine students. Chancellor Hawkins purchased the phone booth from the British Phone Company and donated it to the university.

Tastes and Traditions

Strawberry Banana Split Cake

This recipe is so easy to make, but so impressive to serve. You must use completely ripened strawberries that are naturally sweet.

Crust:
2 cups graham cracker crumbs (about 32 squares)
1/2 cup butter or margarine, melted
1/4 cup sugar

Filling:
1/2 cup butter or margarine, softened
2 cups powdered sugar
1 tablespoon milk
1 teaspoon vanilla extract
3 large firm bananas, cut into 1/4-inch slices
2 (8 ounce) cans crushed pineapple, drained
2 quarts fresh ripe strawberries, sliced

Topping:
2 cups whipping cream
1/4 cup powdered sugar
1 1/2 cups chopped walnuts or pecans

Combine the crumbs, butter and sugar; press into an ungreased 9 x 13 x 2-inch dish. Chill for 1 hour. In a mixing bowl, cream butter, powdered sugar, milk, and vanilla. Spread over crust; chill for 30 minutes. Layer with bananas, pineapple, and strawberries. In a small mixing bowl, beat cream until soft peaks form. Add powdered sugar; beat until stiff peaks form. Spread over fruit. Sprinkle with nuts. Chill until you are ready to serve.

Nelda Chesser Lewis
TSU Parent

Marsha Folsom, a District Four Congressional candidate in 2000 and a former first lady of Alabama, was the keynote speaker for the first Women in Leadership lecture in June 2000.

Desserts

Red Velvet Cake

Cake:
1/2 cup shortening
1 1/2 cups sugar
2 eggs
2 tablespoons cocoa
2 ounces red food coloring
1 teaspoon salt
2 1/4 cups all-purpose flour
1 cup buttermilk
1 teaspoon butter flavoring
1 teaspoon vanilla
1 tablespoon vinegar
1 teaspoon baking soda

Frosting:
1 stick margarine, softened
8 ounces cream cheese, softened
1 box powdered sugar
1 teaspoon vanilla
1 cup chopped nuts, optional

For Cake: Cream shortening, sugar, and eggs. Make a paste with cocoa and food coloring. Add to mixture. Add salt, flour, buttermilk, butter flavoring and vanilla to mixture. Alternately add soda and vinegar. Don't beat hard; just blend. Pour into two greased 9-inch cake pans. Bake 30 minutes at 350 degrees. Remove from oven and cool on wire racks.
For Frosting: Beat margarine, cream cheese and powdered sugar until smooth. Stir in vanilla and nuts, if desired. Spread on cooled cake.

Laura Totty
TSU Student
Chi Omega Sorority

Dump Cake

1 can crushed pineapple
1 cup chopped pecans
1 box yellow cake mix
1 can coconut
1 can cherry pie filling
2 sticks margarine, melted

Dump each item, one on top of the other in order given, into a 9 x 13-inch pan. Do not stir. Bake in preheated 350 degree oven for 35 to 45 minutes.

Hope Hobdy
TSU Student
Kappa Delta Sorority

Tastes and Traditions

Hoosier Cake

2 cups all-purpose flour
2 cups sugar
1 teaspoon baking soda
1/2 teaspoon salt
2 sticks butter
4 tablespoons cocoa
1 cup water
1/2 cup buttermilk
2 eggs
1 teaspoon vanilla
Can of chocolate frosting

In large bowl combine flour, sugar, soda and salt. Stir. In a medium saucepan combine butter, cocoa and water. Heat, stirring, until butter melts. Add to dry ingredients. Beat well to blend. Stir in buttermilk, eggs and vanilla. Beat well. Divide batter between two 9-inch round greased and floured layer cake pans. Bake at 350 degrees for 40 to 45 minutes, until cake tests done. Cool in pan for 10 minutes, then invert onto rack to cool completely. Frost with can of chocolate frosting.

Mary Mitchell
TSU Friend

Crunch Cake

1 box butter recipe yellow cake mix
2 eggs
1 stick butter, softened (do not substitute)
8 ounces cream cheese, softened
1 box powdered sugar

Mix cake mix, 1 egg and butter together, using your hands. Press into 9 x 11-inch pan with your hands. (Tip: Use a little powdered sugar on your hands to keep crust from sticking to them.) Mix cream cheese, 1 egg, and all but 1/4 cup of powdered sugar together. Beat on high until blended. Pour on top of crust. Sprinkle remaining sugar on top. Bake at 350 degrees for 35 to 45 minutes. Cool and cut into squares.

Mandy Dawkins
TSU Student
Phi Mu Sorority

Desserts

Cola Cake

2 cups sugar
2 cups all-purpose flour
1 1/2 cups small marshmallows
1/2 cup butter or margarine
1/2 cup vegetable oil
3 tablespoons cocoa
1 cup Coca-Cola
1/2 cup buttermilk
1 teaspoon baking soda
2 eggs
1 teaspoon vanilla extract

Frosting:
1/2 cup butter
3 tablespoons cocoa
6 tablespoons Coca-Cola
1 (16 ounce) box powdered sugar
1 teaspoon vanilla
1 cup chopped pecans

For Cake: Preheat oven to 350 degrees. In a bowl, sift together sugar and flour. Add marshmallows. In saucepan, mix butter, oil, cocoa, and Coca-Cola. Bring to a boil and pour over dry ingredients; blend well. Add buttermilk, baking soda, eggs and vanilla extract, mixing well. Pour into a well-greased 9 x 13-inch pan, and bake 45 minutes. Remove from oven and frost immediately.
For Frosting: Combine butter, cocoa, and Coca-Cola in a saucepan. Bring to a boil and pour over powdered sugar, blending well. Add vanilla extract and pecans. Spread over hot cake. When cool, cut into squares and serve.

Gloria Edwards
TSU '91

The university's first "extension center" was established in 1951 at Fort Rucker. That program was the genesis of University College, which has grown to serve thousands of students in military and metropolitan locations spread across the globe.

Tastes and Traditions

No-Bake Fruit Cake

This recipe takes the easy way out with no cooking. You can use any size loaf pan, even the very small ones that make gift-size cakes.

2 cups raisins
1 cup candied lemon peel
1 cup candied orange peel
1 cup citron
1 cup candied cherries
1 cup candied pineapple
1 cup dried figs
1 cup dates
1 - 2 cups walnuts
1 - 2 cups pecans
1 pound graham crackers
1 cup butter, softened
2 teaspoons vanilla
1 cup honey
2 teaspoons cinnamon
1 teaspoon mace
1/2 teaspoon nutmeg
1/2 teaspoon allspice

Cut up fruits, chop nuts and mix together. Roll crackers into very fine crumbs. Cream butter and honey, add vanilla and let stand 2 hours. Add spices to cracker crumbs. Combine all ingredients. Pack into loaf pans that have been lined with wax paper. Store in very cool place. (This makes a very large amount, about 5 pounds. You can halve the recipe if you like.)

Deloria Musgrove
TSU Parent

Before Greek-letter sororities appeared on campus in the mid-1920s, the coeds at Troy Normal School enjoyed the social opportunities offered by clubs like the Sleepy Club and the Eat 'Em Up Club, pictured here in 1912.

Desserts

Rum Cake

This cake is extremely easy to fix and looks beautiful when prepared. It is wonderful to serve at holiday meals.

Cake:
1 cup chopped pecans
1 box moist golden cake Mix
1 package vanilla pudding mix
1/2 cup light rum
1/2 cup water
1/2 cup vegetable oil
4 eggs

Glaze:
1 stick margarine
1 cup sugar
1/4 cup rum

For Cake: Grease and flour Bundt pan. Sprinkle nuts over bottom of pan. In a large bowl mix cake and pudding mixes together. Add all other ingredients together and mix for 2 minutes. Pour into prepared pan. Bake at 325 degrees for 50 to 60 minutes. As soon as you take cake out of oven take a dull knife and loosen around edges carefully. Leave in pan and pour hot glaze over cake. Let set in pan for 30 minutes and turn onto a plate. For Glaze: Boil all ingredients for 3 minutes. Pour over hot cake.

Barbara Patterson
TSU

Members of Alpha Delta Pi sorority, which formed at TSU in 1966, can be found offering their Trojan spirit at a number of athletic events.

Tastes and Traditions

Hedgehog Cake

This wonderful cake is often served at receptions for visiting dignitaries and other special events.

Chocolate Sponge:
1/2 pound (2 sticks) unsalted butter, cut into tablespoons
9 ounces bittersweet chocolate, finely chopped
5 large eggs, separated
1/2 cup sugar, divided
1 tablespoon all-purpose flour
Pinch of salt

Chestnut Ganache:
13 ounces extra-bittersweet chocolate, finely chopped
2 cups heavy cream
1 1/2 cups sweetened chestnut puree

Whipped Cream Filling:
1/3 cup heavy cream

Garnish:
Cocoa powder for dusting

Make the chocolate sponge: Preheat oven to 350 degrees. Coat bottom and sides of a 17 1/2 x 12 1/2-inch baking sheet with nonstick spray. Line bottom with parchment paper. Fill a medium saucepan one-third full of water and bring to a simmer. Put butter and chocolate in a medium bowl, place bowl over the simmering water and heat, stirring occasionally, until butter and chocolate are completely melted and mixture is smooth. Remove bowl and allow mixture to cool. Whisk together egg yolks, 1/4 cup sugar, and flour in a medium bowl until pale. Set aside. In bowl of an electric mixer, using whisk attachment, beat egg whites and salt at medium speed until frothy. Gradually add the remaining sugar and beat at high speed until soft peaks form. Whisk the chocolate mixture into the yolk mixture. Using a large rubber spatula, gently fold in beaten whites. Scrape batter into prepared pan and smooth top with spatula. Bake for 25 to 30 minutes, until cake pulls away from sides of pan and a toothpick inserted in center comes out clean. Cool completely in pan. Using a paring knife and plates or lids as guides, cut 3 discs, one measuring 5 inches in diameter, one 6 inches, and one 7 inches, from the cake; leave the discs on the baking sheet.

For Ganache: Put chocolate in a medium bowl. Bring heavy cream to a boil in a medium saucepan. Immediately pour over chocolate. Whisk until chocolate is completely melted and mixture is smooth. Place chestnut puree in a large bowl. Gradually whisk in chocolate mixture, whisking until smooth. Transfer 1 1/4 cups of ganache to a small bowl and reserve. Cover both bowls with plastic wrap and refrigerate, stirring occasionally, until the ganache is firm enough to pipe, about 45 minutes.

Desserts

For Filling: In the bowl of an electric mixer, using whisk attachment, beat cream to stiff peaks.

Assemble the cake: Line an 8-inch-wide bowl with plastic wrap. Scrape 1 cup chestnut ganache into bowl. Using a small offset metal spatula, spread ganache evenly over interior of the bowl. Using a metal spatula, carefully transfer the 5-inch cake disc to bottom of bowl, pressing it lightly into the ganache. Spread 1/3 cup ganache over cake disc. Carefully place 6-inch disc over the ganache-covered disc. Spread another 1/3 cup ganache over cake. Scrape whipped cream filling over ganache and spread it into an even layer. Carefully place 7-inch disc over cream layer and spread with remaining ganache. Cover bowl with plastic wrap and freeze for at least 2 hours and up to 3 days. To unmold cake, carefully immerse bowl in hot water for several seconds, then invert cake onto a serving plate. Frost cake with reserved ganache. Using the back of a spoon or a small spatula, pull out spikes of ganache from cake. Sprinkle cake with sifted cocoa powder.

Sodexho-Marriott
TSU

Honeybun Cake

1 box butter cake mix
8 ounces sour cream
2/3 cup vegetable oil
1/3 cup water
4 eggs
1/2 cup brown sugar
1 teaspoon cinnamon
3/4 cup chopped pecans

Glaze:
1 cup powdered sugar
1/2 teaspoon vanilla
2 tablespoons milk

Mix cake mix, sour cream, oil, water and eggs together. Pour half into an ungreased 9 x 13-inch pan. Mix brown sugar, pecans and cinnamon together. Pour half over mixture in pan. Repeat with remaining batter and pecan mixture. Bake at 350 degrees for 35 to 40 minutes. While still warm drizzle glaze over top.

For Glaze: Combine all ingredients and beat until smooth. Pour into a zip-lock bag and snip one end for an easy drizzle.

Allison Houston
TSU '94

Tastes and Traditions

Thirteen Layer Chocolate Cake

This is a recipe that was given to me by my brother, Ray Jackson, who has cooked this cake many times. A favorite dessert whenever it is served.

1 1/2 cups sugar
1 cup shortening (I prefer butter-flavored shortening)
4 eggs
3 cups self-rising flour
2 1/4 cups milk
1 tablespoon vanilla

Icing:
4 cups sugar
6 tablespoons cocoa
1 cup butter
1 large can evaporated milk
1 tablespoon vanilla

For Cake: Cream sugar and shortening until fluffy. Add eggs one at a time. Sift flour and add alternately with milk to batter. Stir in vanilla. Divide batter between greased 9-inch cake pans (should be enough for thirteen layers). Bake at 375 degrees until lightly brown.
For Icing: In a 4-quart saucepan, mix sugar and cocoa. Add butter and milk. Bring to a rolling boil and cook about 2 minutes, stirring constantly. Remove from heat and add vanilla. The icing is not thick so therefore it runs off the layers onto a larger platter. I also stick holes in my layers so that the icing will drizzle down into the cake layers.

Judy Morgan
TSU

Judy Morgan, a longtime staff member of the TSU Athletic Department, is flanked by two leaders of the 1999 football team: Eric Sloan, left, and Al Lucas.

Desserts

Banana Cake with Peanut Butter Frosting

2 cups sifted all-purpose flour
1 teaspoon baking soda
1 teaspoon baking powder
1/2 teaspoon salt
3/4 cup (1 1/2 sticks) butter or margarine, room temperature
1 1/2 cups sugar
2 eggs
1 cup mashed banana (2 - 3 medium)
1 tablespoon vanilla
1/2 cup buttermilk
1/2 cup finely chopped pecans

Frosting:
4 ounces cream cheese, room temperature
1/4 cup butter or margarine, room temperature
2 - 3 tablespoons milk
1 box powdered sugar
1/2 cup creamy peanut butter
1 tablespoon vanilla

For Cake: Preheat oven to 375 degrees. Coat two 9-inch round cake pans with nonstick spray. Line bottoms with wax paper. Coat paper. Sift together flour, baking powder, soda and salt onto a sheet of wax paper. Beat butter and sugar in bowl at medium speed until light and fluffy. Beat in eggs, banana and vanilla; beat 2 minutes. At low speed, alternately beat in flour mixture with buttermilk, beating after each addition. Fold in pecans. Spread batter in prepared pans. Bake for 25 minutes. Cool cakes in pans on wire racks for 10 minutes. Invert cakes onto racks and cool completely.
For Frosting: Beat cream cheese, butter and 2 tablespoons milk in large bowl until smooth. Gradually beat in powdered sugar until creamy and smooth. Fold in peanut butter. Stir in vanilla and more milk, if needed for smooth texture. Remove wax paper from cake. Stack layers, spreading frosting between layers and over top and sides of cake.

Larita Mitchell
TSU Friend

TSU students voted to change the university's nickname from "Red Wave" to "Trojans" in 1973.

Tastes and Traditions

Christmas Lane Cake

A Southern tradition that's well worth the effort.

Cake:
3 1/4 cups sifted all-purpose flour
3 1/2 teaspoons baking powder
1/2 teaspoon salt
1/4 teaspoon nutmeg
1 cup (2 sticks) unsalted butter, room temperature
2 cups sugar, divided
1 teaspoon vanilla
1 cup milk
8 large egg whites

Filling:
3/4 cup bourbon
3/4 cup dried cherries
3/4 cup finely chopped dried apricots
8 large egg yolks
1 1/3 cups sugar
1/2 cup (1 stick) unsalted butter, room temperature
1 cup chopped toasted pecans
1 cup sweetened flaked coconut
4 ounces semisweet chocolate, chopped, or mini chocolate chips

Frosting:
1 1/2 (3 ounce) packages cream cheese, room temperature
3/4 cup powdered sugar, divided
3 tablespoons bourbon
1 1/2 teaspoons vanilla
1 1/2 cups chilled whipping cream
Pecan halves, optional
Dried apricot halves, optional

For Cake: Preheat oven to 375 degrees. Butter and flour four 9-inch cake pans. Line pans with wax paper. Sift flour, baking powder, salt and nutmeg into medium bowl. Beat butter and 1 1/2 cups sugar in large bowl until smooth. Beat in vanilla. Beat in flour mixture alternately with milk. Beat whites in another large bowl with clean beaters until soft peaks form. Gradually add remaining 1/2 cup sugar, beating until whites are stiff but not dry. Fold whites into batter gradually. Divide batter among pans (batter will be about 1/2 inch deep). Bake cakes until tester inserted into center comes out clean, about 20 minutes. Turn cakes out onto racks; peel off paper. Cool completely.
For Filling: Mix bourbon, cherries and apricots in small bowl. Cover; let stand at room temperature until most of bourbon is absorbed and fruit softens, at least 3 hours and up to 1 day. Using electric mixer, beat yolks and sugar in medium bowl until mixture falls in heavy ribbon when beaters are lifted, about 5 minutes. Beat in butter. Transfer yolk mixture to heavy medium saucepan. Stir over medium-low heat until thermometer

Desserts

registers 160 degrees and mixture is thick, about 15 minutes. Remove from heat; mix in nuts, coconut and fruit mixture. Chill until cold, about 4 hours. Mix in chocolate. (Cake layers and filling can be made 1 day ahead. Wrap cakes; store at room temperature. Cover filling; chill.) Place 1 cake layer on platter. Spread with a third of filling. Repeat layering of cake and filling 2 more times. Top with final cake layer, pressing slightly. Chill cake. For Frosting: Beat cream cheese and 1/4 cup powdered sugar in medium bowl until smooth. Beat in bourbon and vanilla. Beat cream and 1/2 cup powdered sugar in large bowl until soft peaks form. Add cream cheese mixture to whipped cream; beat until stiff enough to spread. Spread frosting over top and sides of cake. Garnish with pecan and apricots, if desired. Store in refrigerator.

Janice Hawkins
TSU First Lady

Lane Cake

My family still prepares this recipe during the Thanksgiving and Christmas holidays. My sister Pearlie Mae Thomas is the only family member who can make this cake the way momma used to. This cake is so good, it makes your mouth water thinking about it.

3 cups flour
2 teaspoons baking powder
1 cup butter, softened
2 cups sugar
1 teaspoon vanilla
8 egg whites
1 cup sweet milk

Filling:
1/2 cup butter, softened
3/4 cup sugar
1 teaspoon cornstarch
8 egg yolks
1 cup raisins
1 cup English walnuts
1 wineglass brandy or sherry
1 teaspoon vanilla

For Cake: Preheat oven to 375 degrees. Butter and flour three 9-inch cake pans. Sift flour and baking powder together. Beat butter and sugar together until smooth. Beat in vanilla. Add flour mixture alternately with milk. Beat egg whites in another bowl with clean beaters until soft peaks form. Gradually fold egg whites into the batter. Divide batter among prepared pans and bake until toothpick comes out clean, about 30 minutes.
For Filling: Cream butter, sugar, and cornstarch; add yolks, raisins, and nuts and cook until very thick. Remove from stove, add brandy and vanilla and spread on cooled cake.

Dejerilyn King-Henderson
TSU '93

Tastes and Traditions

Strawberry Swirl Cheesecake

Crust:
6 chocolate wafers or graham crackers
4 tablespoons butter, melted

Filling:
1 (8 ounce) package cream cheese, softened
1 cup sugar
3 eggs plus 1 egg yolk
3 tablespoons all-purpose flour
1 teaspoon vanilla
3 tablespoons heavy cream

Topping:
8 strawberries

For Crust: Preheat oven to 400 degrees. Crush cookies in a blender or food processor; add melted butter. Press mixture firmly and evenly into bottom of an 8-inch springform pan. Tightly line the outside of the bottom of the pan with aluminum foil.

For Filling: Whip the cream cheese until it is smooth and fluffy. Add the sugar and blend well. Add the eggs and the yolk, one at a time, mixing well with each addition. Blend in the flour, vanilla and cream; mix until smooth. Pour evenly over crust.

For Topping: Puree strawberries and dot the mixture over cream cheese mixture. Using small rubber spatula, gently swirl the puree into the batter. Place the pan in a large baking dish. Fill baking dish with warm water halfway to the top of the cheesecake pan and place in the oven. Bake for 10 minutes, then reduce the heat to 250 degrees. Bake for an additional hour and 30 minutes, until a knife inserted into the middle comes out clean. Once the cheesecake is cooled, cover and refrigerate overnight.

Sodexho-Marriott
TSU

TSU won the prestigious Management Achievement Award from the National Association of College and University Business Officers in August 1996. The award honored the University for its strategic-planning and institutional-effectiveness processes.

Desserts

Peanut Butter Pie

1/3 cup peanut butter
3/4 cup powdered sugar, sifted
1 (9 inch) pie crust, baked
1/3 cup all-purpose flour
1/2 cup sugar
1/8 teaspoon salt
2 cups milk, scalded
3 egg yolks, lightly beaten
2 tablespoons butter or margarine
1 teaspoon vanilla

Meringue:
3 egg whites
1/4 teaspoon cream of tartar
1/2 cup sugar
1 teaspoon cornstarch

For Pie: Blend peanut butter with powdered sugar until mealy. Sprinkle mixture over baked pie shell. Set aside. Combine flour, sugar and salt in top of a double boiler. Stir in scalded milk. Cook over boiling water, stirring constantly, until thickened. Stir a small amount of cooked filling into the egg yolks. Combine with remaining hot mixture and cook several minutes longer. Add butter and vanilla. Pour into pie shell. Top with meringue.
For Meringue: Beat egg whites until stiff. Add cream of tartar. Mix sugar and cornstarch and gradually add to egg whites. Beat until stiff and shiny. Pile on pie and bake in a 325 degree oven until golden brown. Cool pie before serving.

Doug and Rachel Hawkins
TSU Board of Trustees

These members of Chi Omega sorority put on their "game faces" for a pep rally in fall 1999.

Tastes and Traditions

Prize-Winning Cherry Pie

When I was in college I needed a cherry pie to enter in a contest so my sorority chapter could win a trophy for best participation. My mother and I created this one. Neither of us had ever made a cherry pie before, and were very surprised when our pie won first prize!

Pastry for 2-crust pie
1 can dark, sweet cherries, undrained
3/4 cup sugar
4 tablespoons flour
1/2 teaspoon cinnamon
Pinch of salt
1 tablespoon lemon juice
1 1/2 tablespoons margarine
Cinnamon-sugar mixture
1/4 cup blanched, slivered almonds

Pour cherries and juice into saucepan. Mix together sugar, flour, cinnamon and salt. Add to cherries. Add lemon juice. Cook over medium heat, stirring constantly with fork, until thickened. Cool. Pour into pastry-lined pie pan. Dot with margarine. Cut remaining pastry into strips to form lattice crust, place over filling, and seal edges. Sprinkle with cinnamon-sugar and top with almonds. Bake in preheated 400 degree oven until brown, about 30 minutes.

Deb Davis
TSU Spouse

The graduating class of 1908 left Troy Normal School with a quality pedagogical education and a diploma on a rather large scroll of sheepskin. For the sake of comparison: The institution received $15,000 in state funding in 1908; in 1998, TSU was allotted $28 million from state coffers.

Desserts

Key Lime Pie

This key lime pie is served in a restaurant in the Ft. Walton Beach, Florida area. It makes three pies and is super easy to make.

1 can sweetened condensed milk
1 (6 ounce) can frozen limeade
1 1/2 ounces Nellie & Joe's Key West lime juice
2 (16 ounce) containers frozen whipped topping, thawed
3 graham cracker crust pie shells

Combine milk, limeade and lime juice. Fold in whipped topping and mix together well. Divide mixture equally among the crusts. Refrigerate until chilled.

Sara Jones
TSU Spouse

Lemon Meringue Pie

A no-cook, creamy, full-flavored lemon filling that's as easy and quick to fix as a mix. This pie is good for any occasion.

1 (15 ounce) can sweetened condensed milk
1/2 cup lemon juice (fresh, reconstituted or frozen)
2 egg yolks, beaten
1 graham cracker pie crust

Meringue:
2 egg whites, room temperature
1/4 cup sugar
1/2 teaspoon vanilla flavoring

For Pie: In medium-sized mixing bowl, blend together sweetened condensed milk, lemon juice and yolks until thickened. Pour into pie shell. For Meringue: In small-sized mixing bowl whip whites until they hold a soft peak. Gradually add sugar; continue to whip just until whites hold firm peaks. Add vanilla flavoring and pile on to pie filling. Bake in 325 degrees oven until top is golden brown. Refrigerate

Nell Watkins
TSU

Brandi Baker
TSU Student
Phi Mu Sorority

Tastes and Traditions

Chocolate Chip Chess Pie

1 stick margarine, softened
1 1/2 cups sugar
3 eggs
1 1/2 tablespoons corn meal
1 tablespoon vinegar
1 teaspoon vanilla
1/4 teaspoon salt
1/2 cup chocolate chips
1 unbaked pastry shell

Cream margarine and sugar. Add eggs one at a time, beating well after each is added. Add all other ingredients except pastry shell and mix well. Pour into pastry shell. Place in preheated 425 degree oven. Lower temperature to 325 degrees. Bake 45 minutes, until firm.

Anita Jones Davis
TSU '72

Chocolate Chip Pecan Pie

This is a wonderful pie, served hot or cold!

1 cup sugar
1/2 cup self-rising flour
2 eggs, beaten
1/2 cup melted butter
1 cup chocolate chips
1 cup chopped pecans
1 teaspoon vanilla
1 unbaked 9-inch pie shell
Whipped topping, optional

Mix sugar and flour. Beat in eggs. Add butter, chocolate chips, pecans, and vanilla. Mix well. Spoon into pie shell. Bake at 350 degrees for 30 to 40 minutes or until set. Top with whipping topping, if desired.

Jennifer Woodham
TSUD '98

TSU was originally located on a four-acre campus in downtown Troy. It moved to its current location after the 1919 purchase of 275 acres in a pecan grove owned by Troy mayor W. B. Folmar. The purchase was financed by a $35,000 bond issue by the City of Troy.

Desserts

Quick and Easy Chocolate Pie

2 small packages instant chocolate pudding
1 3/4 cups milk
1 (8 ounce) container frozen whipped topping, thawed
1 (6 ounce) graham cracker deep dish crust
1/4 cup toasted sliced almonds

Combine pudding and milk. Beat for one minute on low speed. Fold in whipped topping. Spoon into crust. Chill for at least 4 hours. Garnish with almonds.

April Majors
TSU Student
Alpha Gamma Delta Sorority

Layered Chocolate Pie

1 3/4 teaspoons sugar
1 1/2 cups all-purpose flour
1 1/4 sticks margarine, melted
1 cup chopped pecans
1 large carton Cool Whip, thawed and divided
8 ounces cream cheese, softened
3 cups cold milk
1 cup powdered sugar
2 small packages instant chocolate pudding

Mix sugar, flour, margarine and pecans. Press into bottom of oblong Pyrex dish. Bake at 350 degrees for 25 minutes. Combine a third of Cool Whip, cream cheese, cold milk, powdered sugar and chocolate pudding in a bowl. Whip and pour over crust. Spread remaining Cool Whip over top.

Allison Bassett
TSU Student
Phi Mu Sorority

TSU degree programs can be found in such diverse locations as Guantanamo Bay, Cuba; White Sands Missile Range, New Mexico; Okinawa, Japan; and Hong Kong.

Tastes and Traditions

Chocolate Pie

3 eggs, separated
1 cup sugar
3 tablespoons all-purpose flour
3 tablespoons cocoa
1 1/2 cups milk
1/2 teaspoon vanilla
1 tablespoon butter
1 baked pie crust

Beat 3 egg yolks. Add sugar, flour, and cocoa. Bring milk to a boil in a saucepan. Whisk hot milk into egg mixture. Return to saucepan and cook over low heat until thick, stirring constantly. Add vanilla and butter. Spoon into crust. Beat egg whites until stiff peaks form. Spread over custard and bake at 325 degrees for 12 to 15 minutes.

Stefanie Greene
TSU Student
Phi Mu Sorority

Syrup Pie

1 tablespoon butter
1 cup sugar
3 eggs
1 cup syrup
1 tablespoon flour
1 unbaked pie shell

Cream butter and sugar together. Add eggs, syrup and flour. Beat until smooth and pour into pie shell. Bake slowly until a knife inserted in center comes out clean.

Lucy T. Nall
TSU '20

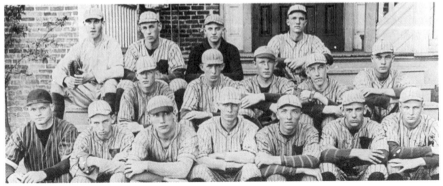

The Troy State Normal baseball team won the league title in 1923.

Desserts

Jim's Pecan Pie

I just started baking this past fall. At 78 years of age, I wanted to see if I could. After looking at several cookbooks, I decided to make my own pecan pie. It worked! Everyone wants the recipe now.

1 box light brown sugar
1 stick butter, softened
4 large eggs
2 tablespoons corn meal
2 tablespoons water
2 cups chopped pecans
Dash of salt
1 teaspoon vanilla
2 unbaked pie shells

Combine all ingredients except pie shells in order listed. Pour into unbaked pie shells. Bake for 1 hour at 325 degrees. Makes 2 pies.

James T. Seymour
TSU Friend

Miss Callie's Pecan Pie

1/2 cup butter, softened
1 cup sugar
3 eggs, lightly beaten
3/4 cup dark corn syrup
1/4 teaspoon salt
1 teaspoon vanilla
1 1/4 cups chopped pecans
1 (8 inch) unbaked pastry shall

Cream butter; add sugar gradually and beat until light and fluffy. Add remaining ingredients except pastry shell and blend well. Pour into pastry shell. Bake on lower shelf in a moderate oven (375 degrees) 40 to 45 minutes.

Eloise Thomas Kirk
TSU Friend

Tastes and Traditions

Honey Crunch Pecan Pie

4 eggs, lightly beaten
1/4 cup firmly packed brown sugar
1/4 cup granulated sugar
1/2 teaspoon salt
1 cup light corn syrup
2 tablespoons butter or margarine, melted
1 tablespoon bourbon, optional
1 teaspoon vanilla
1 cup chopped pecans
1 unbaked (9 inch) pie shell

Topping:
1/3 cup firmly packed brown sugar
3 tablespoons butter or margarine
3 tablespoons honey
1 1/2 cups pecan halves

Heat oven to 350 degrees. Combine eggs, sugars, salt, corn syrup, melted butter, bourbon, vanilla and nuts. Mix well. Spoon into unbaked pie shell. Bake at 350 degrees for 15 minutes. Cover edge of pastry with foil. Bake an additional 20 minutes. Remove from oven.
For Topping: Combine sugar, butter and honey in medium saucepan. Cook about 2 minutes, until sugar dissolves. Add nuts. Stir until nuts are coated. Spoon mixture over pie evenly. Cover edge of pastry with foil. Bake at 350 degrees for 10 to 20 minutes, until topping is bubbly and golden brown. Cool to room temperature before serving.

Lisa Frank
TSU-Fort Bragg

Chocolate Pecan Pie

3 eggs, lightly beaten
1 cup light or dark corn syrup
4 ounces chocolate chips, melted
1/3 cup sugar
2 tablespoon margarine, melted
1 teaspoon vanilla
1 1/2 cups chopped pecans
1 (9 inch) unbaked pie shell

Mix all ingredients except pie shell together. Pour into shell and bake in preheated 350 degree oven for 50 to 60 minutes.

Jean S. Helms
TSU Friend

Desserts

Trojan Best Pecan Pie

One of my favorite things about TSU is the quad with the old Southern pecan trees inviting you to sit under them for a spell between classes and enjoy the breeze. In the fall the ground is covered with large, beautiful pecans. During my second winter break from classes at TSU I took some pecans to my home in northwest Alabama and decided to try them in my own family recipe. Finding just the right recipe to try for Christmas dinner was a challenge so I decided to combine several recipes. In the process I found that my mother's pantry had two kinds of syrup but not enough of either kind for my use, so I combined the two. What resulted was, according to my father, "the best pecan pie ever!" Since I used pecans from my alma mater, I decided to record the recipe and call it "Trojan Best Pecan Pie." Here is the recipe that uses Troy State pecans and won "best pie" by the vote of my daddy.

1 cup sugar
4 teaspoons all-purpose flour
1/2 teaspoon salt
3 eggs, lightly beaten
3 tablespoons melted margarine
1 teaspoon vanilla
2/3 cup light Karo corn syrup
1/2 cup dark Karo corn syrup
1 cup chopped pecans
1 (9 inch) unbaked pie shell

In large bowl, mix together sugar, flour and salt. Add eggs, margarine and vanilla; stir well. Add corn syrup, then chopped pecans, stirring until well mixed. Pour into pie shell. Bake for 10 minutes at 400 degrees, then reduce heat to 350 degrees and bake for 50 minutes, until pie is set.

Rachelle Inman
TSU Student

Bibb Graves Hall is surrounded by dozens of pecan trees. Besides providing the key ingredient for many special recipes, the trees have offered shade and a reprieve for many TSU students.

Tastes and Traditions

The abundance of pecan pie recipes in this volume of "The Tastes and Traditions" can probably be attributed to the abundance of pecan trees on campus, as much of the university has been built amidst an old pecan grove. But the influence of the world-famous Whaley Pecan Company, which is based in Troy and has been harvesting pecans for decades, can't be overlooked.

Southern Pecan Pie

We have been in the pecan shelling business in Troy for more than 60 years and have tried many pecan pie recipes. This one is our favorite. It's easy to make and is a holiday tradition in our family.

1/4 cup melted butter or margarine
3 eggs, beaten
1/2 cup dark corn syrup
1 cup sugar
1 teaspoon vanilla
1 cup Whaley's pecans
1 unbaked pie shell

Mix butter, eggs, corn syrup, sugar and vanilla well. Add pecans. Pour in pie shell. Bake at 350 degrees until firm, about 45 minutes.

Robert and Mary Whaley (Whaley Pecan Co.)
TSU Friends

Jean S. Helms
TSU Friend

Bob and Mary Whaley display some of their tasty wares beneath a pecan tree on the Bibb Graves Quad.

Desserts

Crescent Fruit Pie

This pie is very easy to prepare. When I take it to any event, I always have requests for the recipe.

8 ounces cream cheese, softened
1 (8 count) can refrigerated crescent rolls
1/2 cup powdered sugar
1/2 to 1 can pie filling (blueberry, peach, cherry or apple)

Glaze:
Approximately 1 cup powdered sugar
1 1/2 tablespoons milk

In 9-inch glass pie plate, place the rolls evenly with the points hanging over the edge. Pinch together on bottom and up side. Mix cream cheese and powdered sugar together. Spread over rolls; top with pie filling. Stretch pointed ends to center and pinch together. Bake at 375 degrees for 20 minutes, until brown. Drizzle with glaze made from powdered sugar and milk.

Mary G. Taylor
TSU

Peanut Butter Chiffon Pie

1 cup dark corn syrup
1/2 cup super chunky peanut butter
1/2 cup water
1 envelope unflavored gelatin
3 eggs, separated
1 teaspoon vanilla
3 tablespoons sugar
1 chocolate cookie crust
Whipped cream
Chopped peanuts

In medium saucepan, stir together corn syrup, peanut butter, water, gelatin and egg yolks until well blended. Cook over medium heat, stirring constantly, until thickened. Stir in vanilla. Cool until mixture mounds slightly when dropped from a spoon. In a small bowl with mixer at high speed beat egg whites until soft peaks form. Gradually beat in sugar; continue beating until stiff peaks form. Carefully fold in peanut butter mixture. Chill until mixture mounds. Pile into crust; chill until firm. Garnish with whipped cream and chopped peanuts.

Sonya J. Hubbard
TSU Friend

Tastes and Traditions

Peanut Butter Pie

1 cup powdered sugar
1 (3 ounce) package cream cheese, softened
1/3 cup crunchy peanut butter
1 (16 ounce) container frozen whipped topping, thawed
Graham cracker crust

Cream together powdered sugar and cream cheese. Fold in the peanut butter and then mix in the whipped topping. Pour into crust and refrigerate for several hours or overnight before serving.

Betty Berk
TSU Parent

Hotel Hershey Derby Pie

Pie:
1 cup sugar
4 tablespoons cornstarch
2 eggs, lightly beaten
1/2 cup butter, melted and cooled
3 tablespoons bourbon or 1 teaspoon vanilla extract
1 (6 ounce) package semisweet chocolate chips
1 cup chopped pecans
1 unbaked (9 inch) pastry shell

Derby Whipped Cream:
1/2 cup heavy cream
2 tablespoons powdered sugar
1 teaspoon bourbon or 1/2 teaspoon vanilla extract

Preheat oven to 350 degrees. Combine sugar and cornstarch in a medium bowl. Add eggs, butter and bourbon or vanilla extract; mix well. Fold in chocolate chips and pecans. Pour into unbaked pastry shell. Bake 40 minutes. Cool completely before topping with whipped cream.
For Whipped Cream: Whip heavy cream with powdered sugar. Add bourbon or vanilla extract and beat until stiff peaks form. Spread over pie.

Gloria Edwards
TSU '91

Desserts

Dixie Pie

2 deep dish pie crusts
1 cup margarine, softened
1 cup sugar
5 eggs
1 cup brown sugar
2 teaspoons vanilla
1 can coconut flakes
1/2 package semisweet chips
1 cup chopped pecans

Bake unfilled crusts at 450 degrees for 10 minutes. Cream margarine, sugar, eggs, brown sugar and vanilla. Add coconut, chocolate chips and pecans and stir. Pour into crusts and bake at 350 degrees for 30 to 35 minutes.

Sue McCrimmon
TSU Friend

Coconut Pie

We have lots of TSU friends for lunch at our restaurant every day. This coconut pie is one of Dr. Jack Hawkins' favorites.

4 eggs
1/2 cup self rising flour
2 cups milk
1/4 cup melted butter or margarine
1 1/2 cups of coconut
1 teaspoon vanilla
3/4 cup sugar

Combine all ingredients and pour into greased glass pie plate. Bake 45 minutes to 1 hour at 300 degrees or until golden brown.

Sisters Restaurant
TSU Friend
Troy, Alabama

During the years that followed World War II, male enrollment boomed at Troy State Teachers College, as did the social life. Popular weekend activities included the Frosh Hop, pictured here.

Tastes and Traditions

Buttermilk Pie

1/2 cup butter, softened
1 cup buttermilk
3 tablespoons flour
5 eggs, lightly beaten
2 1/2 cups sugar
1/2 teaspoon lemon extract
1 unbaked pie shell

Combine butter, buttermilk, flour, eggs, sugar and lemon extract, mixing thoroughly. Pour into pie shell and bake at 300 degrees until a knife inserted in the middle comes out clean.

Mrs. Mickey (Susan) Holmes
TSUM

Heather Waters
TSU '93

Julia Wilson
TSUM

Mary Mitchell
TSU Friend

Chess Pie

Another old-time recipe from my mother.

2 cups sugar
1 tablespoon corn meal
1/8 teaspoon salt
5 eggs
5 tablespoons milk
1 tablespoon vinegar
1 teaspoon vanilla
1/2 stick butter, melted
Unbaked pie shell

Mix sugar, corn meal and salt. Beat eggs and add milk, vinegar, vanilla and butter. Add dry ingredients. Pour into unbaked pie shell. Bake at 350 degrees for 45 minutes to 1 hour.

Janice Hawkins
TSU First Lady

Desserts

Aunt Daisy's Egg Custard Pie

My Aunt Daisy was the best cook in Crenshaw County and this is one of her best recipes.

Pie:
2 cups milk, scalded
4 egg yolks
1/2 cup sugar
2 tablespoons margarine
1 unbaked pie shell

Meringue:
4 egg whites
Pinch of salt
1 cup sugar (or more to taste)

For Pie: Combine milk, egg yolks, sugar and margarine thoroughly. Turn into pie shell and bake at 300 degrees until a knife inserted in the middle comes out clean.
For Meringue: Beat egg whites on high until stiff. Add salt and sugar. Spread over partially cooled pie. Brown in oven.

Mrs. Mickey (Susan) Holmes
TSUM

Fudge Pie

This recipe came from my aunt, Mamie Mason. Next to my mom, she's the best cook I know.

1 stick butter
1 ounce unsweetened chocolate
2 eggs
1 cup sugar
1/4 cup sifted flour
1/4 cup cocoa
1 teaspoon vanilla
1 unbaked 9-inch pie shell

Preheat oven to 325 degrees. Melt butter and chocolate, stirring until smooth. Set aside. In bowl, lightly beat eggs. Add sugar and mix. Add flour, cocoa and vanilla. Stir in melted butter and chocolate. Mix well. Pour in pie shell and bake for 45 minutes, until center is firm.

Kelly Hawkins
TSU Student
Phi Mu Sorority

Tastes and Traditions

Lemony Ice Cream Pie

1 quart vanilla ice cream, softened
1 (6 ounce) can frozen lemonade concentrate, partially thawed
1 (9 inch) graham cracker pie crust
Lemon slices, optional

Stir together ice cream and lemonade until blended. Spoon into crust and freeze until firm, about 2 hours. Garnish with lemon slices if desired.

Helen Ricks
TSU

Pineapple Pie

This recipe has been a tradition in my husband's family for years.

Filling:
1 cup milk
3 egg yolks
5 tablespoons flour
3/4 cup sugar
1/2 stick butter (4 ounces)
1 tablespoon vanilla
1(15 ounce) can crushed pineapple

Meringue:
3 egg whites
1/4 teaspoon cream of tartar
6 tablespoons sugar
1/4 teaspoon vanilla

9 inch cooked pie crust

For Filling: Combine all ingredients in a heavy saucepan. Cook over medium heat, stirring frequently, until boiling and thickened. Do not let the filling burn!
For Meringue: Beat egg whites until frothy. Beat in cream of tartar. Add sugar 1 teaspoon at a time while beating. Beat until stiff and meringue holds soft peaks. Beat in vanilla.
Fill pie shell with hot filling. Spread top of the filling with the meringue making sure to cover the entire surface. Bake pie until meringue is golden, 10 to 12 minutes.

Melanie Wood
TSU-Florida Region

Desserts

Little Fried Pies

As a college student, I know what it is like to go home for delicious holiday dinners. Wouldn't it be nice to contribute a little to the preparation of those meals? This recipe will surely impress the family at those occasions.

4 ounces dried apples
1 1/2 cans sweet milk biscuits

Glaze:
1/2 box powdered sugar
1/3 cup boiling water
2 teaspoons vanilla

Cook dried apples according to package directions; cool. Roll out canned biscuits very thin. Place 2 teaspoons of apple in each biscuit. Fold in half and pinch edges together with a fork. Cook in deep fat until golden brown. While pies are hot, dip in glaze made from powdered sugar, boiling water, and vanilla.

Brad Nelson
TSU Student

Jay's Strawberry Pie

This recipe can be prepared easily and keeps well in the refrigerator. It is my boyfriend's favorite dessert and it makes a delicious picnic sweet!

1 ready-made pie crust
2 pints strawberries, washed
1 package strawberry glaze
1 container frozen whipped topping, thawed

Bake crust on 400 degrees for 10 minutes or until golden brown. Arrange strawberries over crust. Pour strawberry glaze over strawberries evenly. Spread whipped topping over strawberries. Garnish with a sliced strawberry.

Dana Lang
TSU Student
Alpha Gamma Delta Sorority

Tastes and Traditions

Strawberry Cheese Pie

1 (8 ounce) package cream cheese, softened
1 box powdered sugar
1 (8 ounce) container frozen whipped topping, thawed
2 baked pie crusts
1 quart fresh strawberries, sliced

Beat cream cheese, powdered sugar, and whipped topping until all ingredients are blended well and mixture is fluffy. Spread a quarter of mixture in each of the pie shells. Top with sliced berries, reserving some for garnish. Cover berries with remaining creamed mixture. Decorate with reserved berries and chill thoroughly.

Jean W. Laliberte
TSU

Strawberry Pie

2 pints strawberries
Baked pie shell
1 cup sugar
1 cup water
3 tablespoons cornstarch
3 tablespoons dry strawberry Jello
1 small container Whipped topping

Slice strawberries, wash and drain well. Put into pie shell. Bring to boil the sugar, water, cornstarch and strawberry Jello. Set aside to cool and thicken. Pour over strawberries and refrigerate until congealed. 2 to 3 hours. Serve with whipped topping.

Brandi Baker
TSU Student
Phi Mu Sorority

The College of Communication and Fine Arts added the cutting-edge Graphic Design program – combining traditional artistic skills with computer technology – in fall 2000.

Desserts

Old-Fashioned Tea Cakes

My children, now grown, still think it isn't Christmas until the tea cakes are baked.

1 cup butter, softened
2 cups sugar
3 eggs
1 teaspoon salt
2 teaspoons vanilla
5 cups all-purpose flour
1 teaspoon baking soda
Flour to roll

Cream butter and sugar. Beat in eggs. Add salt and vanilla. With part of the 5 cups flour, sift in soda and add to mixture. Add remaining flour to dough. Roll and cut with cookie cutter*. Bake on ungreased cookie sheet at 325 degrees until light brown. Remove from sheet immediately. When completely cool, place in an airtight container or freeze.
* In a hurry? Form dough into balls and place on cookie sheet, flatten using a glass that has been dipped in flour.

Dinah Carlisle Kelsey
TSU '71

The Department of Speech and Theatre undertakes four major productions a year, as well as student-produced plays and workshops.

Tastes and Traditions

Five-Star Bread Pudding with Butter Rum Sauce

Bread Slices
3 cups water
2 sticks butter
3 ounces raisins
3 cans sweetened condensed milk
6 eggs, lightly beaten
2 teaspoons vanilla
Cinnamon

Butter Rum Sauce:
2 cups sugar
1 cup water
2 ounces butter
2 ounces rum

Butter 9 x 13-inch pan. Slice bread into 1-inch cubes and fill pan three-quarters full with cubed bread. In a pan, heat water and butter until butter is melted completely. Add raisins. Stir condensed milk into butter mixture and let cool slightly. Add eggs and vanilla and pour over bread, letting it soak. Sprinkle with cinnamon and bake at 350 degrees for 40 minutes. Serve with Butter Rum Sauce.

For Butter Rum Sauce: Heat sugar and water. Add butter and let cool. Add rum. Serve over pudding.

Sara (Sugie) Jones
TSU Friend

Members of Zeta Beta Phi sorority lend their support to a number of campus and community activities, including the annual Homecoming parade.

Desserts

Bailey's Pudding Parfaits with Oatmeal-Walnut Crunch

This dessert was prepared for the reception for Henry Aaron, who visited TSU in spring 1998.

Crunch:
1 cup old-fashioned oats
3/4 cup all-purpose flour
1/2 cup packed golden brown sugar
2 teaspoons instant coffee crystals
1/4 teaspoon allspice
1/4 teaspoon salt
1/2 cup (1 stick) chilled unsalted butter, cut into 1/2-inch pieces
3/4 cup coarsely chopped walnuts

Pudding:
1 1/4 cups chilled whipping cream, divided
12 tablespoons Bailey's Original Irish Cream liqueur, divided
3/4 cup packed golden brown sugar
6 large egg yolks
1/4 teaspoon nutmeg

12 tablespoons dried currants

For Crunch: Preheat oven to 350 degrees. Combine oats, flour, brown sugar, coffee crystals, allspice and salt in large bowl. Add butter and rub in with fingertips until mixture forms moist clumps. Mix in walnuts. Sprinkle mixture onto rimmed baking sheet. Bake until golden brown and crisp, occasionally stirring gently and leaving mixture in clumps, about 35 minutes. Cool completely. (Can be made 2 days ahead. Store in an airtight container.)
For Pudding: Combine 3/4 cup cream, 6 tablespoons liqueur, sugar, yolks, and nutmeg in large metal bowl. Place over saucepan of simmering water. (Do not allow bottom of bowl to touch water). Beat custard until it thickens and thermometer registers 160 degrees, about 8 minutes. Remove from heat and beat until cool, about 8 minutes. Mix in remaining liqueur. Beat remaining cream in medium bowl to medium peaks. Fold into custard. Cover and chill at least 4 hours or overnight.
To Assemble: Layer 1/4 cup pudding, 1 tablespoon currants and 3 tablespoons crunch in each of six 12-ounce goblets; repeat layering 1 more time. Serve immediately or refrigerate up to 1 hour.

Sodexho-Marriott
TSU

Tastes and Traditions

Glorified Rice Pudding

This recipe was one of the favorite foods of Mrs. Bashinsky's children. My mother cooked it very often – we ate "glorified rice pudding" at least once a week.

1/4 cup uncooked rice
1 heaping tablespoon unflavored gelatin
1 pint milk
1 cup sugar
1/2 pint heavy cream, whipped
Raspberry or strawberry fruit topping, optional

Boil rice in 2 cups of salted water until tender. Drain for 20 minutes. In a small bowl, sprinkle gelatin over a tablespoon of cold water to soften. Place bowl over hot water and heat, stirring, until gelatin is dissolved. Combine rice and milk in a saucepan and bring to a boil. Add sugar and gelatin and remove from stove. Pour into a bowl and stir occasionally until cool. Add whipped cream, pour into mold and refrigerate until set, 2 or 3 hours. It may be made the day before. Serve with fruit topping, if desired.

Dejerilyn King-Henderson
TSU '93

In December 1998, Troy arts patron Claudia Crosby donated $1.5 million to renovate Smith Hall Auditorium and fund fine arts scholarships. At the time, her donation was the single-largest gift ever received by TSU. The renamed Claudia Crosby Theater was dedicated during a February 2000 ceremony.

Desserts

Chocolate Bread Pudding

This is Dr. Doug Hawkins' (president pro-tem, TSU Board of Trustees) favorite dessert. Well worth the effort.

12 ounces semisweet chocolate chips
8 ounces dense or toasting white bread, crusts removed
1 cup sugar
1 1/2 cups heavy cream
1/2 stick unsalted butter
6 eggs
2 teaspoons vanilla

Crème Anglaise:
9 egg yolks
2/3 cup sugar
Pinch of salt
3 cups cream
1 tablespoon vanilla

Chocolate Sauce:
4 ounces semi or bitter sweet chocolate
2 ounces heavy cream

For Pudding: Butter a soufflé dish or eight individual dishes. Pulse chocolate, bread and sugar in food processor to crumbs. Heat cream to boil and add to processor with motor running. Add butter. Add eggs one at a time and process for an additional 1 to 2 minutes. Divide into 8 soufflé dishes in an ovenproof pan and fill pan a third to half full with hot water. Bake 50 minutes at 350 degrees. Remove soufflé dishes from hot water. Pour creme anglaise on dessert plate, top with warm chocolate bread pudding and finish with chocolate sauce.

For Crème Anglaise: Beat egg yolks, sugar and salt until ribbons form. Scald cream and slowly add to egg mixture. Transfer mixture to heavy saucepan and cook over moderately low heat, stirring constantly with a wooden spoon, until it begins to thicken. Cool sauce over an ice bath, strain and refrigerate until ready to use.

For Chocolate Sauce: Melt chocolate in cream in double boiler, stirring until smooth.

Janice Hawkins
TSU First Lady

The men's basketball team captured the Trans America Athletic Conference regular season title in 1999-2000. Also capturing honors that season were Detric Golden, who was named Player of the Year, and Don Maestri, who was named Coach of the Year.

Tastes and Traditions

Bread Pudding with Whiskey Custard Sauce

This is a family tradition for dessert on Christmas Eve night. Wonderful taste and very festive. A must for any holiday.

8 large croissants, torn into small pieces
4 cups milk
3 large eggs, beaten
2 cups pecans, toasted and broken into pieces
1 1/2 tablespoons vanilla
1 teaspoon cinnamon
1/2 teaspoon nutmeg
1/2 cup yellow raisins
2 cups sugar

Custard Sauce:
1 cup sugar
1/2 cup butter
1/2 cup half and half
2 tablespoons whiskey (or wine)
1/2 teaspoon vanilla

For Pudding: Place bread pieces in a lightly greased 9 x 13-inch pan. Add milk and let soak for 10 minutes or longer. Blend well using hands. Stir in eggs. Add remaining ingredients. Bake at 325 degrees for 40 to 45 minutes or until firm. Serve warm with Custard Sauce.
For Sauce: Bring sugar, butter and half and half to a boil. Stir in vanilla and whiskey. Simmer until thickened, remove from heat and cool.

Vicki Nutter
TSU Parent

Mississippi Mud

1 package brownie supreme mix
1 jar marshmallow cream
1 tub fudge frosting

Prepare brownies as directed. Heat the marshmallow cream in microwave for 50 seconds, keeping an eye on it as it puffs up a lot! Pour marshmallow over brownies. Heat frosting and pour over marshmallow. Cool 1 hour in refrigerator. Very rich.

Kathy Kallman
TSU-Western Region

Desserts

Ice Cream Dessert

1 box ice cream sandwiches
1 bottle caramel ice cream topping
1 large container frozen whipped topping, thawed
2 cups chopped nuts, optional
3 - 4 crushed Heath bars, optional

Unwrap ice cream sandwiches and place in a 9 x 13-inch pan. Pour caramel topping evenly over sandwiches. Spread whipped topping over caramel and top with nuts or Heath bars, if desired. Cover and freeze for at least 1 hour before serving.

Stephanie Taylor
TSUD '95

Cherry Creighton
TSU Student

Banana Pudding

This recipe was a favorite of my grandchildren.

3/4 cup sugar, divided
3 tablespoons all-purpose flour
Dash of salt
4 eggs
2 cups milk
1/2 teaspoon vanilla
Box vanilla wafers
Fully ripened bananas, sliced

Place 1/2 cup sugar and flour in a double boiler. Mix in 1 egg and 3 egg yolks. Stir in milk and cook uncovered, stirring constantly, until thick. Remove from heat and add vanilla. Spread small amount in bottom of casserole dish. Cover with vanilla wafers and top with bananas. Repeat layers. Whip remaining egg whites until stiff peaks form. Spread on top of pudding. Bake in a 325 degree oven until brown.

Eloise Armstrong
TSU Parent

TSU broadened and increased its international focus in the 1990s: The number of international students grew from 21 (representing 13 countries) in 1989 to 210 (representing 52 countries) in 1999, and the Pace Hall-Rotary International Living and Learning Center opened in 1998.

Tastes and Traditions

Cream Cheese Banana Pudding

1 (8 ounce) package cream cheese, softened
1 can sweetened condensed milk
1 large container frozen whipped topping, thawed
1 large package vanilla instant pudding
1 package vanilla wafers
4 bananas, sliced

Beat cream cheese and milk until smooth. Set aside. Mix vanilla pudding according to directions on package. Combine pudding and cream cheese mixture. Fold in whipped topping. Line a dish with vanilla wafers and sliced bananas. Pour half of pudding over this. Repeat layers. Refrigerate.

Hope Walker
TSU Student
Alpha Gamma Delta Sorority

Sour Cream Banana Pudding

2 (3.4 ounce) packages vanilla instant pudding mix
3 cups milk
1 (8 ounce) container sour cream
1 (12 ounce) container frozen whipped topping, thawed and divided
1 (12) ounce box vanilla wafers
6 bananas, sliced

Whisk together pudding and milk in a large bowl until thickened. Whisk in sour cream; fold in 4 1/4 cups whipped topping. Layer half each of vanilla wafers, sliced bananas and pudding mixture in a 4-quart bowl. Repeat layers. Top with remaining whipped topping. Cover and chill.

Jean S. Helms
TSU Friend

Dr. C. B. Smith is the only TSU alumnus to serve his alma mater as president. Pace, McCartha, Wright, Cowart, Eldridge, Dill and McCartha halls, as well as Memorial Stadium and the campus golf course, were constructed during Smith's tenure from 1937 to 1961.

Desserts

Blueberry Pudding

1 box Dream Whip
1 cup milk
8 ounces cream cheese, softened
1 cup powdered sugar
1 cup granulated sugar
1 teaspoon vanilla
1 prepared angel food cake, cut in 1-inch cubes
2 cans blueberry pie filling

Prepare both envelopes of Dream Whip according to package directions, using 1 cup milk. Add cream cheese and sugars and beat until smooth. Add vanilla. Put a layer of cake cubes in a large bowl. Top with a layer of pie filling. Spread whipped mixture over filling. Continue layering until you have used all ingredients. Refrigerate.

Megan Singleton
TSU Student
Phi Mu Sorority

Chocolate Delight

I made this dish to take to a pot luck. It went super-fast with the ones who tasted it first hurrying back to get seconds. It was all gone in record time with others complaining that they did not get any. It really makes a beautiful dessert besides being delicious.

1 devil's food cake mix
1 large box chocolate instant pudding
1 large container frozen whipped topping, thawed
5 - 6 Skor candy bars, broken in small pieces

Prepare cake mix according to directions. Bake in a 9 x 13-inch pan. When cool, cut into cubes. Prepare pudding mix according to directions. In a clear glass bowl, layer ingredients: cake cubes, pudding, whipped topping, candy bar pieces. Repeat until all ingredients have been used. Chill at least 1 hour or more before serving.

Sara Jones
TSU Spouse

Tastes and Traditions

Cream Puff Dessert

Pastry:
1 stick margarine
1 cup flour
1 cup water
4 eggs

Filling:
3 small boxes vanilla instant pudding
4 cups cold milk
8 ounces cream cheese, softened
1 (8 ounce) container frozen whipped topping, thawed

Chocolate syrup

Heat margarine and water to boil. Remove from heat. Add flour and stir. Add eggs, one at a time, beating after each. Spread in a greased 9 x 13-inch baking dish. Bake 35 minutes in a preheated 350 degree oven. Cool completely.
Filling Directions: Mix pudding with milk. Beat cream cheese into pudding mix. Spread over cooled pastry. Top with whipped topping. Drizzle with chocolate syrup just before serving.

Sara Jones
TSU Spouse

Chocolate Eclair

This is a delicious dessert that can be prepared the night before.

1 package graham crackers
1 large box vanilla pudding
3 cups milk
1 small container frozen whipped topping, thawed
1 can chocolate cake icing

Layer whole graham crackers in the bottom of a 9 x 13-inch pan. Mix pudding with milk and add whipped topping. Spoon mixture over graham crackers. Top with another layer of graham crackers. Warm icing in microwave just until soft, 10 to 15 seconds. Do not overheat! Pour over crackers and refrigerate for up to 24 hours. Served chilled.

Paige Myers
TSU

Desserts

Peach Sparkle

This is one of my husband's favorite desserts. It's not too heavy, not too light.

1 large box peach, pineapple or orange gelatin
2 cups boiling water
2 cups cold water
1 large can crushed pineapple, drained well and juice reserved
1 1/2 cups small marshmallows

Topping:
2 tablespoons margarine
2 tablespoons flour
1/2 cup sugar
1/2 cup reserved pineapple juice
1 egg
1 (8 ounce) package cream cheese, softened
1 container frozen whipped topping, thawed

Dissolve gelatin in boiling water. Add cold water and pineapple. Cover with marshmallows. Refrigerate until hard set.
For Topping: Mix margarine, flour, sugar, pineapple juice and egg in a double boiler. Cook, stirring, until thick. Add cream cheese and beat until smooth. Let cool. Fold in whipped topping. Spread over gelatin mixture and refrigerate.

Debra Grant
TSU

Strawberry Jello Dessert

2 (6 ounce) packages strawberry banana Jello
2 cups boiling water
1 package frozen strawberries, chopped or sliced
1 (#2) can crushed pineapple, including juice
3 ripe bananas, sliced
Whipping cream or Cool Whip
1 (8 ounce) package cream cheese, softened
1 small package slivered almonds

Dissolve Jello in boiling water and fold in fruit. Pour half of mixture into 9 x 13-inch pan. Put in freezer to set. Combine whipped cream and cream cheese and beat until smooth. Gently spread over gelatin. Freeze until set. Top with remaining Jello mixture. Freeze until set. Garnish with almonds before serving.

Stephanie Behrens
TSU Student
Phi Mu Sorority

Tastes and Traditions

English Trifle

The ideal "do-ahead" dessert for a special dinner. The recipe requires three batches of custard, and I recommend that you prepare each batch separately.

36 (1 1/2-inch) almond shortbread cookies
1/3 - 1/2 cup amaretto liqueur
1 (12-ounce) jar strawberry or raspberry jam

Custard (Make 3 batches):
4 egg yolks, divided
4 tablespoons sugar, divided
10 tablespoons milk
1/4 cup whipping cream
2 1/2 teaspoons cornstarch dissolved in 2 tablespoons milk
1/2 teaspoon vanilla
1/8 teaspoon freshly grated nutmeg
1 (12-ounce) pound cake, cut into 1/4-inch slices (homemade is best)
1/2 - 2/3 cup cream sherry
4 (10 ounce) packages frozen raspberries or strawberries, thawed and
    thoroughly drained
2 cups (1 pint) whipping cream
2 tablespoons sugar
1/2 teaspoon vanilla or to taste

Brush flat side of 12 to 15 shortbreads with liqueur. Arrange flat sides around sides of 12-cup glass bowl, then line bottom flat-side up. Spread generously with red raspberry jam, trying not to crush shortbread. For Custard: Whisk yolks in medium saucepan. Gradually add sugar, whisking until mixture is thick and lemon colored, about 1 to 2 minutes. Blend in milk, whipping cream and cornstarch mixture. Place over medium-low heat and cook, stirring constantly, until mixture thickens, about 3 to 5 minutes. Do not boil or mixture will separate. Remove from heat and stir until slightly cooled. Blend in vanilla and nutmeg. Transfer to bowl. Repeat twice, for a total of about 3 3/4 cups custard. Spoon 1 1/4 cups custard over raspberry jam layer. Cover with single layer of pound cake slices. Using pastry brush, soak cake generously with 1/4 to 1/3 cup sherry. Spread thin layer of raspberry jam over cake. Top with half of drained raspberries. Carefully spoon another 1 1/4 cups custard over berries. Repeat layering with remaining pound cake slices, sherry and jam. Cover with remaining berries. Carefully spread remaining custard over top. Brush 8 or 9 shortbread with liqueur and arrange over custard flat-side down. Place plastic wrap directly on surface of trifle. Refrigerate overnight. About 3 to 4 hours before serving, whip cream in medium bowl until foamy. Add sugar and vanilla and continue beating until stiff but not dry. Spoon over shortbread, swirling top. Crush 10 to 12 shortbreads. Sprinkle 1-inch border around outer edge of cream. Refrigerate until serving time.

Janice Hawkins
TSU First Lady

Desserts

Peanut Butter Brownie Trifle

This is rich, so serve small portions. It can be served in goblets or presented in a trifle bowl.

1 package peanut butter brownie mix or chocolate-peanut butter brownie mix
1 package vanilla instant pudding mix
3 cups milk
1/2 cup creamy peanut butter
2 teaspoons vanilla extract
1 cup whipping cream, whipped and divided
2 1/2 cups coarsely chopped peanut butter cup candies, divided

Prepare and bake brownie mix according to package directions, using a buttered and floured 9 x 13-inch pan. Cool. Invert brownies onto a cutting board and cut into 3/4-inch pieces. Combine vanilla pudding mix and milk in a large mixing bowl; beat at low speed of an electric mixer until thickened. Add peanut butter and vanilla; beat until smooth. Gently fold in half of the whipped cream. Set remaining whipped cream aside. For individual trifles, place a layer of brownies in each goblet; top with chopped peanut butter candies and a layer of pudding mixture. Repeat procedure once. Pipe or spoon whipped cream over each trifle. To make one large trifle, place half of brownies in the bottom of a 3-quart trifle bowl; top with half of chopped peanut butter cup candies and half of pudding. Repeat and top with whipped cream.

Anne Boothe
TSU Friend

Chick-fil-A Express is a popular attraction in the Trojan Express Food Court.

Tastes and Traditions

Cream Cheese Soufflé

This unusual soufflé was created by my grandmother, Ruby Collier Thomas, for use at the Red Apple Inn at Eden Isle, Arkansas. The recipe has appeared in Arkansas newspapers.

4 eggs, separated
1/4 teaspoon salt
1 teaspoon flour
6 ounces cream cheese, softened
1 cup sour cream
1/4 cup honey

Beat egg yolks until thick and creamy. Add salt and flour. Combine sour cream and cream cheese; blend until smooth. Add to egg yolks; beat with electric mixer until smooth, Add honey gradually. Beat egg whites until stiff but not dry, and fold in yolk mixture until blended. Pour into a 1 1/2-quart soufflé dish. Place in pan of water and bake in a preheated 300 degree oven for 1 hour.

Jane Varner
TSUM '98

Troy Normal School's first faculty, pictured here circa 1887, included a teacher of methods, a teacher of mathematics and foreign languages, and instructors of music and drawing. Faculty members received an annual salary of $600 and often supplemented their pay by teaching in Troy's public schools.

Desserts

Apple Dapple

3 eggs
1 1/2 cups cooking oil
2 cups sugar
3 cups flour
1 teaspoon cinnamon
1 teaspoon baking soda
1 teaspoon salt
2 teaspoons vanilla
1 cup chopped nuts
3 cups chopped apples
2 cups coconut

Topping:
1 stick margarine
1 cup brown sugar
1/4 cup milk

Beat eggs, oil and sugar. Sift together flour, cinnamon, baking soda and salt. Add to egg mixture 1 cup at a time. Add the vanilla, nuts, apples and coconut. Bake in a 2-quart Pyrex baking dish for 45 minutes at 350 degrees.
For Topping: Mix all ingredients in a saucepan and bring to a boil. Cook for 2 minutes. Pour over the warm cake.

Stefanie Greene
TSU Student
Phi Mu Sorority

Easy Apple Dumplings

1 (8 count) package refrigerated crescent rolls
2 large apples, peeled and quartered
2 tablespoons cinnamon
1 cup orange juice
1 cup sugar
1 stick butter, melted

Heat oven to 350 degrees. Coat cutting board with nonstick spray. Spread crescent rolls out and separate. Place an apple quarter on each roll, sprinkle with cinnamon and roll up. Place in a baking pan. Mix orange juice, sugar, and melted butter in a medium bowl. Pour over apple dumplings. Cook 30 to 40 minutes, basting dumplings occasionally. Serve with ice cream.

Cynthia Henderson
TSU

Tastes and Traditions

Donna's Deep Dish Apple Cobbler

This is a recipe I basically made up. I couldn't find a recipe I liked, so I just added my own ingredients until I got what I wanted. It's good hot or cold.

8 - 10 tart apples, peeled, cored and sliced (about 2 quarts)
Lemon juice
3/4 cup sugar
2 tablespoons flour
1/2 cup brown sugar
1 slightly heaping teaspoon apple pie spice
1 teaspoon cinnamon
1/2 teaspoon allspice
1/2 teaspoon nutmeg
2 packages frozen ready-made crusts, thawed
1 stick butter

Place apples, as you slice them, in bowl of lemon juice and let sit until all are sliced. Lightly toss apples to make sure all are in juice. Drain juice and add sugar. Lightly toss until all apples are coated. Add flour, brown sugar and all spices. Lightly toss again. Arrange 2 pie crusts in bottom of 9x13x2-inch pan. Cut and shape to fill sides and bottom well. Spoon apple mixture over crust. Top with thin slices of butter. Top with 2 more crusts. Crimp edges of crusts together and cut four vents in top crust. Bake at 400 degrees for 50 to 60 minutes, until golden brown.

Donna L. Reynolds
TSU '86

Peach Cobbler

1 stick butter
1 cup sugar
1 cup milk
3/4 cup self-rising flour
1 teaspoon vanilla flavoring
1 medium can sliced peaches, drained and juice reserved

Melt butter in a medium baking dish. Mix sugar, milk, flour and vanilla in a bowl. Pour on top of melted butter. Do not stir. Place peaches evenly throughout batter, making sure they don't bunch together. Pour reserved juice on top. Bake at 350 degrees for 1 hour.

Candi Phillips
TSU Student
Kappa Delta Sorority

Desserts

Blueberry Cobbler

2/3 cup flour
1/2 cup sugar
1 1/2 teaspoons baking powder
2/3 cup low-fat milk
2 tablespoons margarine, melted
2 cups blueberries, cleaned and drained

Preheat oven to 350 degrees. In a medium bowl, combine flour, sugar and baking powder. Stir in milk and mix smooth. Pour melted margarine into a 1 or 1 1/2-quart casserole dish. Pour in batter and sprinkle blueberries on top. Bake 40 to 45 minutes, until lightly browned.

Ashley Wambles
TSU Student
Alpha Gamma Delta Sorority

Mini-Cheesecakes

12 vanilla wafers
2 (8 ounce) packages cream cheese, softened
1 teaspoon vanilla
1/2 cup sugar
2 eggs
Fruit

Place each vanilla wafer in a muffin tin liner. Beat cream cheese, vanilla and sugar in an electric mixer on medium speed until well blended. Add eggs. Mix well. Pour over wafers, filling them three-quarters full. Bake 25 minutes at 325 degrees. Top with fruit.

Jessica Ray
TSU Student
Phi Mu Sorority

A pair of leading celebrities visited Troy State Teachers College in the years following World War II: Renowned poet Carl Sandberg gave a talk at the 1947 Homecoming and Oscar-winning actor Charles Laughton visited campus in 1950.

Tastes and Traditions

Chocolate Turtle Cheesecake

1 (7 ounce) package caramels
1/4 cup evaporated milk
3/4 cup chopped pecans, divided
1 (9 inch) chocolate crumb pie crust
2 (3 ounce) packages cream cheese, softened
1/2 cup sour cream
1 1/4 cups milk
1 (3.9 ounce) package chocolate instant pudding mix.
Fudge topping

Place caramels and evaporated milk in a heavy saucepan. Heat over medium-low heat, stirring continually, until smooth, about 5 minutes. Stir in 1/2 cup chopped pecans. Pour into pie crust. Combine cream cheese, sour cream and milk in blender; process until smooth. Add pudding mix; process for about 30 seconds longer. Pour pudding mixture over caramel layer, covering evenly. Chill, loosely covered, until set, about 15 minutes. (May be made one day ahead to this point. Cover loosely with plastic wrap and refrigerate.) Drizzle fudge topping over pudding layer in a decorative pattern. Sprinkle top of cake with remaining pecans. Chill, loosely covered, until serving time.

Joy Graham
TSU Student
Alpha Gamma Delta Sorority

Mountain Pie

This recipe is easy and delicious. I often took it to dinner-on-the-grounds at Sacred Heart Primitive Baptist Church.

1 stick butter
1 cup sugar
1 cup flour
1 1/2 teaspoons baking powder
1/2 teaspoon salt
1 cup milk
1 quart fruit

Melt butter in casserole dish. Sift sugar, flour, baking powder and salt together. Mix with milk. Pour over butter. Add fruit on top. Cook at 375 degrees for 35 minutes until brown.

Margaret Pace Farmer
TSU '32

Desserts

Three-Step Caramel Pecan Cheesecake

2 (8 ounce) packages cream cheese, softened
1/2 cup sugar
1/2 teaspoon vanilla
2 eggs
20 caramels
2 tablespoons milk
1/2 cup chopped pecans
1 graham cracker crust

Mix cream cheese, sugar, and vanilla with mixer until well blended. Add eggs and mix until blended. Set aside. Melt caramels with milk on low heat, stirring frequently, until smooth. Stir in pecans. Pour caramel mixture into crust. Top with cream cheese mixture. Bake at 350 degrees for 40 minutes. Cool. Refrigerate for 3 hours. If desired, you may garnish with melted caramel and chopped pecans.

Erica Williams
TSU Student
Kappa Delta Sorority

Butter Wafers

These simply melt in your mouth. They freeze well, if they last that long!

1 1/4 cups butter, softened and divided
1/3 cup heavy cream
2 cups flour
Sugar
3/4 cup powdered sugar
1 teaspoon vanilla flavoring

Cream 1 cup butter with cream and flour. Chill about 30 minutes. Preheat oven to 375 degrees. Roll out dough on floured board 1/8-inch thick. Cut with small (donut hole size) cutter . Place on ungreased cookie sheet. Prick with fork and sprinkle with sugar. Bake 7 to 10 minutes. Don't let them get too brown. Meanwhile, blend remaining butter, powdered sugar and vanilla, adding a little cream if too stiff to spread. Make a sandwich cookie by spreading over 1 cookie and topping with another. Good.

Mamie Mason
TSU Friend

Tastes and Traditions

Butter Fingers

Traditional Recipe

Easy to make. Make a double recipe and keep in refrigerator until you need them, then bake.

1/2 pound margarine, softened
5 tablespoons powdered sugar
Pinch of salt
2 1/2 cups all-purpose flour
1 cup chopped pecans
3 teaspoons vanilla

Mix all ingredients together and chill in refrigerator. Roll into small balls and place on an ungreased baking sheet. Bake in a 325 degree oven until lightly browned. Roll in powdered sugar while hot.

Lucy T. Nall
TSU '20

Layered Cranberry Spread

This is one of those recipes you feel you should only make during the Christmas holiday season. Be daring and try it during other times of the year, as long as you can find fresh cranberries.

2 cups cranberries
3/4 cup sugar
1/2 cup orange juice
1 tablespoon grated orange rind
8 ounces cream cheese, softened
2 tablespoons dry sherry
1 cup whipping cream, whipped
3 cups shredded Cheddar cheese

In a 2-quart saucepan combine cranberries, sugar, orange juice and rind. Bring to a boil. Boil 10 minutes, stirring occasionally. Chill. Combine cream cheese and sherry, mixing until well blended. Fold in whipped cream. Layer half of cranberry mixture in a glass pie plate. Top with half of cream cheese mixture and sprinkle with half of cheese. Repeat layers Cover with plastic wrap and chill. Serve with crackers and/or apple slices.

Becky Beall McPherson
TSU '75, '81

In 1999, the third season of soccer at TSU, freshman Andi Tickles led the Lady Trojans with five goals scored and 49 points. Those numbers helped her earn third-team all-conference honors, making her the first TSU soccer player to earn postseason honors.

Desserts

Brickle Dip

8 ounces cream cheese, softened
1 package Brickle chips (called Bits of Brickle, located with the chocolate chips)
1 teaspoon vanilla
1/2 cup packed light brown sugar
1/2 cup sugar

Mix cream cheese with other ingredients. Serve with sliced apples or vanilla wafers.

Ellen Green
TSU Parent

Pineapple Dip

When I was serving as president of Alpha Delta Pi Sorority, we had the dedication of our new home on Sorority Hill. My mom, Mary Shively, prepared a variety of dips and goodies, but the pineapple dip was the favorite of all who attended.

1 large can crushed pineapple, drained
1 cup sugar
1 (8 ounce) package cream cheese, softened
1 tablespoon mayonnaise
1/2 cup chopped nuts

In heavy saucepan, cook pineapple and sugar until thick and golden brown. On medium temperature, mix in softened cream cheese and stir in mayonnaise. Add nuts. Serve with Wheat Thins or crackers.

Amy Shively
TSU Student

The first international chapter of the TSU Alumni Association was chartered in Kirov, Russia in December 1998.

Tastes and Traditions

Peanut Brittle

This is a family favorite. It stores well (in an air-tight container) if you can keep people away from it!

2 cups sugar
1 cup light corn syrup
1/2 cup water
1/2 teaspoon salt
3 cups raw, shelled peanuts
2 tablespoons butter
2 teaspoons baking soda

Heat sugar, syrup, water, and salt to a rolling boil in a heavy 2-quart saucepan. Add peanuts. Reduce heat to medium and stir frequently. Cook to hard crack stage (293 degrees). Add butter, then baking soda. Beat rapidly and pour onto a lightly greased baking sheet, spreading to 1/4-inch thickness. When cool, break into pieces. Store in an airtight container. Makes about 2 pounds.

Willetta Hatcher
TSU Friend

Toffee Candy

This is a special treat. Good to give as a gift. A Christmas tradition at the Dye house. Jay (5) and Jackson (3) love to help make as well as eat them!

1 cup chopped pecans
2 sticks butter (do not substitute)
1 cup sugar
6 ounces semisweet chocolate chips

Spread pecans on buttered aluminum foil. Cook butter and sugar to 300 degrees or just before burned. Mixture will be a light caramel color. Pour evenly over pecans. Sprinkle chocolate chips over pecans while warm and spread evenly. Cool in refrigerator. Break in pieces and store in an airtight container.

Sherry J. Dye
TSU Spouse

Desserts

Pavlova

This is a very special favorite dessert in New Zealand. It is beautiful as well as delicious.

4 egg whites
Few grains of salt
3/4 cup sugar
1/2 teaspoon vanilla
1 teaspoon vinegar
1 teaspoon cornstarch
Whipped cream
Fruit

Preheat oven to 300 degrees. Put a piece of foil on a baking pan. Coat lightly with nonstick spray. Dust with cornstarch. Beat egg whites to a foam. Add salt. Beat to stiff foam. Beat in sugar gradually. Beat until peaks stand up when beater is removed. Add vanilla, vinegar, and cornstarch. Blend. Spoon meringue mixture onto prepared pan, forming a 9-inch circle. Turn oven to 275 degrees. Bake 15 minutes. Lower to 250 degrees; bake 1 to 1 1/4 hours. Allow to cool in oven. Place on flat serving dish. Pile whipped cream on top. Decorate with your favorite fruit: strawberries, kiwi fruit, etc.

Willetta Hatcher
TSU Friend

Butter Crunch Candy

This is a family recipe handed down for three generations. Remember when Hershey bars were a nickel? It's a Christmas tradition in our family.

2 sticks butter (1 oleo, 1 butter)
2 cups sugar
1 cup pecans, lightly toasted
4 Hershey chocolate bars

In heavy skillet melt butter over medium heat. Stir together until well blended. Cook, stirring occasionally, until dark carmel color. Pour immediately into cookie sheet. Spread, break 4 plain Hershey bars (the ones that used to be a nickel!) over the top, when melted, spread over toffee. Finely chop 1 cup pecans and sprinkle over chocolate. Put in cool place to harden, (not refrigerator). Break in pieces, enjoy.

Dee Mason
TSU Friend

Tastes and Traditions

Peanut Butter Fudge

Grandma Newman's fudge, passed down from Kentucky, was a favorite Christmas present from a beloved grandmother.

3 cups sugar
1 1/2 cups milk
1/8 teaspoon salt
4 tablespoons cocoa
1/4 cup corn syrup
1 teaspoon vanilla
1/2 stick margarine
1/4 cup peanut butter

Mix sugar, milk, salt, cocoa in a heavy pan. Bring to a boil on medium heat. Boil until fudge forms a soft ball when a small amount is dropped into a cup of cold water. Remove from heat. Add corn syrup, vanilla, butter and peanut butter. Beat by hand until the fudge begins to thicken. Pour into a buttered 8-inch square cake pan or dish. Cool and cut in 1-inch squares.

Don Forrer
TSU-Florida Region

White Fudge

2 1/2 cups powdered sugar
2/3 cups milk
1/4 cup butter or margarine
12 ounces white chocolate, coarsely chopped
1/2 teaspoon almond extract
3/4 cup coarsely chopped dried cherries, cranberries, or apricots
3/4 cup toasted almond slices

Line 8-inch square pan with foil; grease foil. Mix powdered sugar and milk in a heavy 3-quart saucepan. Over medium heat, add butter and, stirring constantly, bring to a boil. Without stirring, boil for 5 minutes. Over low heat, add white chocolate and almond extract. Stir, then whisk, until chocolate melts and mixture is smooth. Stir in dried fruit and toasted almonds. Pour mixture into prepared pan. Refrigerate 2 hours until firm. Invert pan, peel off foil and cut into 1-inch squares. Garnish as desired.

Bonnie Money
TSU

Desserts

"Trashy" Candy

1 (12 ounce) box Golden Graham cereal
1 cup chopped nuts, optional
1 package vanilla flavor almond bark candy coating

Place cereal and nuts, if desired, in a large bowl. Put almond bark in a microwaveable dish. Heat and stir at 1 minute intervals until completely melted, approximately 4 minutes. Pour melted candy over mixture in bowl. Stir candy mixture until it is completely coated. Drop by spoonfuls on wax paper. Let candy cool for approximately 15 minutes.

Kate Duren
TSU Student
Phi Mu Sorority

Festive Fudge Dreams

This recipe won fourth place in the 1999 National Peanut Festival's annual recipe contest.

1 cup crunchy or creamy peanut butter
1 (17 1/2 ounce) jar marshmallow cream
2 cups sugar
2/3 cup milk

Mix peanut butter and marshmallow cream in mixing bowl. Cook sugar and milk to 250 degrees in large saucepan. Pour sugar and milk over peanut butter mixture and mix well. Pour into greased 9 x 13-inch pan and cool. Cut into small squares.

Kim McNab
TSU '87

TSU's first foreign exchange students, Elizabeth Savage of England and Yumiko Kirino of Japan, arrived on campus in fall 1971.

Tastes and Traditions

Chocolate Fudge

1 2/3 cups sugar
2 tablespoons butter
1/2 teaspoon salt
2/3 cups evaporated milk
1 1/2 cups semisweet chocolate morsels
1/4 pound miniature marshmallows
1/2 cup chopped pecans
1 teaspoon vanilla

Place sugar, butter, salt and evaporated milk in a large saucepan. Stir until mixed and heat to a boil. Boil gently for about 5 minutes, stir continuously. Remove from heat and add chocolate morsels, marshmallows, nuts and vanilla. With a large spoon, beat the candy mixture until chocolate morsels and marshmallows are melted. Pour into a greased 8-inch square pan.

Jean S. Helms
TSU Friend

Scotties

2 sticks (1 cup) butter
1 cup brown sugar
1 cup sugar
2 eggs, beaten
2 cups all-purpose flour, sifted
2 teaspoons baking powder
Dash of salt
2 teaspoons vanilla

Grease and flour a 9 x 13-inch pan. Melt butter. Add both sugars, mixing by hand. Add eggs and mix well. Sift flour, baking powder and salt together. Add to sugar mixture. Mix and add vanilla. Bake at 325 degrees for 25 minutes.

Kelly Miller
TSU Student
Phi Mu Sorority

Desserts

Pecan Crispies

1/2 cup butter, softened
6 teaspoons brown sugar
6 teaspoons sugar
1 egg
1/2 teaspoon vanilla
1/4 teaspoon baking soda
1/4 teaspoon salt
1 1/4 cups sifted all-purpose flour
1 teaspoon baking powder
1 cup chopped pecans

Cream butter and both sugars. Beat in egg and vanilla. Sift together baking soda, salt and flour. Blend into creamed mixture. Stir in nuts. Drop mixture from teaspoon onto ungreased cookie sheet. Bake at 375 degrees for about 10 minutes. Cool cookies slightly before removing from pan. Makes 2 1/2 dozen.

Chandra Myrick
TSU Student

Butterscotch Candy

2 packages butterscotch morsels
1 (10 - 16 ounce) can salted party peanuts
1 (8 - 10 ounce) can Chinese noodles

Melt butterscotch morsels in a double boiler or microwave. Add peanuts and noodles and mix until coated. Drop on wax paper to cool.

Heather Moran
TSU Student
Phi Mu Sorority

WTSU and the Southeastern Public Radio Network began broadcasting in 1976. The network brings public radio programming to an audience of 1.5 million potential listeners in southeast Alabama, southwest Georgia and northwest Florida.

Tastes and Traditions

Potato Candy

1 small potato
2 packages powdered sugar
1 jar smooth peanut butter

Boil potato until skin peels off easily. Gently peel potato and place in a bowl with a little bit of powdered sugar. Mash it while adding more powdered sugar until you have a nice powdered ball that can be rolled out on a flat surface. As you roll out the powdered potato, continue adding powdered sugar until all sticky spots are covered. Roll out into about 1-inch thick. Spread peanut butter over surface until potato is entirely covered. Roll into a pinwheel log, still adding powdered sugar to cover all sticky spots. Slice log 1/2-inch thick and place on a dish. Cover and refrigerate for 1 hour. Then enjoy!

Shana Burke
TSU Student
Alpha Gamma Delta

Pecan Puffs

This is something I bring to our office Christmas party every year and everyone really enjoys them.

1 egg white
1 cup light brown sugar
1/4 teaspoon salt
1/4 teaspoon soda
3 cups pecans

Beat egg white until stiff; add brown sugar, salt and soda and mix well. Add pecans and stir well until pecans are coated. Put puffs on lightly greased cookie sheet about 1 inch apart. Bake at 300 degrees for about 30 minutes until they are brown. These can be frozen after they are cooked.

Bonnie Money
TSU

TSU's Archaeological Research Center is involved in a number of digs and other projects, including a major research project involving a Native American site near Gantt, Alabama.

Desserts

Carnation Custard

Traditional Recipe

This recipe is so simple. Today, people don't have time for the "three-day" recipes – they want something fast. This one is quick and easy. I got it from Dora Wallace Kerns, the best cook I've ever known.

4 eggs
1/2 cup sugar
1/2 teaspoon salt
1 teaspoon vanilla
1 cup water
1 large can Carnation milk

Put all ingredients in bowl and beat to mix well. Pour into 8 custard cups. Put cups into pan of hot water and bake at 350 degrees for 40 to 45 minutes. Remove cups from water and cool.

Margaret Pace Farmer
TSU '32

The 1926 football team

One of TSU's earliest-recorded football games was played on Thanksgiving Day in 1903 at a baseball park in southeast Troy. The "elevens" from Troy Normal lined up against a team from the city that had been assembled the week before. The final score: 10-5, in favor of the city.

Tastes and Traditions

Peanut Crunch

Excellent for tailgating and during the holidays.

24 ounces white almond bark
4 cups corn flakes
1 cup Rice Krispies
1 1/2 cups miniature marshmallows
1 cup roasted or fried peanuts

Melt almond bark in microwave. Add remaining ingredients and mix well. Drop by spoonfuls onto wax paper. Serve when cold.

Coffee County Chapter
TSU Alumni Association

Pralines

This is the recipe of Nellie Hill, a fourth grade teacher at the old Kilby Demonstration School. Her students cooked these pralines in her classroom, so they had to be easy.

2 cups sugar
1 cup Carnation milk
2 cups nuts

Combine sugar and milk in frying pan. Cook until thick and caramel-colored. Add nuts and cook a few minutes more. Drop by spoonfuls on buttered paper.

Margaret Pace Farmer
TSU '32

Archery was an important element in the physical education program at Troy State Teachers College -- these students took aim in November 1943. TSU students were still stringing bows in phys-ed classes in 1999.

Desserts

Buttermilk Pralines

3 cups sugar
1 cup buttermilk
3 tablespoons light corn syrup
1 teaspoon baking soda
1/8 teaspoon salt
2 cups chopped pecans
2 tablespoons butter
2 teaspoons vanilla

In heavy saucepan, place sugar, buttermilk, syrup, soda and salt. Over medium heat, bring to boil. Cook, stirring occasionally, about 40 minutes or until a soft ball forms in cold water. Remove from fire and let stand 5 minutes. Stir in pecans, butter and vanilla. Beat until mixture thickens and loses gloss. Drop quickly by spoonfuls on wax paper. Let stand 30 minutes. Then store in tight container.

Stella Grindley
TSU Friend

Cajun Pralines

1 pound light brown sugar
1/2 pint whipping cream
1/2 stick butter
2 cups chopped pecans

Cook brown sugar and cream in microwave for 13 minutes, stirring half way through. Stir in butter and chopped pecans. Drop on greased cookie sheet. Should yield 36 pralines.

Doug Hawkins
TSU Board of Trustees

TSU students give countless hours of volunteer service to the local community. Two members of Sigma Gamma Rho sorority lent their fishing skills to the annual Catfish Roundup in 1999.

Tastes and Traditions

Cinnamon Logs

1 (16 ounce) loaf thinly sliced white bread
8 ounces cream cheese, softened
1 egg white
1/2 cup powdered sugar
1 cup sugar
1 tablespoon ground cinnamon
1/2 cup butter or margarine, melted

Preheat oven to 350 degrees. Trim crusts from bread slices. Roll slices to 1/4-inch thickness. Beat cream cheese, egg white and powdered sugar at medium speed until smooth. Spread evenly on 1 side of each bread slice. Roll up, forming logs. Stir together sugar and cinnamon in a shallow dish. Dip logs in melted butter and roll in sugar mixture. Place on lightly greased baking sheets. Bake at 350 degrees for 15 minutes. Remove to wire racks to cool.

Jean S. Helms
TSU Friend

The three-year Quest for Excellence capital campaign, the first comprehensive campaign for the TSU System, culminated with special ceremonies in February 2000. The campaign generated $21.2 million for System projects. Pictured from left are Dr. Michael Malone, TSUD president; Ren Jones, TSUM campaign chairman; Dr. Doug Patterson, System vice chancellor; Dr. Jack Hawkins, System chancellor; Dr. Doug Hawkins, president pro-tem of the TSU board of trustees; Harrel McKinney, TSU campaign chairman; and Dr. Cameron Martindale, TSUM president.

Desserts

Alabama Peanut Butter Sour Cream Apple Tort

First Edition Favorite

Since peanuts are a major crop in our area, I adapted this recipe to include them. When Terry and I entertain our Washington friends, serving this pie provides the opportunity to discuss two of our favorite topics — farming and Alabama.

Crust:
2 cups all-purpose flour
3/4 cup crunchy peanut butter
1 cup sugar
2 eggs
1 teaspoon vanilla

Filling:
2 tablespoons flour
1/2 cup sugar
1/4 teaspoon salt
1 teaspoon cinnamon
1 egg, lightly beaten
1 cup sour cream
1 teaspoon vanilla
6 cups peeled and chopped apples (approximately 3 large apples)

Topping:
1 cup brown sugar
1/2 cup all-purpose flour
3 tablespoons melted butter
1/2 cup roasted unsalted chopped peanuts

For Crust: Mix all ingredients together thoroughly and press into a 9-inch springform pan.
For Filling: Sift flour, sugar, salt and cinnamon together. Stir in beaten egg, sour cream and vanilla. Fold in apples and pour into pie crust. Bake at 350 degrees for 30 minutes. Remove from oven and sprinkle with topping. Cool completely before removing from pan.
For Topping: Mix all ingredients together until crumbly.

Barbara Everett
TSU '86, TSUD '88
Wife of U.S. Representative Terry Everett

Tastes and Traditions

Longleaf Anjou Pear Cheesecake

2 Anjou or Bartlett Pears, peeled and diced
1 can Kern's Pear Nectar
2 1/2 cups graham cracker crumbs
1/2 stick melted butter
1 cup finely chopped hazelnuts
3 packages cream cheese softened at room temperature
3 eggs
1 tablespoons sugar
1 tablespoon Frangelico
2 teaspoons vanilla extract or 1 vanilla bean
1/2 teaspoon nutmeg

Cook diced pear in nectar for approximately fifteen minutes. Transfer to bowl to cool. To make crust, melt butter and mix with graham cracker crumbs and hazelnuts. Press into spring form pan that has been lined with wax paper. Bake at 350 degrees for ten minutes. For filling, combine eggs one at a time with softened cream cheese. Add sugar, Frangelico, vanilla extract and nutmeg. Do not over mix. Gently fold pears into mixture with small amount of the nectar. Pour into crust and bake at 350 degrees for 45 minutes or until middle is firm and puffed.

Leslie Schrushy
TSU '90

Alumna Leslie Schrushy and husband Richard, founder of HealthSouth Inc., continue to be special friends to TSU. The Sorrell College of Business provides an Executive MBA program for HealthSouth employees, Mr. Scrushy serves on the TSU board of trustees, and his 1998 gift of $1 million helped renovate Richard M. Scrushy Field at Memorial Stadium.

Desserts

Chocolate Ice Cream Torte

1 cup vanilla wafer crumbs
1/4 cup finely chopped almonds
3 tablespoons butter, melted
1 package (3 3/4 ounce) vanilla instant pudding
1 cup milk
1/2 teaspoon almond extract
1/2 cup whipping cream, whipped
1/2 gallon chocolate ice cream, softened
Whipped cream
Fresh cherries or strawberries

Combine vanilla wafer crumbs, almonds and butter until crumbs are evenly coated. Pack lightly onto the bottom of a nine-inch springform pan. Freeze until firm. Beat pudding mix and milk with mixture on low speed for one minute. Fold in almond extract and whipped cream. Spoon a thin layer of chocolate ice cream over crumb crust in chilled springform pan. Spread half of the pudding mixture over the ice cream. Top with a second layer of ice cream and pudding mixture. Spoon a final layer of ice cream over pudding for the top layer. Cover and freeze at least six hours or overnight. To decorate and serve, let torte stand at room temperature five minutes. Run a thin metal spatula around rim of shell. Remove outside rim of pan. Remove pan and place torte on serving plate. Top with whipped cream in center of torte and garnish with cherries.

Kellie Henderson
TSU Student

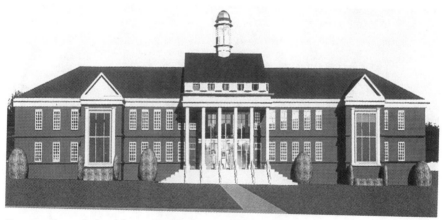

Construction of the Library/Technology Building at Troy State University Dothan began in March 1999 and will be completed in 2001. The $6.5 million facility will include computer laboratories, distance-learning classrooms, a production studio and a 21st-century library.

Tastes and Traditions

Vanilla Cream Pie

3 cups half and half cream
1/2 cup sugar
5 tablespoons cornstarch
1 teaspoon vanilla
4 tablespoons butter

Sweet Dough:
5 cups all-purpose flour
2 cups sugar
5 teaspoons baking powder
1 cup butter
3 eggs
2 tablespoons milk
2 teaspoons vanilla

To make dough: In a large bowl, combine flour, sugar and baking powder. Cut in butter until mixture resembles coarse crumbs. In another bowl, beat together eggs, milk, and vanilla. Gradually add to flour mixture, tossing with fork to distribute. Knead with hands until dough forms a ball. Divide into 4 parts. To make pie crust, roll out 1 portion of dough into a 12 inch round. Ease into 9-inch pie plate, being careful not to stretch pastry. Trim to 1/2 inch beyond edge of pie plate; fold under extra pastry, making an even rim. Fill as directed. (Note: Pastry will puff during baking. Fluting the edge is unnecessary.) Remaining dough can be wrapped in waxed paper and frozen.

In medium saucepan heat 2 1/2 cups of the cream just to boiling. In a mixing bowl combine remaining cream, sugar, and cornstarch. Stir mixture into cream in saucepan. Cook and stir over medium heat until mixture is thick and bubbly. Remove from heat. Stir in vanilla and butter until melted. Pour into prepared, unbaked pie shell. Bake in a 350 degree oven for 25 to 30 minutes or until crust is golden brown. Cool pie on a wire rack for 30 minutes. Cover and refrigerate until serving time. If desired, top pie with fresh fruit, such as sliced peaches, or strawberries.

Janice Malone
TSUD First Lady

Index

Appetizers 17
  "Come Back" Sandwiches 36
  Angels on Horseback 38
  Artichoke Dip 17
  Bacon and Tomato Party Sandwiches 44
  Bacon-Wrapped Dates 35
  Bay Crab Quiche 30
  BBQ Chicken Pizza 37
  Beef Cheese Ball 26
  Black Bean Salsa 31
  Black-eyed Pea Dip 21
  Boursin Cheese Spread 33
  Bread and Butter Pickles 39
  Cheddar Curry Spread 25
  Cheese Ball 26
  Cheese Rounds 43
  Chicken Dip 20
  Chicken Party Dip 21
  Corn Chip Dip 23
  Crab Dip 18
  Crab Mornay 48
  Crawfish & Eggplant Appetizer 48
  Cream Cheese and Caviar 34
  Creamy Cheese Dip 23
  Delicious Hot Mustard 45
  Dill and Cream Cheese Appetizer . . .34
  French Bread Garlic Shrimp 42
  Frozen Cucumber Pickles 47
  Grated Carrot Sandwiches 36
  Green Tomato Pickles 40
  Hot Broccoli Dip 45
  Hot Cheese Dip 22
  Hot Mexi-Corn Dip 19
  Hot Wings With Veggies 42
  Layered Mexican Dip 24
  Mary's Cheese Straws 29
  Mexican Cheese Dip 25
  Orange Marmalade 40
  Pashka 41
  Peach Salsa 31
  Pepperoni and Cheese Crescents . . .29
  Phi Mu Recipe 41
  Watermelon Rind Sweet Pickles 39

Beverages 49
  Champagne Punch 51
  Christmas Instant Spiced Tea 52
  Coffee Punch 49
  Mecosta Fruit Punch 51
  Mint Tea 52
  Old Hotel Vicksburg Punch 50
  Punch .50
  Sangria 53
  Springtime Punch 49

Breads & Breakfast 94
  Apple Bread 98
  Banana Bread 99
  Banana Loaf 99
  Biscuit, Sour Cream 103
  Biscuits, Dawn's 97
  Blueberry Muffins 114
  Bran Muffins 107
  Bread Sticks 106
  Breakfast Casserole 110
  Breakfast Hot Dish 110
  Brunch Ham and Cheese Casserole . 111
  Cheddar Apple Bread 97
  Cheese Biscuits 96
  Cheese Grits Souffle 114
  Cinnamon Rolls 108
  Corn Light Bread 101
  Cornbread Fritters 100
  Cream Cheese Breakfast Squares . . . 111
  Croutons 106
  Danish 109
  Date Bread 102
  Dill Bread 105
  Dinner Rolls 95
  Easy Apple Bread 98
  Gingerbread Muffins 107
  Gingerbread, Fluffy 104
  Hush Puppies 101
  Irish Brown Bread 102
  Muffins, Tropical 108
  Pear Bread 100
  Rolls, Jean's Famous 95

Tastes and Traditions

Sausage and Cheese Casserole 113
Sausage Grits 113
Spinach Cornbread 105
Spoon Rolls 96
Sweet Potato Muffins 103
Tramp Eggs 112

Desserts 221
"Killer" Chocolate Chip Cookies ...225
"Trashy" Candy 307
Apple Cobbler 298
Apple Dapple 297
Apple Dumplings 297
Awesome Chocolate Chip Cookies .226
Bailey's Pudding Parfaits with
  Oatmeal-Walnut Crunch 285
Banana Cake with Peanut Butter
  Frosting 261
Banana Pudding 289
Blueberry Cobbler 299
Blueberry Pudding 291
Bread Pudding 221
Bread Pudding with Whiskey Custard
  Sauce 288
Brickle Dip 303
Brown Sugar Pound Cake 241
Brown Sugar Shortbread 222
Brownie Bonbons 236
Brownies, Craig's Favorite 234
Butter Crunch Candy 305
Butter Fingers 302
Butter Wafers 301
Buttermilk Pie 278
Buttermilk Pralines 313
Butterscotch Candy 309
Cajun Pralines 313
Carnation Custard 311
Cashew White Chocolate Cookies .. 228
Cherry Pie, Prize-Winning 266
Cherry Pound Cake 243
Chess Cake Squares 239
Chess Pie 278
Chocolate Bread Pudding 287
Chocolate Caramel Brownies 234
Chocolate Chip Chess Pie 268
Chocolate Chip Pecan Pie 268
Chocolate Chip Pound Cake 243
Chocolate Chip Treasure Cookies .. 227

Chocolate Delight 291
Chocolate Eclair 292
Chocolate Fudge 308
Chocolate Ice Cream Torte 317
Chocolate Pecan Pie 272
Chocolate Pie 269, 270
Chocolate Pie, Layered 269
Chocolate Pound Cake 244, 245
Chocolate Sheath Cake 249
Chocolate Turtle Cheesecake 300
Christmas Cake 246
Christmas Lane Cake 262
Cinnamon Logs 314
Claxton Fruitcake Cookies 230
Coconut Cake 247
Coconut Pie 277
Coconut Pound Cake 239
Cola Cake 255
Congo Bars 230
Craig's Favorite Brownies 234
Cranberry Spread 302
Cream Cheese Banana Pudding ...290
Cream Cheese Blond Brownies 233
Cream Cheese Pound Cake 245
Cream Cheese Soufflé 296
Cream Puff Dessert 292
Crescent Fruit Pie 275
Crunch Cake 254
Date Nut Balls 231
Deep Dish Apple Cobbler 298
Dixie Pie 277
Do-ee Goo-ee Cake 251
Dump Cake 253
Easy Apple Dumplings 297
Easy Cookie Bars 231
Egg Custard Pie 279
English Trifle 294
Festive Fudge Dreams 307
Five-Flavor Pound Cake 240
Five-Star Bread Pudding with
  Butter Rum Sauce 284
Fresh Apple Cake 250
Fried Pies 281
Fruit Cake, No-Bake 256
Fudge Pie 279
Gingerbread Cookies 224
Heath Bar/Butterfinger Cake 250
Hedgehog Cake 258

Index

Honey Crunch Pecan Pie 272
Honeybun Cake 259
Hoosier Cake 254
Hotel Hershey Derby Pie 276
Ice Cream Dessert 289
Imitation Reese Peanut Butter Bars .232
Key Lime Pie 267
Lane Cake 263
Layered Cranberry Spread 302
Lemon Meringue Pie 267
Lemon Squares 238
Lemon-Orange Pound Cake 242
Lemony Ice Cream Pie 280
Little Fried Pies 281
Mandarin Orange Cake 248
Mini-Cheesecakes 299
Mint Brownies 235
Miss Callie's Christmas Cake 246
Mississippi Mud 288
Mountain Pie 300
Neiman Marcus Bars 238
Oatmeal Cookies 228
Old-Fashioned Tea Cakes 283
Orange Blossoms 221
Pavlova 305
Peach Cobbler 298
Peach Sparkle 293
Peanut Brittle 304
Peanut Butter Brownie Trifle 295
Peanut Butter Brownies 232
Peanut Butter Chiffon Pie 275
Peanut Butter Cookies 229, 237
Peanut Butter Fudge 306
Peanut Butter Nut Chews 237
Peanut Butter Pie 265, 276
Peanut Crunch 312
Pear Cheesecake 316
Pecan Crispies 309
Pecan Pie 271
Pecan Pound Cake 242
Pecan Puffs 310
Pineapple Dip 303
Pineapple Pie 280
Potato Candy 310
Potato Chip Cookies 223
Pound Cake 244
Pound Cake Cookies 224
Pralines 312

Red Velvet Cake 253
Refrigerator Nut Cookies 225
Rice Pudding 286
Rum Cake 257
Scotties 308
Snicker Doodle Cookies 229
Sour Cream Banana Pudding 290
Sour Cream Poppy Seed Cake 247
Southern Pecan Pie 274
Strawberry Banana Split Cake 252
Strawberry Cake 248
Strawberry Cheese Pie 282
Strawberry Jello Dessert 293
Strawberry or Peach Pavlova 226
Strawberry Pie 281, 282
Strawberry Swirl Cheesecake 264
Syrup Pie 270
Tea Cakes, Aunt Claudia's 222
Thirteen Layer Chocolate Cake 260
Three-Layer Banana Cake 246
Three-Step Caramel Pecan
    Cheesecake 301
Toffee Candy 304
Tort, Peanut Butter 315
Trojan Best Pecan Pie 273
Twelve-Minute Pound Cake 241
Vanilla Cream Pie 318
Vanishing Oatmeal Raisin Cookies . 227
White Fudge 306

Main Dishes 117
African Chop 120
Baba's Steak 119
Barbecue Chicken Cubes 141
Barras Cajun Gumbo 171
Beef and Baked Bean Casserole . . .152
Beef Stir-Fry 124
Beef Stroganoff Casserole 152
Brisket, Barbecue 123
Broccoli-Chicken-Ham Pizza 144
Brunswick Stew 165, 166
Cabbage Rolls 173
Cajun Jambalaya 169
Chicken à la King 136
Chicken and Broccoli Casserole . . .135
Chicken and Broccoli Ring 133
Chicken and Dressing 136
Chicken Breast, Spinach-Stuffed
    with Bearnaise Sauce 131

Tastes and Traditions

Chicken Breasts Florentine 128
Chicken Casserole .. 129, 130, 135, 138
Chicken Casserole, Three-Cheese ..134
Chicken Kiev 125
Chicken Mornay 129
Chicken Pie 137
Chicken Pilaf 142
Chicken Spaghetti 157
Chicken Tetrazzini 133
Chicken, Baked Italian 132
Chicken, Creamy Skillet 132
Chicken, East Indian 181
Chicken, Mexican 134
Chicken, Roast 137
Chili Chicken Stew 166
Classic Roast Chicken 137
College-Style Quesadillas 144
Creamy Skillet Chicken 132
Crock Pot Stew 164
East Indian Chicken 181
Easy-Do Veggie Stew 164
Enchiladas, Sour Cream 183
Flank Steak 118
Garlic Mushroom Chicken Breast ..140
Goulash 182
Gumbo, Barras Cajun 171
Hamburger Casserole 154
Hamburger Noodle Bake 153
Hamburger Pie 155
Homemade Pizza 179
Italian Baked Chicken 132
Italian Sausage and Peppers 185
Lamar's Jambalaya 170
Lasagna, Low-fat 161
Lasagna, Slow-Cooker 161
Last-Minute Supper 172
Linguine Primavera 179
Low Country Boil 151
Mandarin Pork Stir-Fry 174
Marzetti 156
Meatloaf 117
Meatloaf, Little-Bit-of-Texas 117
Mexican Casserole 153
Mexican Chicken 134
Mexican Mary 154
Mickey's Chili 168
Moroccan-Spiced Chicken with
    Rosemary Oil 146

Mushroom Chicken 138
Pahari Chicken 143
Pakistani Chicken Marsala 142
Party Chicken 143
Pepper Steak 123
Pheasant 175
Pizza Italiano 178
Pork Chops, Orange-Cranberry 121
Pork in Balsamic Vinegar 119
Pork Tenderloin Elizabeth 184
Pork Tenderloin with Jezebel Sauce 176
Pork Tenderloin, Peachy 118
Roast and Gravy 124
Rotel Chicken Casserole 139
Rotel Chicken Spaghetti 158
Roy's Tacos 187
Salmon Croquettes 150
Salmon Steaks with Caper Sauce ..151
Seafood Alfredo 177
Sesame Chicken 140
Shrimp & Broccoli 186
Shrimp and Noodles 149
Shrimp Casserole 149
Shrimp Newburg 185
Shrimp or Chicken Casserole 148
Shrimp Pasta 148
Sour Cream Chicken 141
Sour Cream Chicken Squares 139
Sour Cream Enchiladas 183
Spaghetti Arrabiatta 159
Spaghetti Carbonara 156
Spaghetti Pie Casserole 159
Spaghetti, Cajun 157
Spareribs, Barbecued and Sauce ...122
Spareribs, Steamed Barbecued 121
Spatzle (Noodles) 181
Steak Bake 122
Steak, Baba's 119
Stir-Fry, Pork 174
Stuffed Peppers 180
Szechwan Chicken 145
Taco Rice 175
Tagliarini 172
Tailgate Chili 167
Three-Cheese Chicken Casserole ..134
Tortilla Rolls 180
Turkey Lasagna 163
Twenty-Minute Spaghetti 158

Index

Veal Roll-Ups 178
Vegetarian Lasagna 162
Veggie Stew 164
Venison Stew 167
White Bean Turkey Chili 186
White Chili 188
Winter-Style Barbecue Brisket 123
Zucchini Lasagna 160

Salads .74
Avocado and Grapefruit Salad 92
Bing Cherry Salad Mold 90
Blueberry Congealed Salad 83
Broccoli and Cauliflower Salad 88
Caesar Salad 75
Calico Slaw 85
Chicken Salad 77
Chicken Salad, Royal Curried 76
Colonial Cranberry Salad 79
Cranberry Salad 80
Creamy Congealed Salad 93
Endive and Pear Salad with
    Gorgonzola Cream Dressing 74
English Country Salad 86
Gazpacho Salad 82
Green Bean Salad 90
Hot Chicken Salad 78
Lime Congealed Salad 83
Mandarin Romaine Salad with
    Praline Pecans 91
Marinated String Bean Salad 84
Onion Slaw 85
Pasta and Chicken Salad 88
Pasta Salad 79
Rice Salad 87
Salad Dressing 81
Salad, Nina Fraser's 89
Seven Cup Salad 80
Shoepeg Corn Salad 84
Smoked Chicken Salad 78
Snow Pea Salad 92
Strawberry Pretzel Salad 81
Taco Salad 82
Turkey, Mandarin and Poppy Seed
    Salad 87
West Indies Salad 77
Wilted Spinach Salad 91

Soups & Sauces 54
Adelaide's White Cream Sauce 64
Apricot Pork Tenderloin 73
Baked Potato Soup 59
Barbeque Sauce 65
Bisque, Crab 69
Broccoli Soup 59
Carrot Soup 69
Cheddar Chowder Soup 56
Corn and Shrimp Chowder 70
Cream of Mushroom Soup 68
Cream of Peanut Soup 67
Cucumber Sauce 72
Curried Cream Cheese Soup 67
Curry Dressing 70
Divine Dressing for Fruit Salad 71
Fruit Salad Dressing 71
Gumbo, Steven's 55
Mango Vinaigrette Salad Dressing . .72
Marinade for Beef Tenderloin 73
Mustard Sauce for Shellfish 72
Orange Sauce 63, 64
Pea Soup 60
Pear Relish 66
Potato Soup 58
Quick Crab Bisque 69
Santa Fe Soup 57
Spaghetti Sauce 62, 63
Taco Soup 54
Turkey Soup 56, 61
Vegetable Soup 60

Vegetables & Side Dishes 189
Acorn Squash 203
Apple Cheese Casserole 217
Apples, Onions, and Red Cabbage
    Sauté 214
Asparagus Bread Pudding 215
Asparagus Casserole 202
Baked Cheesy Macaroni Casserole . 208
Baked Fruit 218
Baked Ziti 207
Broccoli and Rice Casserole 190
Broccoli and Spaghetti Casserole . . 191
Broccoli Casserole 191
Brussels Sprouts 206
Candied Sweet Potatoes 200

Tastes and Traditions

Cheese and Tomato Casserole 210	Mexican Corn Casserole 193
Cheese Potato Casserole 196	Mushroom-Stuffed Mushrooms . . .190
Cheese Soufflé 218	Pasta and Vegetable Toss 194
Corn Casserole 192	Pineapple Soufflé 209
Corn Fritters 192	Potato Casserole 196
Corn Pudding 193	Rice Ring with Creamed Mushrooms 213
Eggplant and Cheese Casserole . . .189	Risotto with Gold 211
Eggplant Creole 217	Spinach and Artichokes 205
Green Bean and Corn Casserole . . .201	Spinach Casserole 205
Green Bean Casserole 194	Spinach Madeline 206
Green Beans, Red Wine Vinegar . . .195	Spinach Mold 214
Hashbrown Casserole 197	Squash Casserole 202
Herbed Mushrooms & Artichokes . . 216	Squash Fritters 204
Holiday Spinach Mold 214	Stir-Fry, Five-Vegetable 212
Layered Macaroni and Cheese 209	Stuffed Baked Potatoes 199
Leek Casserole 207	Sweet Potato Casserole 199
Macaroni and Cheese 208	Twice Stuffed Baked Potatoes 198
Mama's Stuffing 210	Vegetable Casserole 201
Marinated Vegetable Salad 195	Vidalia Onion Pie 204

NOTES

Notes

Tastes and Traditions

The *Tastes and Traditions*
of
Troy State University

Troy State University Foundation
253 Adams Administration Building
Troy, Alabama 36082

Please send me _____ copies   @ $19.95 each _____
    Alabama residents add 7% sales tax   @ $ 1.40 each _____
    Postage and handling   @ $ 3.00 each _____
                Total amount for order _____

Make checks payable to: Troy State University Foundation

Name: _____
Address: _____
City _____ State _____ Zip _____

The *Tastes and Traditions*
of
Troy State University

Troy State University Foundation
253 Adams Administration Building
Troy, Alabama 36082

Please send me _____ copies   @ $19.95 each _____
    Alabama residents add 7% sales tax   @ $ 1.40 each _____
    Postage and handling   @ $ 3.00 each _____
                Total amount for order _____

Make checks payable to: Troy State University Foundation

Name: _____
Address: _____
City _____ State _____ Zip _____